CAMBRIDGE
UNIVERSITY PRESS

Cambridge Lower Secondary
Science

TEACHER'S RESOURCE 9

Mary Jones, Diane Fellowes-Freeman & Michael Smyth

CAMBRIDGE
UNIVERSITY PRESS

University Printing House, Cambridge CB2 8BS, United Kingdom

One Liberty Plaza, 20th Floor, New York, NY 10006, USA

477 Williamstown Road, Port Melbourne, VIC 3207, Australia

314–321, 3rd Floor, Plot 3, Splendor Forum, Jasola District Centre, New Delhi – 110025, India

103 Penang Road, #05–06/07, Visioncrest Commercial, Singapore 238467

Cambridge University Press is part of the University of Cambridge.

It furthers the University's mission by disseminating knowledge in the pursuit of education, learning and research at the highest international levels of excellence.

www.cambridge.org
Information on this title: www.cambridge.org/9781108785228

First published 2013
Second edition 2021

20 19 18 17 16 15 14 13 12 11 10 9 8 7 6 5 4 3 2

Printed in Great Britain by CPI Group (UK) Ltd, Croydon CR0 4YY

A catalogue record for this publication is available from the British Library

ISBN 978-1-108-78522-8 Paperback with Digital Access

Additional resources for this publication at www.cambridge.org/delange

> Contents

Digital resources

The following items are available on Cambridge GO. For more information on how to access and use your digital resource, please see inside front cover.

Active learning

Assessment for Learning

Developing learner language skills

Differentiation

Improving learning through questioning

Language awareness

Metacognition

Skills for Life

Letter for parents – Introducing the Cambridge Primary and
Lower Secondary resources

Curriculum framework correlation

Mid-point test and answers

End-of-year test and answers

Answers to Learner's Book questions

Answers to Workbook questions

Answers to English Language Skills Workbook questions

Glossary

You can download the following resources for each unit:

Differentiated worksheets and answers

Language worksheets and answers

Resource sheets

End-of-unit tests and answers

〉 Introduction

Welcome to the new edition of our Cambridge Lower Secondary Science series.

Since being launched, Cambridge Lower Secondary Science has been used by teachers and children in over 100 countries around the world for teaching the Cambridge International Lower Secondary Science Curriculum Framework.

This exciting new edition has been conceived and designed by speaking to Lower Secondary Science teachers all over the world, looking to understand their needs and difficulties, and then carefully designing and testing the best ways of meeting these needs. As a result of this research, we've made some important changes to the series. This Teacher's Resource has been carefully redesigned to enhance its usability and accessibility to teachers, with careful focus on navigation and the incorporation of pages from the Learner's Book. This Teacher's Resource is also available digitally through our Cambridge GO platform, along with extra support and more teaching resources.

The series is built around well-known teaching pedagogies, and we provide full guidance within this Teacher's Resource for using child-centred teaching approaches which develop active learning and metacognition, and which are brought to life in the classroom through illustration and questioning.

Get to know your learners better with frequent and effective formative assessment opportunities and guidance, starting with clear learning objectives and success criteria as well as an array of assessment actions, including advice on self- and peer assessment.

Ensure that all learners are able to progress in the course with clear, consistent differentiation in the form of tiered activities, differentiated worksheets and advice about supporting learners' different needs.

All our resources are written for teachers and learners who use English as a second or additional language. This has meant the careful avoidance of unnecessarily complex vocabulary and expression, while the series provides a major focus on building up functional and subject vocabulary.

We hope you enjoy using this course and that it is beneficial in advancing the learning of your students. Please get in touch if you have any questions for us, as your views are essential for us to ensure our schemes meet your needs as a teacher.

Eddie Rippeth
Head of Primary and Lower Secondary Publishing, Cambridge University Press

> About the authors

Mary Jones

Mary obtained an MSc in Zoology from the University of Oxford. She has worked as a teacher and a lecturer in different types of educational institution, teaching students of all ages.

Mary's greatest interest is in sharing her love of science with young learners. She has written many textbooks, in which she aims to encourage learners to 'think like a scientist'. Her long involvement in examining and in international training has given her insight into the difficulties that learners all over the world have in understanding some topics in science, and this has informed her writing approach. She is passionate about the need to develop skills rather than just accumulating knowledge – skills that are vital for students to be successful as they move into higher education or the world of work.

Diane Fellowes-Freeman

Diane was a teacher for almost 40 years, mostly as Head of the Science Department at several large state schools in the south of England. She has taught all three sciences to students of all abilities up to GCSE and biology and chemistry to A Level. With so many changes in science courses over this time she has developed many new resources to meet the new specifications and to help her students. When her own children were young she spent some time teaching (mainly science) at their primary school, which was a new, fascinating and enjoyable experience.

She is passionate about engaging students in science so that they are able to understand and appreciate more about the world around them. It is important they see the relevance of science to their future.

Throughout her career she loved learning from other teachers and trying new techniques. One of the most enjoyable and rewarding parts of her job was mentoring many teacher training students and teachers who were newly qualified.

Whilst still teaching full time she did some work for Cambridge University Press but the first big project was for the previous Cambridge Checkpoint Science edition. She has been fortunate to be invited to speak at a number of Cambridge overseas training events in Dubai, Malaysia, Indonesia and Vietnam. It is always a delight to meet so many teachers and share ideas and skills.

Her hope is that teachers will find this new edition gives them more help to develop their skills and provide an excellent foundation in science for all their learners.

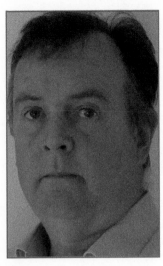

Michael Smyth

Michael graduated with a PhD in Biophysics and began his career in research at the University of Oxford. His enthusiasm for both science and education then led him into full-time teaching. Michael spent most of his teaching career as a Head of Science in a leading UK private school, which taught across the age ranges from kindergarten to A Level. He significantly raised attainment in the sciences at this school.

With publications spanning four decades, Michael's work includes articles in high-impact journals and secondary science learning aids for the 11–19 age groups. His work has been featured in major newspapers and he has won international awards for his work in science education. A senior examiner for over 20 years, Michael currently writes and marks exam papers, trains teachers and examiners and writes books and articles on science.

Michael remains passionate about the sciences and science education, realising that teachers of today are preparing the scientists of tomorrow. He feels this series will greatly benefit teachers and learners alike. The Learner's Books give clear explanations with accompanying pictures and diagrams. The Workbooks give learners practice at answering test-style questions, and these questions are fully differentiated. Taken together, Michael believes these components conspire to be the most powerful learning tool available for the 11–14 age group.

> How to use this series

The Learner's Book is designed for students to use in class with guidance from the teacher. It contains nine units which offer complete coverage of the curriculum framework. A variety of investigations, activities, questions and images motivate students and help them to develop the necessary scientific skills. Each unit contains opportunities for formative assessment, differentiation and reflection so you can support your learners' needs and help them progress.

The Teacher's Resource is the foundation of this series and you'll find everything you need to deliver the course in here, including suggestions for differentiation, formative assessment and language support, teaching ideas, answers, unit and progress tests and extra worksheets. Each Teacher's Resource includes:

- a print book with detailed teaching notes for each topic
- Cambridge GO edition with all the material from the book in digital form, plus editable planning documents, extra guidance, downloadable worksheets and more.

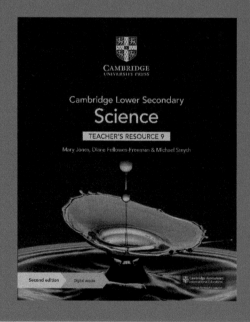

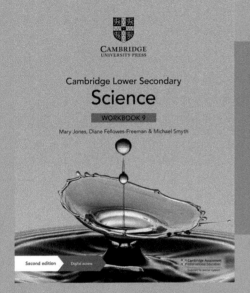

The skills-focused, write-in Workbook provides further practice of all the topics in the Learner's Book and is ideal for use in class or as homework. A three-tier, scaffolded approach to skills development promotes visible progress and enables independent learning, ensuring that every learner is supported.

English language skills are the single biggest barrier to students accessing international science. The English Language Skills Workbook helps learners understand scientific terms and express themselves effectively in English. Activities range from choosing the right word in a list of possible answers to writing longer responses.

A letter to parents, explaining the course, is available to download from Cambridge GO (as part of this Teacher's Resource).

> How to use this Teacher's Resource

This Teacher's Resource contains both general guidance and teaching notes that help you to deliver the content in our Cambridge Lower Secondary Science resources. Some of the material is provided as downloadable files, available on **Cambridge GO**. (For more information about how to access and use your digital resource, please see inside front cover.) See the Contents page for details of all the material available to you, both in this book and through Cambridge GO.

Teaching notes

This book provides **teaching notes** for each unit of the Learner's Book and Workbook. Each set of teaching notes contains the following features to help you deliver the unit.

The **Unit plan** summarises the topics covered in the unit, including the number of learning hours recommended for the topic, an outline of the learning content and the Cambridge resources that can be used to deliver the topic.

Topic	Approximate number of learning hours	Outline of learning content	Resources
9.1 Parallel circuits	3-4	The difference between series and parallel circuits; how current flows in a parallel circuit	**Learner's Book:** Questions 1–5

The **Background knowledge** feature explains prior knowledge required to access the unit and gives suggestions for addressing any gaps in your learners' prior knowledge.

Learners' prior knowledge can be informally assessed through the **Getting started** feature in the Learner's Book.

BACKGROUND/PRIOR KNOWLEDGE

Learners should recall the circuit symbols for a cell, lamp, buzzer, ammeter, switch and how to represent connecting wires. Learners should also recall how to draw series circuits with these components and the functions of each of these components.

The **Teaching skills focus** feature covers a teaching skill and suggests how to implement it in the unit.

TEACHING SKILLS FOCUS

Giving feedback
Many teachers say that giving feedback to every learner during every lesson is very time-consuming and so is not possible.

Reflecting the Learner's Book, each unit consists of multiple sections. A section covers a learning topic.

At the start of each section, the **Learning plan** table includes the learning objectives, learning intentions and success criteria that are covered in the section.

It can be helpful to share learning intentions and success criteria with your learners at the start of a lesson so that they can begin to take responsibility for their own learning

LEARNING PLAN

Learning objectives	Learning intentions	Success criteria
9Pe.01 Describe how current divides in parallel circuits.	• Recognise and understand the difference between series and parallel circuits.	• Recognise and draw circuit diagrams for parallel circuits.

There are often **common misconceptions** associated with particular learning topics. These are listed, along with suggestions for identifying evidence of the misconceptions in your class and suggestions for how to overcome them.

Misconception	How to identify	How to overcome
Current is the same in all parts of a parallel circuit.	After learning about current in parallel circuits, ask learners to comment on the current through the cell and through the branches of a simple parallel circuit.	Learners may have had difficulty grasping that current is the same in all parts of a series circuit. This may now be committed to memory, so dealing with the difference in parallel circuits could be challenging. Main teaching idea 3 should help to overcome this.

For each topic, there is a selection of **Starter ideas**, **Main teaching ideas** and **Plenary ideas**. You can pick out individual ideas and mix and match them depending on the needs of your class. The activities include suggestions for how they can be differentiated or used for assessment. **Homework ideas** are also provided.

Starter idea

1 Getting started (5 minutes)

Learning intention: To recall information about circuits from Stage 7.

Description: At Stage 7, the word 'series' may not have been used because the distinction with parallel circuits was not needed. At this stage, learners can just be told to draw circuit diagrams just as they did before.

Main teaching ideas

1 Activity: Measuring current in parallel circuits (15–30 minutes, depending on number of circuits)

Learning intention: To allow learners to connect ammeters in various positions in parallel circuits and determine how current divides.

Resources: See Learner's Book.

Description: See Learner's Book.

Thinking and Working Scientifically skills are woven throughout the Learner's Book. In the teaching notes, the *Thinking and Working Scientifically* **guidance** identifies these sections from the Learner's Book and provides more detail about the skills that it supports.

Science in Context skills are addressed in the Projects at the end of each unit in the Learner's Book, where learners can use what they have learned in the context of the wider world, and these Projects are supported by the *Project Guidance* sections in the Teaching Notes.

The **Language support** feature contains suggestions for how to support learners with English as an additional language. The vocabulary terms and definitions from the Learner's Book are also collected here.

LANGUAGE SUPPORT

Learners will use the following words:

connected in series: components that are attached in a circuit end-to-end with no branches so that all the current flowing out of one component flows into the next; there are no branches in a series circuit

Digital resources to download

This Teacher's Resource includes a range of digital materials that you can download from Cambridge GO. (For more information about how to access and use your digital resource, please see inside front cover.) This icon ⬇ indicates material that is available from Cambridge GO.

Helpful documents for planning include:

- **Letter for parents – Introducing the Cambridge Lower Secondary resources:** a template letter for parents, introducing the Cambridge Lower Secondary Science resources.
- **Curriculum framework correlation:** a table showing how the Cambridge Lower Secondary Science resources map to the Cambridge Lower Secondary Science curriculum framework.

Each unit includes:

- **Differentiated worksheets:** these worksheets are provided in variations that cater for different abilities. There are 3 levels of Worksheet: A, B and C. 'A' support the less confident, and 'C' are designed to challenge the more confident. Answer sheets are provided.
- **Language worksheets:** these worksheets provide language support and can be particularly helpful for learners with English as an additional language. Answer sheets are provided.
- **Resource sheets:** these include templates and any other materials that support activities described in the teaching notes.
- **End-of-unit tests:** these provide quick checks of the learner's understanding of the concepts covered in the unit. Answers are provided. Advice on using these tests formatively is given in the Assessment for Learning section of this Teacher's Resource.

Additionally, the Teacher's Resource includes:

- **Mid-point test and answers:** a test to use after learners have studied half the units in the Learner's Book. You can use this test to check whether there are areas that you need to go over again.
- **End-of-year test and answers:** a test to use after learners have studied all units in the Learner's Book. You can use this test to check whether there are areas that you need to go over again, and to help inform your planning for the next year.
- **Answers to Learner's Book questions**
- **Answers to Workbook questions**
- **Answers to English Language Skills Workbook questions**
- **Glossary**

In addition, you can find more detailed information about teaching approaches.

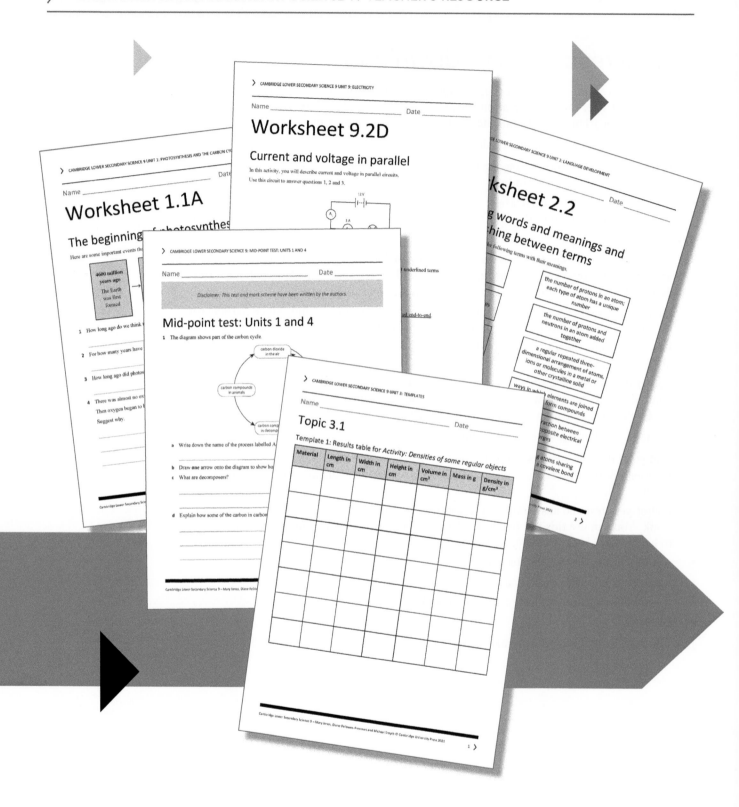

> About the curriculum framework

Cambridge International have developed their Cambridge Lower Secondary Science curriculum framework to support learners in developing their understanding about the natural world, particularly how to explain and investigate phenomena.

The curriculum framework incorporates three components:

- four content strands (Biology, Chemistry, Physics, and Earth and Space)
- a skills strand called Thinking and Working Scientifically
- a context strand called Science in Context.

Biology, Chemistry, Physics and Earth and Space provide the scientific knowledge content, which gradually develops from stage 7 to stage 9 and provides a smooth progression towards Cambridge IGCSE™ study.

The Thinking and Working Scientifically learning objectives focus on the key scientific skills that are developed throughout the course. This strand is split into three types of scientific enquiry:

- Models and representation
- Scientific enquiry
- Practical work.

Science in Context allows for personal, local and global contexts to be incorporated into scientific study, making science relevant to the contexts that learners are familiar with. This element of the curriculum offers great flexibility to teachers and learners around the world, exploring development of scientific knowledge over time; the evaluation of issues; ideas of peer review and the ideas surrounding specific environmental impacts from the uses of science..

The Cambridge Lower Secondary Science curriculum framework promotes a learner-led, enquiry-based approach. Practical work is a valuable part of science learning and develops learners' investigation skills such as observation, measurement and equipment handling.

⟩ About the assessment

Information about the assessment of the Cambridge International Lower Secondary Science curriculum framework is available on the Cambridge Assessment International Education website: https://www.cambridgeinternational.org/lowersecondary

⟩ Approaches to learning and teaching

The following are the key pedagogies underpinning our course content and how we understand and define them.

Active learning

Active learning is a pedagogical practice that places the learner at its centre. It focuses on how learners learn, not just on what they learn. We, as teachers, need to encourage learners to 'think hard', rather than passively receive information. Active learning encourages learners to take responsibility for their learning and supports them in becoming independent and confident learners in school and beyond.

Assessment for Learning

Assessment for Learning (AfL) is a teaching approach that generates feedback which can be used to improve learners' performance. Learners become more involved in the learning process and, from this, gain confidence in what they are expected to learn and to what standard. We, as teachers, gain insights into a learner's level of understanding of a particular concept or topic, which helps to inform how we support their progression.

Differentiation

Differentiation is usually presented as a teaching practice where teachers think of learners as individuals and learning as a personalised process. Whilst precise definitions can vary, typically the core aim of differentiation is viewed as ensuring that all learners, no matter their ability, interest or context, make progress towards their learning outcomes.

It is about using different approaches and appreciating the differences in learners to help them make progress. Teachers, therefore, need to be responsive, willing and able to adapt their teaching to meet the needs of their learners.

Language awareness

For many learners, English is an additional language. It might be their second or perhaps their third language. Depending on the school context, students might be learning all or just some of their subjects through English.

For all learners, regardless of whether they are learning through their first language or an additional language, language is a vehicle for learning. It is through language that students access the learning intentions of the lesson and communicate their ideas. It is our responsibility, as teachers, to ensure that language does not present a barrier to learning.

Metacognition

Metacognition describes the processes involved when learners plan, monitor, evaluate and make changes to their own learning behaviours. These processes help learners to think about their own learning more explicitly and ensure that they are able to meet a learning goal that they have identified themselves or that we, as teachers, have set.

Skills for Life

How do we prepare learners to succeed in a fast-changing world? To collaborate with people from around the globe? To create innovation as technology increasingly takes over routine work?

To use advanced thinking skills in the face of more complex challenges? To show resilience in the face of constant change? At Cambridge, we are responding to educators who have asked for a way to understand how all these different approaches to life skills and competencies relate to their teaching.

We have grouped these skills into six main Areas of Competency that can be incorporated into teaching, and have examined the different stages of the learning journey and how these competencies vary across each stage.

These six key areas are:

• Creativity – finding new ways of doing things, and solutions to problems

• Collaboration – the ability to work well with others

• Communication – speaking and presenting confidently and participating effectively in meetings

• Critical thinking – evaluating what is heard or read, and linking ideas constructively

• Learning to learn – developing the skills to learn more effectively

• Social responsibilities – contributing to social groups, and being able to talk to and work with people from other cultures.

Cambridge learner and teacher attributes

This course helps develop the following Cambridge learner and teacher attributes.

Cambridge learners	Cambridge teachers
Confident in working with information and ideas – their own and those of others.	**Confident** in teaching their subject and engaging each student in learning.
Responsible for themselves, responsive to and respectful of others.	**Responsible** for themselves, responsive to and respectful of others.
Reflective as learners, developing their ability to learn.	**Reflective** as learners themselves, developing their practice.
Innovative and equipped for new and future challenges.	**Innovative** and equipped for new and future challenges.
Engaged intellectually and socially, ready to make a difference.	**Engaged** intellectually, professionally and socially, ready to make a difference.

Adapted from Approaches to learning and teaching series, courtesy of Cambridge University Press and Cambridge Assessment International Education: cambridge.org/approachestolearning.

More information about these approaches to learning and teaching is available to download from Cambridge GO

Series-specific approaches

Cambridge Lower Secondary Science has been developed with scientific investigation at its heart, to support learners to understand and explain the world around them. *Think like a scientist* features offer engaging opportunities for learners to predict, observe and identify the patterns in what they see. Encouraging learners to see and investigate for themselves promotes active learning and deep understanding.

Opportunities for active learning are included throughout the series, in Activities and Questions at every point. Learners are also encouraged to self-assess and reflect on their learning, to develop their metacognitive skills and their awareness of their own progress.

Projects provide valuable opportunities to delve deeper into learners' own personal and local contexts, as well as global contexts as they progress through the course. This ensures that scientific learning is relevant for every learner.

$>$ Setting up for success

Our aim is to support better learning in the classroom with resources that allow for increased learner autonomy while supporting teachers to facilitate student learning.

Through an active learning approach of enquiry-led tasks, open-ended questions and opportunities to externalise thinking in a variety of ways, learners will develop analysis, evaluation and problem-solving skills.

Some ideas to consider to encourage an active learning environment are as follows:

- Set up seating to make group work easy.
- Create classroom routines to help learners to transition between different types of activity efficiently, e.g. move from pair work to listening to the teacher to independent work.
- Source mini-whiteboards, which allow you to get feedback from all learners rapidly.
- Start a portfolio for each learner, keeping key pieces of work to show progress at parent–teacher days.
- Have a display area with learner work and vocab flashcards.

Planning for active learning

We recommend the following approach to planning.

1 Plan learning intentions and success criteria: these are the most important feature of the lesson. Teachers and learners need to know where they are going in order to plan a route to get there.

2 Plan language support: think about strategies to help learners overcome the language demands of the lesson so that language doesn't present a barrier to learning.

3 Plan starter activities: include a 'hook' or starter to engage learners using imaginative strategies. This should be an activity where all learners are active from the start of the lesson.

4 Plan main activities: during the lesson, try to: give clear instructions, with modelling and written support; coordinate logical and orderly transitions between activities; make sure that learning is active and all learners are engaged; create opportunities for discussion around key concepts.

5 Plan assessment for learning and differentiation: use a wide range of Assessment for Learning techniques and adapt activities to a wide range of abilities. Address misconceptions at appropriate points and give meaningful oral and written feedback which learners can act on.

6 Plan reflection and plenary: at the end of each activity and at the end of each lesson, try to: ask learners to reflect on what they have learnt compared to the beginning of the lesson; build on and extend this learning.

7 Plan homework: if setting homework, it can be used to consolidate learning from the previous lesson or to prepare for the next lesson

For more guidance on setting up for success and planning, please explore the Professional Development pages of our website www.cambridge.org/education/PD

> Acknowledgements

The authors and publishers acknowledge the following sources of copyright material and are grateful for the permissions granted. While every effort has been made, it has not always been possible to identify the sources of all the material used, or to trace all copyright holders. If any omissions are brought to our notice, we will be happy to include the appropriate acknowledgements on reprinting.

Thanks to the following for permission to reproduce images:

Cover Mehmet Hilmi Barcin/Getty Images

Worksheet 4.1

DigitalGlobe/ScapeWare3d/Contributor/Getty Images; End-of-year Test tombaky/Getty Images

> 1 Photosynthesis and the carbon cycle

Unit plan

Topic	Learning hours	Learning content	Resources
1.1 Photosynthesis	3-4	Introduction to photosynthesis	**Learner's Book:** Questions 1–4 Think like a scientist: Collecting the gas produced in photosynthesis Think like a scientist: Investigating how light intensity affects the rate of photosynthesis (extension material) Activity: Words beginning with photo- Activity: Photosynthesis and respiration **Workbook:** Exercise 1.1A, How light level affects photosynthesis Exercise 1.1B, The effect of different colours of light on the rate of photosynthesis Exercise 1.1C, Turning an idea into an hypothesis that can be tested **Teacher's Resource:** Worksheets 1.1A–C, The beginning of photosynthesis Template 1: Results table for *Think like a scientist: Investigating how light intensity affects the rate of photosynthesis* (extension material)
1.2 More about photosynthesis	3-4	Chloroplasts and chlorophyll; leaves; minerals required by plants.	**Learner's Book:** Questions 1–6 Activity: Which surface of a leaf has most stomata? Think like a scientist: Testing a leaf for starch Think like a scientist: Planning an investigation into the effect of fertilisers on plant growth **Workbook:** Exercise 1.2A, Duckweed experiment Exercise 1.2B, Testing a variegated leaf for starch Exercise 1.2C, Floating discs experiment **Teacher's Resource:** Template 2: Planning record for *Think like a scientist: Planning an investigation into the effect of fertilisers on plant growth*

Topic	Learning hours	Learning content	Resources
1.3 The carbon cycle	2.5-3	How carbon atoms move between organisms and the air	**Learner's Book:** Questions 1–4 Think like a scientist: How do plants and animals affect carbon dioxide concentration? Activity: Modelling the carbon cycle **Workbook:** Exercise 1.3, Completing a carbon cycle diagram **Teacher's Resource:** Worksheets 1.3A–C, Building a carbon cycle Template 3, Results chart for *Think like a scientist: How do plants and animals affect carbon dioxide concentration?*
1.4 Climate change	2.5-3	The effects of greenhouse gases and asteroid collisions on the Earth's climate	**Learner's Book:** Questions 1–6 Think like a scientist: How do rising temperatures affect sea level? Activity: The carbon cycle and climate change **Workbook:** Exercise 1.4, Interpreting graphs about climate change **Teacher's Resource:** Worksheet 1.4, Impacts of climate change
Cross-unit resources			**Learner's Book:** Check your Progress **Project:** What happened to the dinosaurs? **Teacher's Resource:** Language development worksheets 1.1 Completing sentences about the carbon cycle 1.2 Making predictions

BACKGROUND/PRIOR KNOWLEDGE

It is likely that learners will already know something about photosynthesis. Learners who have followed a science curriculum programme may have learnt at Primary level that plants get energy from light, and they will also know that plants are the producers in food chains, a concept that was addressed at Stages 7 and 8. They should know something about energy changes, which were covered in the Physics units in Stage 7.

Learners will also need to be confident with word equations. These are first dealt with in the chemistry topics in Stage 8, and learners are also likely to remember using the word equation for respiration in Stage 8.

The work on the carbon cycle requires an understanding of the concept of elements and compounds, which was covered in chemistry at Stage 7. Learners will revisit their earlier work on decomposers from Stage 7, and integrate this with their previous knowledge of respiration, as well as the new work on photosynthesis. They are likely to have met combustion reactions in their chemistry lessons, probably in Stage 8.

The climate change topic builds on earlier work on greenhouse gases in the chemistry topics in Stage 8. Learners are also likely to remember something about asteroids from Stage 8.

TEACHING SKILLS FOCUS

Assessment for learning

As teachers, we all want to know how our learners are progressing. The learners themselves also want to know this, as do their parents. We give learners tests to find out. You may also enter your learners for externally marked tests.

These assessments can be thought of as summative assessments. Their purpose is to find out what learners have learnt and how well they understand the material. Their results in summative assessments can be used to help them to move into further or higher education courses, or to employment.

However, this is not the only type of assessment that teachers use. Formative assessment – also known as assessment for learning – is a type of assessment that can be used almost all of the time. Its purpose is to find out what our learners can do, so that we can adjust our teaching and the tasks and support that we provide to the learners, to help them to move on and up from their current position. There is much evidence that using assessment for learning can have a significant impact on the standards that can be achieved by learners.

Good formative assessment is at the heart of successful teaching. However well we plan a lesson, and however well we teach a topic, we cannot know how successful we have been until we find out how well the learners have understood what we have taught. As every teacher knows, what we teach is not the same as what our learners learn. If we find that their understanding is not as good as we hoped, then we need to adjust the planned teaching, to take this into consideration. Perhaps we need to revisit the topic in the next lesson for the whole class, approaching it in a different way. Perhaps some learners need to be given a further challenge, while others need more support to help them to grasp the concepts we have been teaching.

How is assessment for learning done? There are several things that you can try to do.

- Find out where individual learners are now – what do they understand? What do they feel less confident about? A good teacher does this constantly – using questioning in class, listening to learners as they talk to each other during group work, watching them doing an experiment, as well as marking written work.

- Share learning intentions and success criteria with learners. Learners need to know what they are supposed to be able to do, and how to judge when they have done it well. Using self- and peer assessment can really help here, as it gives them clear targets to focus on.

- Give focused, specific and personal feedback to learners to make clear to them what is good about their work and what they can do to improve. Make sure that these targets are achievable, not so broad or ambitious that they are beyond the learner's capability. Develop your learners' confidence to make sure that everyone understands that they can improve.

In the Teacher's Resource for Units 2, 5 and 8, you will find more guidance on using self- and peer assessment. Units 3, 6 and 9 give advice on giving feedback to learners. In Unit 4, there are suggestions about how to set achievable targets for learners, while Unit 7 includes ideas on how to use reflection to help learners to think about how they learn and how they can improve. There is advice on using questioning in Units 2, 5 and 8 at Stage 8.

In this unit, you could try:

- watching and listening to learners as they work on *Think like a scientist: Investigating how light intensity affects the rate of photosynthesis*, to check how well everyone understands what they are doing, and what is happening

- using questioning when everyone has finished and is sitting down, to find out what they understand about what they have done

- using peer assessment to help learners to focus on how to design a good results chart

- using what you find to make adjustments to your teaching plans, if need be.

Topic 1.1 Photosynthesis

LEARNING PLAN

Learning Objectives	Learning intentions	Success criteria
9Bp.06 Know that photosynthesis occurs in chloroplasts and is the process by which plants make carbohydrates, using the energy from light.	• Learn what happens during photosynthesis, and be able to use and understand the word equation.	• Be able to write the photosynthesis equation, and use it to name reactants and products.
9Bp.07 Know and use the summary word equation for photosynthesis (carbon dioxide + water ⊠ glucose + oxygen, in the presence of light and chlorophyll).	• Collect the gas produced in photosynthesis, and test it.	• Collect and test gas produced by a water plant.
9TWSa.01 Evaluate the strength of the evidence collected and how it supports, or refutes, the prediction.	• Carry out a fair test experiment, to find out how light intensity affects the rate of photosynthesis.	• Collect results in the light intensity experiment, draw a graph using these results, and write a conclusion
9TWSa.02 Describe trends and patterns in results, identifying any anomalous results and suggesting why results are anomalous.		
9TWSa.03 Make conclusions by interpreting results, explain the limitations of the conclusions and describe how the conclusions can be further investigated.		
9TWSa.04 Evaluate experiments and investigations, including those done by others, and suggest improvements, explaining any proposed changes.		
9TSWa.05 Present and interpret results, and predict results between the data points collected.		
9TWSc.01 Sort, group and classify phenomena, objects, materials and organisms through testing, observation, using secondary information, and making and using keys.		
9TWSc.02 Decide what equipment is required to carry out an investigation or experiment and use it appropriately.		

CONTINUED

Learning Objectives	Learning intentions	Success criteria
9TWSc.03 Decide when to increase the range of observations and measurements, and increase the extent of repetition, to give sufficiently reliable data.		
9TWSc.04 Take appropriately accurate and precise measurements, explaining why accuracy and precision are important.		
9TWSc.05 Carry out practical work safely, supported by risk assessments where appropriate.		
9TWSc.06 Make an informed decision whether to use evidence from first-hand experience or secondary sources.		
9TWSc.07 Collect, record and summarise sufficient observations and measurements, in an appropriate form.		
9TWSp.01 Suggest a testable hypothesis based on scientific understanding.		
9TWSp.02 Describe examples where scientists' unexpected results from enquiries have led to improved scientific understanding.		
9TWSp.03 Make predictions of likely outcomes for a scientific enquiry based on scientific knowledge and understanding.		
9TWSp.04 Plan a range of investigations of different types to obtain appropriate evidence when testing hypotheses.		
9TWSp.05 Make risk assessments for practical work to identify and control risks.		

Learners will use the following words:

photosynthesis: a series of chemical reactions that take place inside the chloroplasts of plants, in which carbon dioxide and water react together using light energy; the products are glucose (and other carbohydrates) and water

chlorophyll: a green pigment present in chloroplasts, which absorbs energy from light and helps to transfer it to the carbohydrates made in photosynthesis

light intensity: a measure of the quantity of light energy falling onto an object

Common misconceptions

Misconception	How to identify	How to overcome
Learners often say that photosynthesis is the way that plants respire.	Difficulties with this concept are likely to be brought out in *Activity: Photosynthesis and respiration*.	Throughout this unit, make sure that reference is made to respiration in plants.

Starter ideas

1 **Getting started (10 minutes, including sharing ideas)**

Resources: Two plants, or sets of plants; one that has grown in the light and one that has been in the dark. If these are not available then learners can look at the photographs in the Learner's Book.

Description: Ask learners to work with a partner to make a list of any differences they can see. Use their observations to discuss why plants need light.

2 **Words beginning with photo- (5 minutes)**

Description: Organise learners into teams. Ask them to follow the instructions for *Activity: Words beginning with photo-*.

Main teaching ideas

1 **Collecting the gas produced in photosynthesis (10 minutes to set up; leave for one day; another 10 minutes to test the gas collected)**

Learning intention: To observe photosynthesis in a water plant; to obtain first-hand evidence that plants release oxygen gas.

Resources: Per group: a large beaker; a glass funnel; blocks or modelling dough to hold the funnel off the bottom of the beaker; test tube; pond water (tap water can contain chemicals that harm the water plant); a water plant such as *Elodea* or *Cabomba* –

these can be obtained from pet shops or aquarium shops (these plants should not be introduced to ponds or rivers unless they are native to the area).

Description: Learners can set up the apparatus as shown in the diagram in the Learner's Book.

> **Practical guidance:** Before the lesson, keep the water plants in the water that you will use for the experiment, in bright light, so that they are already photosynthesising. Choose short pieces of plant and cut diagonally across the stem – this makes it easier for the bubbles to emerge. When assembling the apparatus, place the pieces of plant upside down, so that the cut end is pointing upwards.

Raising the funnel above the bottom of the beaker enables good water circulation.

Learners can often be clumsy in placing the test-tube full of water over the funnel without the water spilling, and again when removing it at the end of the experiment. Practise this yourself first, then show the learners how to do it correctly.

> **Differentiation ideas:** All learners should be able to assemble the apparatus, but some may need support with removing the tube and testing the gas at the end.

Questions 1 and 2 are likely to be challenging for some learners, who will need support in thinking out possible answers for them.

Learners who need a challenge could be asked if they think that the gas that has collected is likely to be pure oxygen (it is not) and perhaps suggest what other gases might be present.

⟩ **Assessment ideas:** You could assess learners on their ability to work safely, by watching them as they assemble the apparatus and test the gas.

2 Think like a scientist: Investigating how light intensity affects the rate of photosynthesis (40–45 minutes)

Learning intention: To increase confidence in handling apparatus, collecting and analysing results; to practise designing and completing their own results chart. Note: studying the intensity of light goes beyond Stage 9.

Resources: Per group:

- a piece of water plant, pre-treated as described in the previous activity

- a large test tube in which the piece of water plant easily fits

- a means of supporting the test tube – for example, a beaker (whatever is used must not prevent light from passing from the lamp to the tube)

- some pond water

- a lamp – make sure that this is safe, as it will be used close to water (though there is no need at all for any water to come into contact with the lamp, if learners obey safety instructions)

- a ruler to measure the distance between the test-tube and the lamp

- if necessary, a paperclip to weigh down the piece of plant in the tube of water

- a timer.

Description: Ask learners to follow the instructions in the Learner's Book. They should already be familiar with the idea of a water plant giving off bubbles, if they have done the previous activity.

Emphasise the importance of keeping all electrical components away from the water.

It is best to begin with the tube as close as possible to the lamp, as this will give the plant plenty of light so that photosynthesis should be reasonably rapid. If learners start with the lamp far away, nothing at all may happen.

Learners should make three bubble counts at each distance of the tube from the lamp, so that they can later calculate a mean number.

⟩ **Differentiation ideas:** Some learners are likely to need help with setting up their apparatus and collecting results. They may also need help in designing their results chart. Template 1 is provided for this, which you could hand out to any individual or group that needs it.

Learners who need a challenge could be asked to look at the three readings they have made at each distance. Are the three readings the same? If they are not, what does that indicate? They may be able to see that this could mean that another variable might be affecting the number of bubbles, not only the light intensity (which does not change throughout the three readings) – what could this be, and what does it mean for their experiment? It is likely to be something internal to the plant, which we cannot see or measure.

⟩ **Assessment ideas:** There are many skills that could be assessed here, but perhaps it is best to concentrate on the results charts that learners are asked to construct.

3 Activity: Photosynthesis and respiration (15 minutes)

Learning intention: To begin to appreciate the relationship between photosynthesis and respiration.

Description: Organise learners into pairs. Ask them to follow the instructions in the Learner's Book.

Similarities that they might suggest include:

- they are both chemical reactions

- they both have reactants and products

- we can write equations for both

- they both happen inside living cells

- they both involve energy changes

- they both involve carbon dioxide, water, glucose and oxygen.

Differences they might suggest include:

- respiration happens in all cells, but photosynthesis only in some plant cells

- aerobic respiration happens in mitochondria, but photosynthesis happens in chloroplasts

- photosynthesis needs sunlight, but respiration does not

- photosynthesis needs chlorophyll, but respiration does not

- photosynthesis needs an energy input, while respiration releases energy.

⟩ **Differentiation ideas:** All learners can attempt this task. Differentiation will be by outcome, with some pairs providing few or very basic ideas, while others may show greater insight.

Plenary ideas

1 Sharing results charts (15 minutes)

Resources: Everyone's results charts from *Think like a scientist: Investigating how light intensity affects the rate of photosynthesis.*

Description: Put all the results charts onto the wall. Ask learners to bring a chair so that everyone sits in front of the display and can see the charts. Join the group (also sitting on a chair) and ask each group in turn to explain their chart to you all. Use questioning to check how well everyone understands what was happening during the experiment: that they know the photosynthesis equation; that they know how to construct a results chart, and so on. You can also ask the class to suggest one good point about each results chart that is discussed, and ideas about how each results chart could be improved

> **Assessment ideas:** As included in the Description above.

2 Mastermind (5 minutes)

Resources: A card for each learner, with a tick on one side and a cross on the other side.

Description: Choose a learner (or ask for a volunteer) to be Mastermind. You ask the Mastermind a question about photosynthesis based on the work done in this lesson. The Mastermind gives an answer – they can purposefully give a wrong answer if they like. The other members of the class hold up their cards to show whether the answer is correct or incorrect. You can then question the rest of the class to find the correct answer if necessary, or to find out why a learner has identified a correct answer as a wrong one.

Repeat with more questions to the same Mastermind.

> **Assessment ideas:** Use responses of the class to point out any misunderstandings.

Homework ideas

1 Workbook Exercises 1.1A–C

2 Worksheets 1.1A–C

Topic worksheets

- Worksheets 1.1A–C, The beginning of photosynthesis

Topic 1.2 More about photosynthesis

LEARNING PLAN		
Learning Objectives	**Learning intentions**	**Success criteria**
9Bp.06 Know that photosynthesis occurs in chloroplasts and is the process by which plants make carbohydrates, using the energy from light. 9Bp.07 Know and use the summary word equation for photosynthesis (carbon dioxide + water ⬚ glucose + oxygen, in the presence of light and chlorophyll). 9Bp.05 Know that plants require minerals to maintain healthy growth and life processes (limited to magnesium to make chlorophyll and nitrates to make protein).	• Learn about the role of chlorophyll in photosynthesis. • Think about the relationship between structure and function in leaves. • Find out why plants need magnesium and nitrates. • Plan a fair test experiment about the effect of fertilisers on plant growth.	• Explain why chlorophyll is needed for photosynthesis, including explaining the results of testing a variegated leaf for starch. • Answer questions 1 and 2 following *Activity: Which surface of a leaf has most stomata?* • Produce a workable plan for *Think like a scientist: Planning an Investigation into the effect of fertilisers on plant growth.*

CONTINUED

Learning Objectives	Learning intentions	Success criteria
9TWSc.01 Sort, group and classify phenomena, objects, materials and organisms through testing, observation, using secondary information, and making and using keys.		
9TWSc.02 Decide what equipment is required to carry out an investigation or experiment and use it appropriately.		
9TWSc.03 Decide when to increase the range of observations and measurements, and increase the extent of repetition, to give sufficiently reliable data.		
9TWSc.04 Take appropriately accurate and precise measurements, explaining why accuracy and precision are important.		
9TWSc.05 Carry out practical work safely, supported by risk assessments where appropriate.		
9TWSc.06 Make an informed decision whether to use evidence from first-hand experience or secondary sources.		
9TWSc.07 Collect, record and summarise sufficient observations and measurements, in an appropriate form.		
9TWSp.01 Suggest a testable hypothesis based on scientific understanding.		
9TWSp.02 Describe examples where scientists' unexpected results from enquiries have led to improved scientific understanding.		
9TWSp.03 Make predictions of likely outcomes for a scientific enquiry based on scientific knowledge and understanding.		

CONTINUED

Learning Objectives	Learning intentions	Success criteria
9TWSp.04 Plan a range of investigations of different types to obtain appropriate evidence when testing hypotheses. 9TWSp.05 Make risk assessments for practical work to identify and control risks.		

LANGUAGE SUPPORT

Learners will use the following words:

stomata (singular: stoma): a microscopic hole in the surface of a leaf (usually on the underside) through which gases diffuse into and out of the air spaces inside the leaf

fertiliser: a substance containing minerals required by plants, which can be added to soil

yield: the quantity of useful crop obtained at harvest

Common misconceptions

Misconception	How to identify	How to overcome
Learners often state that chlorophyll 'attracts' light, rather than absorbing energy from it.	Oral questioning about the role of chlorophyll, and question 4 in *Think like a scientist: Testing a leaf for starch.*	Constant use of the correct term yourself, and careful checking of learners' spoken and written statements.

Starter ideas

1   **Getting started (10 minutes, including sharing ideas)**

    Resources: A complete plant with roots, stem, leaves and flowers.

    If this is not available, learners can look at the diagram in the Learner's Book instead.

    Description: Ask learners to work individually to answer the questions in the Learner's Book. Then ask for ideas from some of them, and discuss their answers.

2   **What is happening? (5–10 minutes)**

    Description: Show the class a video clip of chloroplasts moving within mesophyll cells. Ask them: What are these structures? (They are cells.) What kind of cells are they? (Plant cells) What are the green objects?

(Chloroplasts). Do you know what happens inside chloroplasts? Can you suggest why they are moving around inside the cells? (It is thought that they move to control the amount of light they receive.)

Main teaching ideas

1   **Think like a scientist: Testing a leaf for starch (25 minutes)**

    Learning intention: To appreciate that plants produce starch and store it; to work safely and observe carefully.

    Resources: Per group:

    *   access to a plant, preferably one with variegated leaves

    *   a burner and beaker to heat water

    *   a tripod and gauze (see diagram in the Learner's Book)

- a large test tube
- forceps (tweezers) to handle the leaves
- iodine in potassium iodide solution, in a small bottle with a dropper
- a white tile.

Per class:

- ethanol – keep this on your desk and provide it to learners only when they have turned off their burner.

Description: Ask learners to follow the instructions in the Learner's Book.

> **Practical guidance:** The day before the lesson, place a potted plant such as a geranium (*Pelargonium*) in a place where it will get plenty of light, and make sure it is watered. If at all possible, use a plant with variegated leaves.

As burners and ethanol are used in this experiment, it is important that everyone is aware that ethanol is flammable and must not be taken close to a flame. Ensure that the burners are turned off before ethanol is collected and taken back to the working area.

Have a damp cloth to hand, so that if a tube of ethanol does catch light you can quickly and simply drop the cloth over it. The flame will go out immediately.

> **Differentiation ideas:** Some learners may need help to follow the instructions carefully, so it would be a good idea to organise groups so that less confident learners can work with those who will find this easier.

Questions 1 to 4 are quite challenging, so you may want to ask some learners to try these on their own, while you provide a little more support (perhaps in the form of scaffolding questions) to others.

> **Assessment ideas:** This is a good opportunity to assess the ability of learners to follow instructions carefully, to work safely and to observe carefully.

2 Activity: Which surface of a leaf has most stomata? (10 minutes)

Learning intention: To relate a diagrammatic drawing of a leaf to a real leaf, and to think about how it exchanges gases with its environment.

Resources: A fresh leaf and a container, such as a cup or beaker with some warm water.

Description: Ask learners to follow the instructions in the Learner's Book.

> **Differentiation ideas:** Everyone can do this activity. Differentiation is likely to be in the outcome of the discussion questions. Use scaffolding questions to help learners who are having difficulty working their way through to some answers.

Assessment ideas

3 **Think like a scientist: Planning an investigation into the effect of fertilisers on plant growth (30 minutes if done just as planning exercise; about 30 minutes to set up experiment, and then 10 minutes every week for a few weeks to collect results)**

Learning intention: To suggest a testable hypothesis; to practise planning a fair test experiment to obtain evidence to test the hypothesis.

Resources: If done as a planning exercise only:

- pictures or specimens of duckweed plants.

If done as an experiment:

- duckweed plants
- small containers such as Petri dishes
- distilled water
- several different types of fertiliser
- top pan balance
- spatulas
- forceps.

Description: Ask learners to follow the instructions in the Learner's Book to construct their plan.

If you are able to let learners do the experiment, tell them what fertilisers will be available before they write their plans. Check the completed plans. We recommend that you do not 'correct' mistakes unless they involve safety – it is better for learners to discover faults in their plan when they try to implement it, which they very often manage to do for themselves. You may, however, need to suggest changes to the apparatus or quantities of materials, if you cannot supply them.

This is not the most reliable of experiments, although, if done carefully, learners are likely to find measurable differences in the growth rates of the plants in different types or concentrations of fertiliser. The plants grow quite quickly, so results should be obtained within three or four weeks, but you may like to leave the experiment running for longer.

> **Differentiation ideas:** All learners can attempt the planning task, and can also make an attempt at carrying out the experiment. Some will need help with planning, and you may like to provide a copy of Template 2. Otherwise, differentiation will be by outcome, with more competent and confident learners producing more robust plans, and working sufficiently carefully to obtain a set of results that they can analyse.

Plenary ideas

1 Sentence starters (5–15 minutes)

Resources: Small cards with words used in Topics 1.1 and 1.2 written on them.

Description: Organise learners into groups of three or four. Put all the cards into a bag. Take the bag to the first group and ask them to pick a card. The group then has to make up a sentence that includes that word.

> **Assessment ideas:** Use the sentences to determine how well learners understand what they have learnt in Topics 1.1 and 1.2.

2 Commentary (20–25 minutes)

Resources: Video clip of photosynthesis.

Description: Show the class a video clip showing water and carbon dioxide entering a leaf, and oxygen being released. Organise learners into groups and ask each group to produce a commentary for the video clip. Then ask each group in turn to give their commentary as the clip plays.

> **Assessment ideas:** Use their commentaries to check understanding of photosynthesis.

Homework ideas

1 Workbook Exercises 1.2A–C

2 Writing the plan for *Think like a scientist: Planning an investigation into the effect of fertilisers on plant growth* makes a good homework task.

Topic worksheets

• There are no worksheets for this topic

Topic 1.3 The carbon cycle

LEARNING OBJECTIVES

Learning Objectives	Learning intentions	Success criteria
9ESc.01 Describe the carbon cycle (limited to photosynthesis, respiration, feeding, decomposition and combustion).	• Be able to describe how carbon atoms move between organisms and the environment.	• Complete a diagram of the carbon cycle, and answer questions about it.

LANGUAGE SUPPORT

There is no new vocabulary in this topic.

Common misconceptions

Misconception	How to identify	How to overcome
Learners may not understand the concept of a compound, and not appreciate that carbon atoms can exist on their own, or within compounds.	Try the Getting started task in the Learner's Book.	Discuss any incorrect answers to the Getting started task. *Activity: Modelling the carbon cycle* will also help.

Starter ideas

1 Getting started (10 minutes, including sharing ideas)

Resources: None.

Description: Ask learners to work with a partner and follow the instructions in the Learner's Book.

After a few minutes, ask some of them for their responses to the questions. Check that everyone appreciates that carbon atoms are always carbon atoms, no matter where they are or what they are combined with.

2 Why is carbon dioxide important? (10 minutes)

Description: Organise learners into groups of three or four. Ask each group to think of two things that they know about carbon dioxide. Allow two or three minutes.

Then ask each group for their suggestions, writing them down on a flip chart. Leave them there, so that they can be referred to at appropriate points during the rest of this topic.

Main teaching ideas

1 Building up a diagram of the carbon cycle (30–40 minutes)

Learning intention: To gradually construct the carbon cycle.

Resources: Text and diagrams in the Learner's Book.

Description: Work through the text and diagrams in the Learner's Book to slowly build up a complete diagram of the carbon cycle. Involve learners in each step, using questioning to engage them in thinking about what the boxes and arrows mean. Building up the cycle together greatly helps with understanding; the cycle can be overwhelming if presented in its entirety.

> **Differentiation ideas:** This is a whole-class activity. Make sure that each learner is involved in answering questions or making suggestions.

Some learners may be reluctant to answer questions, but you can help them to increase their confidence by specifically targeting them with relatively straightforward questions that you think they can answer. Include some questions involving higher order thinking skills to provide a challenge.

2 Think like a scientist: How do plants and animals affect carbon dioxide concentration? (20 minutes to set up the experiment; 10 minutes to collect results, which can be done at the end of the same lesson, or learners can come back to look at their tubes several hours later)

Learning intention: To bring together earlier work on respiration and photosynthesis.

Resources: Per group:

- six large test tubes, each fitted with a little platform made out of perforated metal (or you can give the pieces of metal to the learners and ask them to make the platforms), and each with a rubber bung to fit tightly
- hydrogencarbonate indicator solution; this must be fresh, and preferably kept with air bubbling through it to ensure it is in equilibrium with the carbon dioxide concentration in the air
- water plants that have been kept in the light and are photosynthesising
- small invertebrate animals; for example, you may be able to obtain fly larvae (maggots) from shops that sell fishing equipment
- blunt forceps
- black paper and sticky tape.

Description: Show learners how to set up the experiment. Ask them to predict the results. Then ask them to follow the instructions in the Learner's Book.

> **Differentiation ideas:** Some learners will need further support in setting up their experiment.

The questions at the end of this task are quite challenging, and it is likely that not all learners will be able to work their way through to question 5 to give successful answers. Be prepared to give more support if necessary.

> **Assessment ideas:** Answers to the questions will give a good indication of how well learners understand the relationship between the gases used and emitted during respiration and photosynthesis.

3 Activity: Modelling the carbon cycle
(20–25 minutes)

Learning intention: To make the abstract concept of the carbon cycle more concrete and, hence, deepen understanding.

Resources: Coloured card and marker pens for making labels; see the instructions about this in the Learner's Book.

Description: Explain to learners that each of them is going to be a carbon atom. Talk through the instructions with them and explain what they are all going to do. Write the processes that match each number on the die on the board so that everyone can see them clearly.

Place all the 'carbon atoms' in the five labelled places, with roughly equal numbers in each place.

Roll a die and call out the number on it (or you can ask a learner who is not a carbon atom to do this). The learners who are affected by the process indicated by this number move to the appropriate place. Watch them carefully — there is likely to be confusion to start with, but this is all part of the learning process!

Continue until you feel that enough has been done, or all the carbon atoms have ended up in the same place.

⟩ **Differentiation ideas:** Everyone can do this activity. Some learners may find it difficult to link the number to a process, and to link a process to what they are supposed to do; they are likely to cope by following others. Learners who need a challenge can think about the shortcomings of this model, in particular the way in which every carbon atom in one place moves to another at the same time. They could be asked to try modifying the model so that it works better.

Plenary ideas

1 Events in the carbon cycle (10 minutes)

Resources: Images of stages in the carbon cycle from the Learner's Book or from an online search, or a video clip of events in the carbon cycle from an online search.

Description: Show learners the pictures of the different stages, or show learners a video clip of the carbon cycle. Ask learners how what they can see in each image (or each stage if using a video clip) relates to a stage in the carbon cycle.

⟩ **Assessment ideas:** Use questioning about the images or the video clip, and answers, to determine how well learners understand the events in the carbon cycle.

2 Fill in the blanks: carbon cycle
(10 minutes)

Resources: Whiteboard and markers

Description: Set this up as a class exercise. Organise learners into pairs or threes. On the whiteboard, write one stage of the carbon cycle in a box and draw an arrow leading from the box. Ask the first group of learners to suggest which stage comes next. Then move on to the next group to suggest another stage or an arrow, and so on until the whole cycle has been completed.

Homework ideas

1 Workbook Exercise 1.3
2 Worksheets 1.3A–C

Topic worksheets

• Worksheets 1.3A–C, Building a carbon cycle

Topic 1.4 Climate change

LEARNING PLAN

Learning Objectives	Learning intentions	Success criteria
9ESc.02 Describe the historical and predicted future impacts of climate change, including sea level change, flooding, drought and extreme weather events. 9ESs.01 Describe the consequences of asteroid collision with the Earth, including climate change and mass extinctions.	• Be able to relate understanding of the carbon cycle to the causes of global warming. • Explain some of the consequences of climate change. • Describe the effects of asteroid collisions with the Earth.	• Be able to list current and predicted impacts of climate change. • Explain how asteroid collisions have affected life on Earth.

LANGUAGE SUPPORT

Learners will use the following words:

slush: partly-melted snow

mass extinction: the complete loss of a very large number of species

meteoroids: objects in space that are smaller than an asteroid

meteors: a meteoroid when it moves through the Earth's atmosphere

meteorite: part of a meteor that reaches the Earth's surface

Common misconceptions

Misconception	How to identify	How to overcome
It is very common for learners to think that the greenhouse effect is a 'bad thing'.	Use questioning after the Getting started activity to ask: What would the Earth be like if there was no carbon dioxide in the atmosphere? What happens if there is too much?	Take care to use the term 'enhanced greenhouse effect' when you mean the result of increased carbon dioxide in the atmosphere.

Starter ideas

1 **Getting started (5–10 minutes)**

   Resources: Diagram in the Learner's Book.

   Description: Ask learners to work in pairs to match the statements to the diagram. Then ask for their suggestions and determine the correct label for each arrow.

2 **What do you know about climate change? (5–10 minutes)**

   Description: Ask learners: 'Tell me one thing about climate change.'

   Go round the class, asking each learner to tell you what they have thought of. Make sure that you limit each learner to only one statement. You may like to write the statements on the board or a flip chart to refer to as you work through the rest of the topic.

This activity will elicit preconceptions and help you to determine where you are starting from as you work through this topic.

Main teaching ideas

1 Climate change in the past (20–30 minutes)

Learning intention: To understand that climate change is not 'new', and how and why the climate has differed in the past.

Resources: Text and images in the Learner's Book.

Description: Use the Learner's Book as a scaffold for discussing how and why the Earth's climate has changed in the past. You could ask learners for spoken answers to questions 1, 2, 3 and 4.

> **Differentiation ideas:** Use questioning to involve everyone in the discussion, ensuring that even the least confident learners are encouraged to make a contribution. All learners can contribute, and differentiation will be by the type of questions that they ask and answer.

2 Think like a scientist: How do rising temperatures affect sea level? (30–40 minutes)

Learning intention: To understand how melting ice affects sea level.

Resources: Per group:

- two large measuring cylinders
- a large funnel (to hold at least 10 ice cubes)
- access to at least 20 ice cubes
- a conical flask, fitted with a two-hole bung, with a thermometer in one hole and a glass or plastic tube in the other (see the diagram in the Learner's Book); just before the activity begins, fill each flask right to the top with cold water
- a lamp
- a timer (optional)

Description: Instructions for this experiment are given in the Learner's Book. You may like to demonstrate how to set up each experiment before asking learners to do so themselves.

> **Practical guidance:** Try to ensure that all the ice cubes are roughly the same size. It is a good idea to trial the experiments yourself, to get an idea of how long it will take the ice to melt. If this takes too long use smaller cubes.

For the second experiment there is no need to record the time at which readings were taken. It is the relationship between temperature and the water level that is being investigated. However, learners may want to make sure that they take readings at roughly the same time intervals, and it is fine for them to do this.

> **Differentiation ideas:** Some learners may need help with constructing the graph, and could be given axes, perhaps with scales, to start them off.

Learners who need a further challenge could be asked to suggest how well these experiments represent what happens in the real world, and how they might modify them to make their models more realistic.

> **Assessment ideas:** Use the results tables, graphs and answers to questions to assess learners.

3 Activity: The carbon cycle and climate change (20–30 minutes)

Learning intention: To think about how the carbon cycle affects climate; to begin to think about how we might be able to reduce the negative impacts of climate change.

Note that there is no requirement in the Curriculum Framework to discuss actions that can be taken to mitigate climate change, but it is important to give learners the idea that we *can* do something about it.

Resources: Diagram of the carbon cycle from the Learner's Book. You could also use the video of events in the carbon cycle.

Description: Organise learners into groups of three or four, and ask them to answer the two questions about activities that increase and decrease carbon dioxide concentration. Then, in their groups, they should write a list of suggestions about how the increases in carbon dioxide concentration can be halted or even reversed.

You can then chair a discussion, allowing each group to put forward their views.

> **Differentiation ideas:** Everyone should be able to take part in this activity. Working in groups will give confidence to less self-assured learners. More confident learners are likely to suggest a wider range of ideas and have deeper insights into the difficulties in implementing targets that could reduce the impacts of climate change.

Plenary ideas

1 Impacts of climate change
   (20–25 minutes)

   Resources: Learners' responses to Worksheet 1.4, Impacts of climate change.

   Description: As you approach the end of this topic, set learners Worksheet 1.4. This could be done individually or in small groups, in class or for homework. Each learner puts themselves in the place of one of the people listed on the worksheet, or someone else of their own choosing, and describes how climate change is affecting their life.

   During this plenary session, ask for volunteers to share their descriptions with the rest of the class. Use these descriptions to stimulate discussion of climate change impacts.

   ⟩ **Assessment ideas:** The descriptions given by the learners, and the discussion, will show how well learners understand the impacts that climate change is having and will have in the future.

2 Team quiz (20–30 minutes)

   Description: Organise learners into teams of three or four.

   Remind them of the topics they have covered in this unit: photosynthesis, the carbon cycle and climate change.

Ask each group to write one question about each of these topics (three questions in all). They must also write the answers.

The first group asks their first question and the other groups try to answer it. The person who gives the correct answer then asks their first question, and so on.

If any group does not answer enough questions to be automatically able to ask their questions, you can intervene to give them the opportunity to do so.

⟩ **Assessment ideas:** Both the questions and the answers to them will indicate how well learners remember and understand the facts and concepts covered in this unit.

Homework ideas

1 Workbook Exercise 1.3

2 Worksheet 1.4; this could be done for homework before the final lesson in this topic, and answers used in a plenary session.

Topic worksheet

• Worksheet 1.4, Impacts of climate change

PROJECT GUIDANCE

This project addresses the following learning objectives:

9ESs.01 Describe the consequences of asteroid collision with the Earth, including climate change and mass extinctions.

9SIC.01 Discuss how scientific knowledge is developed through collective understanding and scrutiny over time.

9SIC.04 Describe how people develop and use scientific understanding as individuals and through collaboration, e.g. through peer review.

This project provides learners with the opportunity to work together to discover more about the events that we believe happened about 67 million years ago when an asteroid collided with Earth.

It is best if you, or the class, decide at an early stage what form the final presentation will take. It could be a display of posters to put onto the wall, or a series of talks or perhaps a video containing presentations from each group.

The guidance in the Learner's Book suggests five different issues to research. Depending on the size of your class, you might like to reduce this number, or possibly add more (or split some of these to make more). You may also like to do your own research first, using the suggested search terms. If learners are not very confident in using the internet and finding reliable information, you may like to suggest some specific websites for them to look at.

The size and make-up of your class will determine how best to organise the groups. Groups of three or four generally work well, ensuring that everyone can be actively involved, and that the workload on any one person is not too great. For this project you may prefer to have mixed-ability groups so that less confident learners can be supported by others in the group.

>2 Properties of materials

Unit plan

Topic	Learning hours	Learning content	Resources
2.1 Atomic structure and the Periodic Table	2-3	The structure of the atom and Periodic Table	**Learner's Book:** Questions 1–7 Activity: A model of an atom **Workbook:** Exercise 2.1, Atomic structure **Teacher's Resource:** Worksheets 2.1A–C, Matching terms and facts Template 1: Peer assessment of *Activity: A model atom*
2.2 Trends in Groups within the Periodic Table	2-3	Trends in Groups 1, 7 and 8 in the Periodic Table linked with the atomic structures of the elements	**Learner's Book:** Questions 1–23 Think like a scientist: Observation of the reactions of Group 1 metals with water **Workbook:** Exercise 2.2A, Elements in the same group Exercise 2.2B, Trends in groups in the Periodic Table Exercise 2.2C, Comparing trends in Groups 1 and 7 **Teacher's Resource:** Worksheets 2.2A–C, Elements in Group 1 and Group 8 Template 2: Observations and explanations sheet for *Think like a scientist: Observation of the reactions of Group 1 metals with water*
2.3 Why elements react to form compounds	2-3	Why elements react to form compounds; formation of ionic and covalent bonds	**Learner's Book:** Questions 1–16 Activity: Forming ionic compounds **Workbook:** Exercise 2.3A, Atoms and ions Exercise 2.3B, Why do ions form? Exercise 2.3C, Forming ionic compounds **Teacher's Resource:** Worksheets 2.3A–C, Ionic and covalent bonds Template 3: Peer assessment sheet for *Activity: Forming ionic compounds*

Topic	Learning hours	Learning content	Resources
2.4 Simple and giant structures	3–4	Simple and giant structures; details of the structures and the link between the structures and the properties	**Learner's Book:** Questions 1–12 Activity: Building giant structures Think like a scientist: Ionic compounds conducting electricity **Workbook:** Exercise 2.4A, Ionic or covalent bonds Exercise 2.4B, Properties of ionic and covalent substances Exercise 2.4C, Giant structures of carbon **Teacher's Resource:** Template 4: Peer assessment sheet for *Building giant structures*
Cross-unit resources			**Learner's Book:** Check your Progress **Project:** Building the Periodic Table **Teacher's resource:** Language development worksheets 2.1 Using the correct word 2.2 Matching words and meanings and distinguishing between terms

BACKGROUND/PRIOR KNOWLEDGE

Learners will have some idea of the structure of the atom and the Periodic Table from Stage 8, Unit 5. They should be able to build on this knowledge of the parts of the atom and the fact that each type of atom is different. This unit develops the ideas and gives details of the improvement in the model of the atom they met in Stage 8. There may need to be some discussion of why the idea of structure covered in Stage 8 is different and it is worthwhile spending some time going over the fact that scientists' ideas change when they have more information. Learners will have some idea that elements in the same group of the Periodic Table have properties in common, but will need to link this to their electronic structures.

You will need to spend some time going over the electronic structures of various atoms in preparation for the section on why atoms join together to form compounds. Learners may find it difficult to grasp the ideas of ion formation and molecule formation, so the repeated use of various examples and some practice may be needed.

Learners will have experience, from earlier stages, of the idea that atoms can join together to form compounds and can use the more detailed information in this unit to explain how and why bonds form.

The section on giant structures will be new to learners, but some experience of building 3D models of diamond and graphite will help them to understand the great differences in properties of two substances that are made of the same element.

TEACHING SKILLS FOCUS

Moving towards peer- and self-assessment

When a teacher assesses the work of a learner, they may be looking for a number of things, such as:

- what the learner has understood and can explain
- where the learner may have misconceptions
- how the teacher can prepare the next steps for the learning of this particular learner
- what the learner needs to do in order to overcome any misconceptions
- what the teacher needs to do to improve their teaching of this topic
- how much effort this learner has made.

Often the teacher needs to have a dialogue with the learner to address the points above, so only putting a grade on a piece of work is of limited value in helping learners improve their knowledge and understanding. As a result, teachers often write a great deal on learners' work in order to help them. However, many learners are more interested in the grade and not in comments made by the teacher. One way of addressing this is to return work to learners with no grades but only comments. Some teachers may require learners to respond to their written feedback and then check this and make another comment. This can take a significant amount of teacher time. Some teachers choose to highlight points in the work but give class feedback where the teacher addresses common issues raised by the marking.

Moving towards peer- and self-assessment ensures that the learners take a more active part in their progress and an active responsibility for their own and their peers' learning. It also has the benefit of giving the teacher feedback on the learners' knowledge and understanding in a less time-consuming manner.

To establish these modes of assessment, the learners could be encouraged to listen to responses to questions in class and decide if an answer is reasonable; can they add anything to the answer or would they give another answer?

You could use this idea with actual answers given by class members or you could use answers that you have heard when you asked this question to other classes. This allows learners to decide how valid answers are or how detailed they need to be and to discuss common misunderstandings. It also gives them an idea of the standard of answer required and helps to build confidence in their understanding.

There are examples of peer-assessment templates throughout this course that encourage learners to look at the criteria for assessment and to identify where they or their partner have done well and what it is they need to focus on to improve. Using some of these to feedback to the entire class and to discuss the assessment provides an opportunity for whole class discussion about the topic and where the misconceptions are. For presentations that have been done by a group, you could take questions about the work from the class and you could act as the chairperson passing on each question to the most suitable member of the group. This provides a means of addressing areas the class are unsure about.

You could give your class a question, a mark scheme and some answers from anonymous learners to assess and ask them to suggest how the answers could be improved. You could also ask them to suggest what the answer tells them about the knowledge and understanding of the learner who wrote it and how this could be improved. By sharing these ideas with others, your learners will begin to focus on what they need to do to improve.

Another suggestion for learners to assess their own level of confidence with a particular piece of work is for them to decide if they are 'green' (happy with their understanding), 'amber' (not quite sure) or 'red' (very unsure). By assessing the colours in the room you can match greens with ambers or reds, or if there are a lot of reds it may mean that more in-depth teaching is needed.

Topic 2.1 Atomic structure and the Periodic Table

LEARNING PLAN

Learning Objectives	Learning intentions	Success criteria
9Cm.01 Understand that the structure of the Periodic Table is related to the atomic structure of the elements and the Periodic Table can be used to predict an element's structure and properties. 9Cp.02 Describe how the density of a substance relates to its mass in a defined volume. 9TWSm.01 Understand that models and analogies reflect current scientific evidence and understanding and can change. 9TWSm.02 Describe some important models, including analogies, and discuss their strengths and weaknesses. 9TWSm.03 Use symbols and formulae to represent scientific ideas.	• Describe the Rutherford–Bohr model of the atom. • Use the Periodic Table to describe and/or draw the atomic structures of the first 20 elements. • Understand how the elements are arranged in the Periodic Table. • Use the Periodic Table to predict an element's structure and properties. • Understand how the density of a substance relates to its mass in a defined volume.	• Be able to draw and label the structure of an atom using the Rutherford–Bohr model. • Be able to draw the atomic structure of the first 20 elements using the data from the Periodic Table. • Describe how the elements are arranged in the Periodic Table. • Predict the structure and properties of an element using the Periodic Table. • Be able to explain what is meant by, and calculate the density of, a substance.

LANGUAGE SUPPORT

Learners will use the following words:

Periodic Table: a table of all the elements placed in order of their atomic number

atomic number: the number of protons in an atom: each type of atom has a unique atomic number

mass number: the number of protons and neutrons in an atom added together

electron shells: the layers of electrons arranged around the nucleus of an atom

energy levels: the layers or shells of electrons are referred to as being at different energy levels

electronic structure: the arrangement of electrons in the shells or levels around the nucleus of an atom

electrostatic forces: forces of attraction between particles with opposite electrical charges

Common misconceptions

Misconception	How to identify	How to overcome
Many learners do not understand how small atoms are. Learners do not believe that most of the atom is empty space.	Ask learners directly what they think is between the electrons or between the nucleus and the electrons.	Spend some time drawing the models of the atoms and drawing the learners' attention to the amount of relative space. This needs to be reinforced at every opportunity.
Some of the learners find it difficult to remember which particle goes where.	Ask learners to label models of the atom.	Spend some time drawing the models of the atoms and drawing the learners' attention to the location of the particles.

Starter ideas

1 Getting started (10 minutes)

Learning intention: To revise the structure of the atom.

Description: Ask learners to list the parts of an atom. Ask learners to give at least one fact about each part. Then ask them to use the names of the parts and the facts to write a description of the atom. You could ask learners to do this on their own and then compare with a partner or they could do it in pairs and then feedback to the whole class.

2 Finding a word (10 minutes)

Learning intention: To improve vocabulary.

Resources: Learner's Book.

Description: Write the word 'neutron' vertically on the board. Challenge learners to find scientific words starting with those letters. You could restrict learners to words connected with this particular topic or give them a wider choice of vocabulary, deciding whether or not to allow access to the Learner's Book.

Allow a fixed time (5 minutes or less) and ask for ideas from the learners. Check that learners have an idea what each word means. You can award points for a correct word and extra points if no one else has this word.

Make sure learners do not just go for difficult words they do not know the meaning of, although some learners love to find the hardest words they can. This can be a real boost to their scientific vocabulary, especially if this technique is used regularly.

Main teaching ideas

1 The Periodic Table (15–20 minutes)

Learning intention: To look at the arrangement of elements in the Periodic Table and to explain the terms mass number and atomic number.

Resources: A large poster of the Periodic Table (or an electronic version) and/or the Learner's Book.

Description: Draw the learners' attention to the Periodic Table and ask them about where they would find the metals/non-metals or the symbols for the elements, building on the knowledge from previous stages. Explain the meanings of the numbers in each square (mass number and atomic number) and go over what these numbers tell you. You could work through the worked example in the Learner's Book and ask learners to complete the details for other elements.

The idea that the larger the mass number, the more mass an element has, is not difficult for the learners to grasp. However, the idea of density could be very difficult to grasp for some learners. Reference to density has been made here as it addresses one of the two learning objectives for chemistry that involve density. The details of these learning objectives are covered fully in Unit 3, Topic 3.1.

You could spend some time measuring blocks of different materials to calculate the densities to reinforce the ideas for learners.

〉 **Differentiation ideas:** You could use elements with lower atomic numbers with learners who need support and use those with higher atomic numbers for learners who need a challenge. You could write the symbols of all these elements on card and ask learners to choose one to do.

You could colour-code the symbols on card to assign suitable elements to those learners who need a challenge.

> **Assessment ideas:** You could use the answer from the different elements and their number of protons, neutrons and electrons to assess learners' understanding.

2 Arranging the electrons (15–20 minutes)

Learning intention: To compare the Rutherford model of the atom with that of Bohr and to explain the distribution of electrons in the different atoms.

Resources: Learner's Book.

Description: Revise the structure of the atom from Stage 8 and discuss the changes to this model that were made by Bohr. This is a good opportunity to discuss the way that models change when scientific knowledge and understanding changes. Spend some time going through the idea of the shells or energy levels and explaining that the electrons move around within that shell. Give the learners practice in writing out the electronic structures.

> **Differentiation ideas:** Use those elements with lower atomic numbers with learners who have less confidence and use elements with higher atomic numbers with those who need a challenge.

> **Assessment ideas:** You could use questions 1–7 to assess progress and understanding.

3 Activity: A model atom (at least 40 minutes)

Learning intention: To understand and reinforce the structure of the atom.

Resources: Scissors, hole punch, string, glue, card in different colours (red, blue, green and another colour for the shells), coloured paper could be used for the electrons, protons and neutrons if preferred.

Description: You could assign one of the first twenty elements to each of your learners or you could ask them to choose by picking a piece of paper, marked with one of these twenty elements, from a box. Ensure that you have more pieces of paper than learners so that everyone feels that they have a choice. Learners could work on their own or in pairs.

It is useful to have a number of strong card templates for the learners to use. These will have to be prepared well in advance. The nucleus could be the size of a glass or approximately 5–6 cm in diameter. The first shell for electrons could be a ring based on the size of a small plate; the ring needs to be between 1–2 cm wide. The second shell could be based on a larger plate and the final one even larger. You could use a drawing pin, string and a small pencil to draw the nucleus and concentric circles for the electron shells from one sheet of strong card.

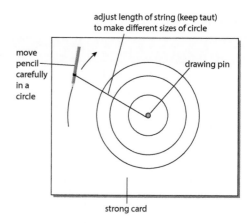

The small circles for the electrons, protons and neutrons should be cut out in different colours. Cut twice as many, so that they can be stuck on both sides of the nucleus and shells. Build up the shells and nucleus first. Then make a hole in the nucleus card and the inner edge of the first shell and use a piece of string to join them. Then make another hole in the outer edge of the first shell and join it to the second shell. The shells should hang freely. Use a string from the top of the final shell to hang the model from the ceiling. It is also useful to hang a label from the bottom of the model that lists the name of the element, the electronic structure and the numbers of protons, neutrons and electrons.

These models can be used to provide an interesting display in a corridor or display area within the school.

> **Differentiation ideas:** You could assign the lower atomic number elements to learners who are less dextrous. It may be necessary to have some learners do more than one element.

You could assign the higher atomic numbers to those learners who need a challenge.

> **Assessment ideas:** You could use Template 1 to assess the models.

Plenary ideas

1 Pyramid ideas (10 minutes)

Resources: None.

Description:

Ask learners to complete the pyramid and use it as an exit card so that you have a chance to see what, if anything, they need to have explained to them in the next session.

⟩ **Reflection ideas:** Use the reflection point idea about reviewing the models of the atom and their use.

2 Quick-fire atomic structure (10 minutes)

Resources: Periodic Table.

Description: Select elements at random and ask learners to give the number of protons, number of neutrons, number of electrons and the electronic structure for each element. You could do this as a class activity or as an 'in the hot seat' activity where a confident learner can be in the hot seat and can choose to give the correct or an incorrect answer and the class challenge them if they think they have given an incorrect answer.

⟩ **Assessment ideas:** You could use the answers to the previous activity as an assessment of knowledge and understanding.

CROSS-CURRICULAR LINKS

Maths : learners use basic operations to find the number of neutrons in an atom, and to find the relative masses of different atoms.

Homework ideas

1   Workbook Exercise 2.1

2   Worksheets 2.1A–C

Topic worksheets

•   Worksheets 2.1A–C, Matching terms and facts

Topic 2.2 Trends in groups within the Periodic Table

LEARNING PLAN

Learning Objectives	Learning intentions	Success criteria
9Cm.01 Understand that the structure of the Periodic Table is related to the atomic structure of the elements and the Periodic Table can be used to predict an element's structure and properties. 9Cp.01 Understand that the groups within the Periodic Table have trends in physical and chemical properties, using Group 1 as an example. 9TWSm.03 Use symbols and formulae to represent scientific ideas.	• Learn about the similarities between different elements in the same groups in the Periodic Table. • Relate the structure of the Periodic Table to the structure of the elements. • Use the Periodic Table to predict the structure and properties of elements.	• Describe the similarities between different elements in the same groups in the Periodic Table. • Relate the structure of the Periodic Table to the structure of the elements. • Use the Periodic Table to predict the structure and properties of elements.

LANGUAGE SUPPORT

Learners will use the following words:

alkali metals: metals in Group 1 of the Periodic Table that produce alkalis when they react with water

halogens: the elements found in Group 7 of the Periodic Table

noble gases: the elements found in Group 8 of the Periodic Table

Common misconceptions

Misconception	How to identify	How to overcome
Some learners may find the atomic structures difficult to understand and thus to compare them.	Listen to the learners as they try to compare the structures of the various elements.	Reinforce the structures by giving learners lots of opportunities to draw out the structures for themselves.

Starter ideas

1 Getting started (10 minutes)

Learning intention: To familiarise the learners with the Periodic Table and to revise the terms group and period.

Resources: A copy of the Periodic Table.

Description: Use a copy of the Periodic Table and ask learners to find a metal in the same group as magnesium; a metal in the same period as magnesium; a non-metallic solid in the same period as magnesium and a gas in the same period as magnesium.

Learners should compare their answers with a partner and then use both their answers to include all the elements that apply in each case.

2 First to find ... (10 minutes)

Learning intention: To familiarise the learners with the Periodic Table.

Resources: A copy of the Periodic Table for each learner.

Description: Make sure each learner has a copy of the Periodic Table within reach. Call out an element and ask the learners to place their index finger on this square in the table and raise their hand when they have done so. You can vary this by asking for the element with atomic number 10 or 14 or with the mass number 7 or 39.

This can become loud, but it is worth doing so that the learners become familiar with the Periodic Table and makes them look more closely than they might otherwise have done.

Main teaching ideas

1 Think like a scientist: Observation of the reactions of Group 1 metals with water (30 minutes)

Learning intention: To show the differences in the behaviour of elements within the same group in the Periodic Table, in order to be able to relate them to the atomic structure of the elements.

Resources: Safety glasses for everyone present in the room, large trough of water, safety screen or screens large enough to protect everyone in the class (including the teacher), white tile, scalpel or knife, long forceps, samples of the three metals (lithium, sodium and potassium) stored under oil, paper towels, filter paper (optional), universal indicator solution (optional).

Description: This activity should be an observed demonstration. It could be illustrated by using clips from the internet but nothing is as good as actually being there when this demonstration is done.

Learners are impressed by these reactions and are always keen to see them again and to film them if they have the necessary equipment.

You can use this opportunity to discuss the properties of metals, especially as the Group 1 metals are not like most of the metals learners will have met before.

Start with lithium since it is the least reactive. Remove a small piece from the stock bottle with the forceps. It would be useful to discuss with the learners both the way lithium is stored and why it is handled using forceps. Cut a small piece off on the white tile using the scalpel. Return any unused pieces to the bottle as soon as possible. Use paper towels to mop up any spills from the oil.

Point out the shiny surface of the newly cut metal to the learners and discuss with them why the surfaces that have not been newly cut are not shiny. (This is because these metals are very reactive and react with the oxygen in the air to form a compound, an oxide, which covers the surface). Link this to the properties of metals that they would normally expect.

A small piece of lithium, no bigger than a pea, can then be placed on the surface of the water of the trough and the reaction observed. (Alternatively, some teachers like to place the metal on a piece of filter paper before floating it on the water.) Note that if you do this with sodium the temperature reached is sufficient to ignite the hydrogen because heat is not dissipated by the metal skating around on the surface. Extra care is needed as a glassy bead of sodium hydroxide is formed which may catch fire and spit, so stand well back.

You will probably have to draw learners' attention to the finer details, such as the metal getting hot and forming a ball. Once the reaction has been observed you may want to repeat it after adding universal indicator solution to a fresh trough of water to show a change in pH and discuss the reaction that has taken place. This would be a good opportunity to remind the learners of the use of word equations.

Repeat the above using sodium and then potassium. Ensure that the piece of sodium used is smaller than used for lithium and the piece of potassium is even smaller. This is because of the heat generated and the explosive nature of the reactions, especially with potassium, which can lead to pieces of the metal being thrown out over great distances.

The purpose of this activity is to illustrate the trends in a group in the Periodic Table, so ensure that you allow learners to compare the reactions of the three metals.

> **Practical guidance:** There are real safety concerns about this demonstration. Ensure that the learners are far enough back from the trough, they are all wearing safety glasses and that they do not touch the metals. Ensure that the learners are behind the safety screen; you need to be protected by a safety screen too. Use long forceps to place the small piece of metal in the trough and keep your face on the safe side of the safety screen (this is why you may need more than one safety screen). Ensure there is good ventilation. Do not touch the metals with bare hands as they may react with moisture on the hands and cause burns; wear surgical gloves.

> **Differentiation ideas:** You could use Template 2 with some learners who need support to help them record the observations.

Learners who need a challenge could be asked to complete Workbook Exercise 2.2C.

> **Assessment ideas:** You could use Template 2 to assess the explanations of the observations made in this activity.

2 Atomic structures in Group 1 metals (15–20 minutes)

Learning intention: To relate the atomic structure of the elements in Group 1 to their behaviour.

Resources: Learner's Book, large copy of the Periodic Table.

Description: Draw learners' attention to Group 1 on the Periodic Table and use the information about atomic and mass numbers to construct diagrams to show the atomic structure. Discuss the similarities and differences in atomic structure and link them to

the data shown in the table in the Learner's Book and to the demonstration of the reactions with water.

> **Differentiation ideas:** You could ask learners to draw their own atomic structures for the Group 1 metals to reinforce the ideas if they are finding it a challenge to see the differences and similarities.

Learners who need a challenge could be asked to predict the behaviour of other Group 1 metals. Avoid asking them to predict the atomic structure of other Group 1 metals, such as rubidium, as this will cause confusion and is a level of detail not required at this stage.

> **Assessment ideas:** You could use the questions in the Learner's Book to assess knowledge and understanding.

3 Looking at Group 7 and Group 8 (30 minutes)

Learning intention: To relate the atomic structure of elements in the same group to their properties.

Resources: Learner's Book.

Description: Draw learners' attention to Group 7 on the Periodic Table and then work through the table of data about these elements and link that to the atomic structures of the elements concerned. Then do the same for the elements in Group 8 of the Periodic Table.

> **Differentiation ideas:** You could ask learners to draw their own atomic structures for Group 7 and Group 8 elements to reinforce the ideas if they are finding it a challenge to see the differences and similarities.

> **Assessment ideas:** You could use the questions in the Learner's Book to assess knowledge and understanding.

Plenary ideas

1 More or less / larger or smaller (10 minutes)

Resources: Periodic Table.

Description: Choose one of the elements in Groups 1, 7 or 8. Ask learners to decide if this element is more or less reactive than the one above or below it in the Periodic Table. For example, if you choose sodium, the question could be 'Is sodium more or less reactive than lithium?'. You could ask 'Does sodium have a higher or lower atomic number than potassium?'

You could ask learners to do this as individuals and then compare their answers with a partner, or you could ask learners to work with a partner.

> **Reflection ideas:** Ask learners: How does the atomic structure of an element relate to its position in the Periodic Table?

2 Quick-fire atomic structures
(10 minutes)

Description: Ask learners to draw the atomic structures of lithium, sodium and potassium. This could be done on mini white boards or on paper and then reviewed by a partner.

Homework ideas

1 Workbook Exercises 2.2A–C

Topic worksheets

- Worksheets 2.2A–C, Elements in Group 1 and Group 8

Topic 2.3 Why elements react to form compounds

LEARNING PLAN

Learning Objectives	Learning intentions	Success criteria
9Cm.02 Understand that a molecule is formed when two or more atoms join together chemically, through a covalent bond. 9Cm.03 Describe a covalent bond as a bond made when a pair of electrons is shared by two atoms (limited to single bonds). 9Cm.04 Describe an ion as an atom which has gained at least one electron to be negatively charged or lost at least one electron to be positively charged. 9Cm.05 Describe an ionic bond as an attraction between a positively charged ion and a negatively charged ion. 9Cc.01 Use word equations and symbol equations to describe reactions (balancing symbol equations is not required). 9TWSm.03 Use symbols and formulae to represent scientific ideas.	• Describe the structure of an ion and compare it with that of an atom. • Understand how ionic and covalent bonds are formed. • Understand what a molecule is. • Write the formulae of some ionic compounds.	• Show the differences between the structure of an ion and an atom. • Be able to explain how ionic and covalent bonds are formed. • Be able to explain what a molecule is. • Be able to write the formulae of some ionic compounds.

LANGUAGE SUPPORT

Learners will use the following words:

stable: firmly fixed

chemical bond: ways in which elements are joined together to form compounds

ion: an atom with a net electric charge due to the loss or gain of one or more electrons

ionic bond: a link formed between two or more ions to form a compound

ionic compound: a compound formed when the ions of a metal and a non-metal react together

molecule: a particle formed when atoms are bonded together with covalent bonds

covalent bond: a link formed when atoms share electrons to form a molecule

dot and cross diagram: a way of showing atoms sharing electrons to form a covalent bond

Common misconceptions

Misconception	How to identify	How to overcome
Some learners think that an atom and an ion are the same thing.	Ask learners to explain the differences between the structure of atoms and ions of various elements.	Ask learners to draw examples of atoms and ions.

Starter ideas

1 Getting started (10 minutes)

Learning intention: To revise the structure of the atom.

Resources: Learner's Book.

Description: Ask learners to draw the structure of lithium and fluorine atoms. Then ask them to compare them with a partner. Ask learners to discuss which group in the Periodic Table each of these elements is in. Ask the class to share their thoughts.

2 Five things I remember (10 minutes)

Learning intention: To revise last lesson's content.

Resources: None.

Description: Ask learners to list five things they remember from the last lesson. If necessary, you could allow them to consult their books. (They could do this on sticky notes and arrange them on a suitable board so that you could select some to discuss with the class.)

Feed back to the class and use the remembered items to set the scene for the start of this lesson.

Main teaching ideas

1 Ionic bonds (30–40 minutes)

Learning intentions: To be able to describe the structure of the atoms and ions of various elements and explain why ions are more stable than some atoms.

To look at the details of forming ionic compounds where more than one electron is lost or gained.

Resources: Learner's Book.

Description: Revisit the structure of an atom and compare the structure of elements in Group 1 and Group 7 with those in Group 8 and relate this to their reactivity. Explain how atoms in these groups can become more stable by losing or gaining electrons. Work your way through the diagrams and the notations. It would be useful if you involved

learners by asking them to draw similar diagrams on the board under direction.

Work your way through the structures involved in the reaction of sodium with chlorine and then discuss the differences in the reactivity of lithium and potassium and the reasons for this.

Other ionic compounds: Work your way through the examples given in the text. Concentrate on the idea that more than one electron can be lost or gained. Take care with the example of magnesium and chlorine, where more than one atom of chlorine is involved. Use this example to explain the formula for magnesium chloride as $MgCl_2$. You could use other examples or ask some of your learners to try some. Note that this is extension material.

〉 **Differentiation ideas:** Much of the first part of this is really a class activity, so you may have to set learners who need support more diagrams to draw for themselves, as this will help to ensure they understand the ideas. When you come to the section about other ionic compounds, you could ask learners who need more of a challenge to try to work through other examples, such as calcium and fluorine or chlorine or oxygen and sodium.

〉 **Assessment ideas:** You could use questions 9–12 in the Learner's Book to assess progress and understanding.

2 Activity: Forming ionic compounds (30 minutes)

Learning intention: To reinforce the structure and formation of ions and ionic compounds.

Resources: Learner's Book. Poster-making equipment: coloured paper and/or card, glue, scissors, large sheet of paper, ruler, pair of compasses (and/or string and a drawing pin).

Description: Organise learners into groups of two and allow each group to choose one of the following metals and non-metals:

- Metals: calcium, magnesium, lithium, sodium or potassium
- Non-metals: fluorine, chlorine or oxygen.

Ask learners to make a poster to illustrate the structure of the atoms of the chosen elements and show how an ionic bond is formed to make an ionic compound. You could suggest materials to make their posters 3D.

Ensure the learners add the name of the elements and their symbols, and the name of the compound and its formula.

You could use Template 3 for the groups to peer-assess their work.

> **Differentiation ideas:** You could allocate the elements to the various groups. For example, the use of a Group 2 metal with chlorine or fluorine or a Group 1 metal with oxygen is more of a challenge than the use of a Group 1 metal with a halogen.

> **Assessment ideas:** Use Template 3 for the groups to peer-assess their work.

3   Covalent bonding (30–40 minutes)

Learning intention: To explain covalent bonding.

Resources: Learner's Book.

Description: Show learners the structures of the two non-metals hydrogen and chlorine and show how the atoms are able to share electrons to form a more stable structure as they form a molecule of hydrogen chloride. Stress that the formation of covalent bonds occurs when non-metal atoms join together. Work through examples of this, including the formation of a molecule of hydrogen and ammonia. Ask the learners to practice drawing the dot and cross diagrams to show covalent bonding. Draw their attention to the coloured representations of molecules.

> **Differentiation ideas:** For those learners who need a challenge you could ask them to draw dot and cross diagrams of other molecules. Take care which molecules you choose, as only single bonds are required at this level.

Learners who need support would benefit from being led to draw the diagrams step-by-step. You could do this with a small group on the board.

> **Assessment ideas:** You could use questions 13–16 to assess knowledge and understanding.

Plenary ideas

1   Charge me (10 minutes)

Resources: Periodic Table.

Description: You choose an element (could select at random) and ask what charge the ion has.

Look for positive or negative and ±1 or ±2.

You could add in protons and neutrons and electrons.

> **Reflection ideas:** Why do elements react?

2   Ionic or covalent (10 minutes)

Description: Ask learners to decide if a chemical is ionic or covalent: you could select a mixture of the compounds and elements named in the Learner's Book, or choose your own. You could use 'thumbs up, thumbs down' or some other variant so that every learner is involved. This will provide you with a quick guide to how well the class has understood these ideas.

> **Reflection ideas:** How do I know if a compound is ionic or covalent?

Homework ideas

1   Workbook Exercises 2.3A–C

Topic worksheets

*   Worksheets 2.3A–C, Ionic and covalent bonds

Topic: 2.4 Simple and giant structures

LEARNING PLAN

Learning Objectives	Learning intentions	Success criteria
9Cp.04 Know that elements and compounds exist in structures (simple or giant), and this influences their physical properties.	• Learn how giant structures are formed. • Compare the properties of ionic and covalent substances. • Understand how the structures of these substances relate to their properties.	• Explain how giant structures are formed. • Compare the properties of ionic and covalent substances. • Relate the structures of these substances to their properties.

LANGUAGE SUPPORT

Learners will use the following words:

lattice: a regular, repeated, three-dimensional arrangement of atoms, ions or molecules in a metal or other crystalline solid

intermolecular forces: the forces between molecules

macromolecules: giant molecules

graphite: a form of carbon used as the 'lead' in pencils

layers: a form of material where one sheet of material is placed on top of another

Common misconceptions

Misconception	How to identify	How to overcome
Some learners do not understand that diamond and graphite are both built of carbon atoms.	Ask learners to describe directly the structures of diamond and graphite.	You could spend some time building the structures from modelling materials.

Starter ideas

1 Getting started (10 minutes)

Learning intention: To ensure the learners all understand the differences between an ionic and a covalent substance.

Description: Ask learners to explain how atoms of sodium and chlorine join together to make the compound sodium chloride. Ask them to draw diagrams if it helps them to explain. Allow them a fixed time to do this on their own. Then ask them to share their ideas with a partner, again, for a fixed time. Then ask them to work together to explain how this is different from the way that two oxygen atoms join together to form an oxygen molecule. Share answers with the class.

2 Give me five (10 minutes)

Learning intention: To ensure learners are familiar with the substances that have ionic and covalent bonds.

Description: Give learners 2 minutes to list five ionic and five covalent substances. Then ask them to share their lists with a partner and make a longer list (2 minutes). This pair should then share their lists with another pair (2 minutes).

Feed back to the whole class, award points for correct answers and extra points for answers that no one else has.

Main teaching ideas

1 Introducing the idea of giant and simple structures (40 minutes)

Learning intention: To introduce the facts about simple and giant structures and relate these to the properties of the materials.

Resources: Learner's Book. Giant crystals, large piece of graphite, a pencil, diamond-tipped cutting tool if available.

Description: Work thorough the factual content in the Learner's Book, stressing the strength of the forces between the ions in sodium chloride, within the molecules of substances such as carbon dioxide, and between the molecules of carbon dioxide. Relate these to the properties of the substances.

Work thorough the factual content in the Learner's Book about the giant structures of diamond and graphite, stressing the fact that they are both formed from atoms of carbon, but that the arrangements of the atoms are different, with differences in the forces holding the atoms in place. Relate the differences in structure to the difference in properties. Demonstrate these if possible. You could compare writing with a soft pencil and using a diamond tipped cutting tool. You could allow learners to touch a large piece of graphite so that they can feel how slippery it is.

> **Differentiation ideas:** All learners need to understand these facts, so you may find it useful to ask plenty of questions as you circulate around the class to find out which learners need support; asking learners to describe the structures they see can help to reveal this. You can use more confident learners to demonstrate or to describe the structures they see to the class.

> **Assessment ideas:** You could use questions 1–12 to assess progress and understanding.

2 Building giant structures (40–60 minutes or longer if you choose to feed back to the whole class)

Learning intention: To reinforce the ideas of giant structures.

Resources: Poster-making materials, such as coloured paper, card, glue and sticky tape. Construction materials such as paper straws or wires to make covalent bonds; small polystyrene or foam balls or sponge to make particles or modelling materials to make particles, such as atoms or ions.

Description: Ask learners to construct a giant structure of sodium chloride, graphite or diamond. They could do this in a group of three with each person taking responsibility for one of the structures. They should discuss how they would do this before they start construction. Each model should have an explanation of the structure with relation to the properties of the structure.

You could share each group's work and assessments with the whole class.

> **Differentiation ideas:** You could consider how you group the learners for this task. In this case it might be useful to put some of the more creative learners with those who are less creative and to mix those learners who are more dextrous with those who are not.

> **Assessment ideas:** You could use Template 4: Peer assessment to assess the quality of the work.

3 Think like a scientist: Ionic compounds conducting electricity (40 minutes)

Learning intention: To demonstrate conductivity in ionic substances.

Resources: Safety glasses, surgical gloves, electrical wires, a battery, a lamp, carbon electrodes, a beaker, a selection of crystals and solutions of ionic compounds, such as copper sulfate and sodium chloride.

Description: You may need to demonstrate the set-up of the apparatus before the learners do this task. If you do, use learners to set it up so that the whole class can see. Stress the health and safety considerations.

Ensure that learners know which solutions they are testing; stress organisation and good labelling. Ensure they know that they need to clean the electrodes between each test.

As learners work, circulate and reinforce good practical skills and organisation.

> **Practical guidance:** Hint: Ensure learners set up the apparatus without the solution and test to check that the bulb is working before they start the test.

Safety: Some crystals and solutions such as copper sulfate are irritants. Take care when using these and avoid touching them with bare hands. Wear surgical gloves and safety glasses.

2 PROPERTIES OF MATERIALS

> **Differentiation ideas:** Use the learners with least confidence to help with the demonstration as they are being shown what to do without any pressure. As none of the learners has done this before, it may help them gain confidence.

If more confident learners bring up the fact that carbon is a non-metal and it is conducting electricity, remind them that they came across this in earlier work, and you could explain about the strange structure of graphite that means there are some electrons that are free to move and carry the charge.

> **Assessment ideas:** You could use *Think like a scientist* questions 1–5 to assess progress and understanding. You could also use the time you circulate to assess practical skills.

Plenary ideas

1 Five fingers (10 minutes)

Resources: None.

Description: Learners draw around their hand on a scrap of paper or in their book and write the answers to the following questions along each finger.

- Thumb: What have you learnt? What do you understand?
- Index finger: What skills have you used today?

- Middle finger: Which skills did you find difficult today?
- Ring finger: Who did you help today?
- Little finger: What will you make sure that you remember from today's lesson?

It will be useful to collect these in and use them to help you decide what you need to concentrate on in the next lesson.

This type of plenary is a way of structuring learners' reflection time. It allows those who need the most support to celebrate what they have done well and encourages those who need a challenge to think about the next steps in learning.

2 Exit ticket emoji (10 minutes)

Resources: Sticky notes or paper.

Description: Ask learners to draw an emoji for how they feel they did in the lesson and to answer the following:

- How well did you understand today's material?
- What did you learn today?
- What did you find difficult today?

Homework ideas

1 Workbook Exercises 2.4A–C

PROJECT GUIDANCE

This project addresses the following learning objectives:

9SIC.01 Discuss how scientific knowledge is developed through collective understanding and scrutiny over time.

9SIC.04 Describe how people develop and use scientific understanding as individuals and through collaboration, e.g. through peer review.

This project is another that concentrates on the idea that scientists collaborate and build on the ideas of others to move ideas forward. Put learners into groups of two or three. You could consider how you will group them, either with similar abilities together or a spread of abilities. You need to ensure that all learners participate in the task. There is enough information to start groups off if they do not have access to the internet. There is a list of suggested questions to start off their internet search, but these should not be regarded as the only questions they should attempt to answer. You will need to be sure that all learners are contributing by explaining that all learners are expected to take part in the actual presentation. You will need to circulate whilst the learners are working and perhaps prompt them with the questions from the Learner's Book or additional ideas to stretch them. The focus should be on the way that scientists collaborate, building on the work of others and changing their ideas once they have more information.

You could set a time limit for the presentation or leave it to the learners. It would be a good idea to allow one group to present to another and for them to give feedback using Template 4. If you try to allow all groups to feed back to the class, it may become repetitive and a challenge for learners to maintain interest. You could ask a few groups to present to the class, especially if you have some different ways of presentation, such as slide presentations, reports and posters.

> 3 Forces and energy

Unit plan

Topic	Learning hours	Learning content	Resources
3.1 Density	3-4	What is meant by density; how to calculate density; compare the densities of solids, liquids and gases; understand and predict whether objects will float or sink in water	**Learner's Book:** Questions 1–9 Activity: Densities of some regular objects Think like a scientist: Densities of some irregular objects **Workbook:** Exercise 3.1A, Comparing densities Exercise 3.1B, Understanding and calculating density Exercise 3.1C, Density, floating and sinking **Teacher's Resource:** Worksheets 3.1A–C, Density Template 1: Results table for *Activity: Densities of regular objects* Template 2: Results table for *Think like a scientist: Densities of irregular objects*
3.2 Heat and temperature	2-2.5	Understand the difference between heat and temperature	**Learner's Book:** Questions 1–5 Activity: The Mpemba effect Think like a scientist: Measuring heat and temperature **Workbook:** Exercise 3.2A, Heat or temperature? Exercise 3.2B, Comparing heat and temperature Exercise 3.2C, Measuring heat and temperature **Teacher's Resource:** Worksheet 3.2, Heat and temperature Template 3: Results table and graph axes for *Think like a scientist: Measuring heat and temperature*
3.3 Conservation of energy	1.5-2	Energy cannot be created or destroyed; when energy is conserved, there is no increase or decrease in energy; thermal energy is dissipated from hotter places to colder places	**Learner's Book:** Questions 1–4 Activity: Conservation of energy Think like a scientist: Bottle racers **Workbook:** Exercise 3.3A, What does conservation of energy mean? Exercise 3.3B, The law of conservation of energy Exercise 3.3C, Calculating energy changes **Teacher's Resource:** Worksheet 3.3, Conservation of energy

Topic	Learning hours	Learning content	Resources
3.4 Moving from hot to cold	1-1.5	Thermal energy always transfers from hotter places to colder places; what is meant by heat dissipation	**Learner's Book:** Questions 1–5 Activity: Hot coffee Think like a scientist: Temperature change from heat dissipation **Workbook:** Exercise 3.4A–C, Direction of thermal energy transfer
3.5 Ways of transferring thermal energy	2-3	How thermal energy can be transferred by conduction; how thermal energy can be transferred by convection; how thermal energy can be transferred by radiation	**Learner's Book:** Questions 1–4 Think like a scientist: Conduction of thermal energy in different materials Think like a scientist: Observing convection Think like a scientist: Emitting thermal energy by radiation **Workbook:** Exercise 3.5A, Describing thermal energy transfers Exercise 3.5B, Comparing thermal energy transfers Exercise 3.5C, Variables affecting thermal energy transfer
3.6 Cooling by evaporation	1.5-2	How evaporation causes cooling	**Learner's Book:** Questions 1–5 Think like a scientist: Making an air cooler Activity: Feeling the effects of evaporation **Workbook:** Exercise 3.6A, How evaporation works Exercise 3.6B–C, Evaporation and cooling
Cross-unit resources			**Learner's Book:** Check your Progress **Project:** Load lines **Teacher's resource:** Language development worksheets 3.1 Forces and energy vocabulary 3.2 Correcting the units

BACKGROUND/PRIOR KNOWLEDGE

Learners need to understand the difference between weight and mass for Topic 3.1. The ability to use a formula triangle or to rearrange an equation will be helpful. Knowing how to calculate the volume of a cuboid is also useful for this topic. Learners must also understand that quantities must be substituted correctly into equations and that large numbers are not always divided by small numbers.

For Topic 3.2, learners should recall energy stores and changes from Stage 7. The particle theory of matter should be understood, and so should how the movement of the particles in matter depends on temperature. The units of temperature and of energy must also be recalled.

The concepts of energy changes from Stage 7 should be recalled for Topic 3.3, as should the idea of energy dissipation. Some understanding of percentages may also be helpful.

The difference between heat and temperature should be understood for Topic 3.4, along with the idea of energy being transferred from place to place.

TEACHING SKILLS FOCUS

Giving feedback

Giving effective feedback to learners is an essential part of the process that helps them to make improvement and development in their learning. However, feedback that is delivered incorrectly can have a very negative effect.

To get started, think about feedback that you have received. This can be either recently or when you were at school. What made feedback effective for you?

Here are some things to do, and some things not to do, when delivering feedback:

DO make feedback positive. Rather than saying that work or an answer is 'unsatisfactory', focus on what can be done to make the work better. For example, 'You would greatly improve this by…' or 'Your score on the next test will be much better if…'

DO make feedback specific. Rather than saying that work is 'good' or 'excellent', explain what is good or excellent about the work. For example, 'You chose the scale on the graph very well, so your graph turned out to be excellent' or 'You remembered to give the correct unit with every answer – that was very good.'

DO give feedback on the processes involved in the learning rather than a learner's natural ability. Praising effort raises motivation. Praising ability leads to learners making comparisons between themselves and their fellow learners that can be demotivating.

DON'T ever give insincere feedback. If a learner has made many attempts without success, it can be tempting to offer some sort of praise when they achieve even a very modest level of success. Learners can easily detect a lack of sincerity and this can be very demotivating because it suggests to them that you have low expectations of what they should be able to achieve.

DO give feedback in the class, but consider doing so in a way that only the one learner can hear the feedback. Teenagers can be very sensitive about what others in the class think of them. If learners think that peers will hear feedback, then learners can develop avoidance strategies. This can be due to fear of perceived failure or peer perception of over-performance.

DON'T make comparisons with other learners. Being positively compared to others can lead to an elevated sense of their own ability. Being negatively compared to others can be damaging to confidence and lead to anxiety.

As a challenge, you could ask a class to give you feedback! This should be structured with the use of questions asking what they liked, what they did not like and how they might deliver the lesson or topic differently if they were the teacher. Learners should be given the opportunity to do this anonymously. Of course, it is up to you whether to act on the feedback, but the feedback should not be discussed with the class.

Topic 3.1 Density

LEARNING PLAN

Learning Objectives	Learning intentions	Success criteria
9Pf.01 Use density to explain why objects float or sink in water. **9Cp.02** Describe how the density of a substance relates to its mass in a defined volume. NOTE: this a Chemistry Learning Objective but is best covered in this unit. **9Cp.03** Calculate and compare densities of solids, liquids and gases. NOTE: this a Chemistry Learning Objective but is best covered in this unit. **9TWSp.03** Make predictions of likely outcomes for a scientific enquiry based on scientific knowledge and understanding. **9TWSp.04** Plan a range of investigations of different types to obtain appropriate evidence when testing hypotheses. **9TWSc.01** Sort, group and classify phenomena, objects, materials and organisms through testing, observation, using secondary information, and making and using keys. **9TWSc.02** Decide what equipment is required to carry out an investigation or experiment and use it appropriately. **9TWSc.04** Take appropriately accurate and precise measurements, explaining why accuracy and precision are important. **9TWSc.07** Collect, record and summarise sufficient observations and measurements, in an appropriate form. **9TWSa.02** Describe trends and patterns in results, identifying any anomalous results and suggesting why results are anomalous. **9TWSa.04** Evaluate experiments and investigations, including those done by others, and suggest improvements, explaining any proposed changes.	• Recall the equation for density in terms of mass and volume. • Use the equation for density and give the unit of density. • Understand the concept of density as mass per unit volume. • Understand how density can be used to predict whether objects will float or sink in water. • Compare densities of different substances, including solids, liquids and gases.	• Calculate densities from given masses and volumes. • Correctly give the unit for density, given the units of mass and volume. • Describe, using examples, the difference between density and weight. • Make correct predictions about whether objects will float or sink in water, given the density of the object and the density of water. • State that gases are less dense than solids or liquids and explain this in terms of particle arrangements.

LANGUAGE SUPPORT

Learners will use the following words:

hollow: an object that has a space filled with air on the inside

solid: in this context, an object that has no space filled with air on the inside

density: the property of a material or object that is mass per unit volume; calculated as $\dfrac{\text{mass}}{\text{volume}}$ and usually has the units g/cm³ or kg/m³

regular: of a three-dimensional shape, such as a cube or a cuboid, having a volume that can be calculated using a simple equation

irregular: of a three-dimensional shape, having a volume that cannot be calculated using a simple equation

Common misconceptions

Misconception	How to identify	How to overcome
Density is a measure of how heavy something feels.	After learning about density, ask learners to describe what density means (rather than how to calculate it).	Provide a large object of low density that learners can lift; examples could be polystyrene packing or soft wood, such as balsa, pine or spruce. Provide another object of much higher density that is much smaller and so has less mass than the previous object; examples could be an iron nail or a small rock. Ask which object is heavier (be careful with the use of terms weight and mass). Use a balance if necessary. Learners should see that the object that is less dense has more mass, and so is actually heavier. Finish the activity by showing (approximately) the same volume of the two materials to prove that density is mass per unit volume and not just mass (or weight).
Light things float and heavy things sink (in water).	Ask learners what determines whether something floats or sinks in water. This question can be asked before or after learning about density and floating and sinking.	Either, show images of very large ships, such as cruise liners or cargo ships. Compare this to a small rock. The ship floats, but the rock sinks. Which is heavier? Or, use metal foil or modelling clay to show that shape (with no change in mass) affects floating and sinking. A ball of metal foil will sink, but a 'boat' made from the same mass of the same material will float. The latter activity can be explained in terms of average density, as the shape that floats includes air.

Starter ideas

1 Getting started (5 minutes)

Learning intention: To assess prior knowledge for the density topic.

Description: Learners should recall the use of the word volume, perhaps from mathematics topics. Both rock and feathers should be familiar, as should iron. If learners are not familiar with polystyrene, then an example or picture can be shown. Some learners may recognise polystyrene by the brand name *Styrofoam*™.

Misconceptions are possible here as learners often confuse weight with density, so their use of the terms mass and weight may be incorrect.

2 Floating or sinking (5–10 minutes)

Learning intention: To assess what learners think affects floating or sinking.

Resources: Modelling clay, bowl of water.

Description: Start with the modelling clay rolled into a solid ball. Ask learners whether it will float or sink in water. Demonstrate that the ball sinks. Then ask if there is any way in which it can be made to float. Suggest reducing the mass by removing some of the clay, but keeping the ball shape. Then demonstrate that if the same mass of clay is modelled into a thin bowl shape, it floats. Ask what has changed. If learners recognise that the shape has changed then that is sufficient.

Misconceptions are possible here as some learners think that weight (or mass) determines floating or sinking. This activity shows that shape has more of an effect on floating or sinking than mass.

Main teaching ideas

1 Activity: Densities of some regular objects (15 minutes or more, depending on number of objects)

Learning intention: Measuring lengths, widths and heights of objects, calculation of volume, measuring mass and calculating density.

Resources: See Learner's Book.

Description: See Learner's Book.

> **Differentiation ideas:** Learners needing more support could be reminded of the equation for density and could be provided with the unit.

Question 3 is suitable for learners needing more challenge.

Learners needing more challenge could be asked to convert their densities in g/cm^3 to kg/m^3, although some support may be needed with this process.

> **Assessment ideas:** Learners could be asked to describe what density means in their own words, using examples of their objects.

2 Think like a scientist: Densities of irregular objects (20–30 minutes, depending on number of objects)

Learning intention: To use the displacement method to determine densities.

Resources: See Learner's Book.

Description: See Learner's Book.

> **Differentiation ideas:** All learners can be asked to suggest ways to determine the densities of irregular objects that do not fit into a measuring cylinder.

If small air bubbles are seen on the submerged object, learners who need more challenge can be asked how these would affect the density result.

> **Assessment ideas:** Learners can be asked questions about how exactly to read the volume on a measuring cylinder and the importance of making sure the balance is set to zero before taking readings.

3 Density of air (20+ minutes)

Learning intention: To show that air has mass and, therefore, density.

Resources: Balloons, tape measure or string, digital balance.

Description: Learners often consider that air has no mass, so this activity can deal with that misconception.

Learners measure the mass of the balloon before inflation. Learners then blow up the balloon and tie it to seal the air inside. The larger the balloon, the better the results will be. The mass of the inflated balloon is measured and the difference is the mass of air inside.

The balloon can be assumed to be a sphere. Use the string or measuring tape to measure the circumference. Divide the circumference by 2π (6.28) to get the radius, r. Then use $V = \frac{4}{3}\pi r^3$ followed by density $= \frac{mass}{volume}$.

Answers

The density of air at sea level and room temperature is 0.0012 g/cm³ giving a mass of between 2 and 4 g in a typical balloon, but learners' results do not have to be close to this value. It is sufficient that they understand that air has mass and density.

⟩ **Differentiation ideas:** Learners needing support can have the volume of the inflated balloon calculated for them.

Learners needing more challenge could be asked how to ensure there is no air in the balloon before inflation and how any air present at the start would affect the result.

⟩ **Assessment ideas:** Learners can be asked to predict how the density of the gas used to fill balloons that float (helium) would compare with air.

Learners who need more challenge could be asked why a gas only slightly less dense than air may not make a balloon float. (The balloon will only float if the average density of the balloon and the gas inside is less than the density of air).

Plenary ideas

1 What did I learn (3–5 minutes)

Resources: Small, rectangular pieces of paper, approximately 10 cm by 5 cm.

Description: Learners are asked to list five things that they learned in the lesson or topic.

⟩ **Assessment ideas:** By reading the responses, any misconceptions or gaps in learning could be identified.

2 Describing density (5 minutes)

Resources: Paper, pens.

Description: Learners are shown two objects with very different densities, for example a feather and a steel ball. Learners are asked to choose one of these objects and explain (in writing or orally) why, in terms of mass and volume, its density differs from the other object.

⟩ **Assessment ideas:** This activity can be done in notebooks for assessment at the same time as the next homework or as exit slips.

Homework ideas

1 Questions from the Learner's Book

2 Workbook Exercises 3.1A–C

3 Worksheets 3.1A–C

Topic worksheets

• Worksheets 3.1A–C, Density

Topic 3.2 Heat and temperature

LEARNING PLAN

Learning Objectives	Learning intentions	Success criteria
9Pf.02 Describe the difference between heat and temperature. 9TWSp.01 Suggest a testable hypothesis based on scientific understanding. 6TWSp.03 Make predictions of likely outcomes for a scientific enquiry based on scientific knowledge and understanding.	Understand the difference between heat and temperature.	• Describe what is meant by heat. • Describe what is meant by temperature. • Compare the heat and temperature of different objects.

CONTINUED

Learning Objectives	Learning intentions	Success criteria
9TWSp.05 Make risk assessments for practical work to identify and control risks.		
9TWSc.01 Sort, group and classify phenomena, objects, materials and organisms through testing, observation, using secondary information and making and using keys.		
9TWSc.03 Decide when to increase the range of observations and measurements, and increase the extent of repetition, to give sufficiently reliable data.		
9TWSc.04 Take appropriately accurate and precise measurements, explaining why accuracy and precision are important.		
9TWSc.05 Carry out practical work safely, supported by risk assessments where appropriate.		
9TWSc.07 Collect, record and summarise sufficient observations and measurements, in an appropriate form.		
9TWSa.01 Evaluate the strength of the evidence collected and how it supports, or refutes, the prediction.		
9TWSa.02 Describe trends and patterns in results, identifying any anomalous results and suggesting why results are anomalous.		
9TWSa.03 Make conclusions by interpreting results, explain the limitations of the conclusions and describe how the conclusions can be further investigated.		
9TWSa.04 Evaluate experiments and investigations, including those done by others, and suggest improvements, explaining any proposed changes.		
9TSWa.05 Present and interpret results, and predict results between the data points collected.		

Some people think that the C in the unit of temperature means centigrade. The temperature scale was originally called centigrade, meaning 100 steps (by Anders Celsius himself) in the 18th century. However, the scale was officially re-named Celsius in 1948 and that is now the internationally accepted unit. The word centigrade, therefore, should not be used with learners.

Common misconceptions

Misconception	How to identify	How to overcome
Heat and temperature are the same thing.	After learning about heat and temperature, provide learners with lists of pairs of terms. Include 'heat and temperature' with others such as 'weight and mass' and 'force and energy'. Ask whether any of the terms in a pair are the same.	Ask learners how they would measure the temperature of a liquid. They should use the word *thermometer*. Ask for the unit of temperature. Then ask how the temperature of the liquid could be increased. Prompt for the term *energy*, then ask for the unit of energy. Compare °C and J showing that these are not the same. This topic is conceptually quite challenging, so some learners may need extra support with this.

Starter ideas

1 **Getting started (5 minutes)**

   Learning intention: To allow learners to think about temperature and thermal energy.

   Resources: Paper and pens, Learner's Book.

   Description: Ask learners to answer the questions from the 'Getting started' task in the Learner's Book in groups. Learners may think that the energy required to raise the temperature of a substance depends only on the temperature change and not on the quantity of substance.

2 **Heating comparison (5–10 minutes)**

   Learning intention: To allow learners to think about heat and temperature.

   Resources: Two identical beakers as large as possible, water, two identical heat sources and a thermometer.

   Description: Put a small volume of water in one beaker to a depth of about 1 cm. Fill the other beaker with water to about $\frac{3}{4}$ full. Tell learners that you will use the same type of heat source to heat both volumes of water. Ask which will increase by, for example, 10 °C quickest.

Ask for reasons for the learners' predictions. Once learners have had time to think about their predictions, prompt for ideas about particles. (In order for temperature to increase, particles need to gain energy. There are more particles in the larger volume, so the process will take longer.)

Main teaching ideas

1 **Activity: The Mpemba effect (30 minutes)**

   Learning intention: To investigate how the starting temperature of water affects the time taken to freeze the water.

   Resources: See Learner's Book.

   Description: See Learner's Book.

   It could be mentioned that Mpemba was a learner working in a school in East Africa and was carrying out the same investigation in 1963.

   > **Differentiation ideas:** Learners needing a challenge could be asked to try to explain the results. If warmer water was seen to freeze in a shorter time, learners can discuss reasons why. It should be pointed out that scientists are still not in complete agreement as to why this happens.

> **Assessment ideas:** Learners can be asked questions about changes of state and particle arrangements in solids and liquids.

2 Think like a scientist: Measuring heat and temperature (20–30 minutes including graph plotting)

Learning intention: To link thermal energy supplied to a substance and the temperature change of that substance.

Description: See Learner's Book.

This investigation is similar to the one used at higher learning stages for specific heat capacity. Specific heat capacity is beyond Stage 9 and so should not be introduced.

> **Practical advice:** If a joule meter is not available, an ammeter can be connected in series with the immersion heater and a voltmeter connected across the heater in parallel. The teacher (not the learners) can then calculate the power delivered to the heater as current in amps multiplied by voltage. The energy supplied is power in watts multiplied by time in seconds. Again, this calculation should be done by the teacher as it is beyond Stage 9.

> **Differentiation ideas:** Learners who need more support can be asked questions about changes in particle movement in the water as the temperature increases.

Learners that need more challenge could be asked whether other liquids would give exactly the same results as water. When the same quantity of energy is supplied to two different liquids of the same mass for the same time, will the temperature changes be equal?

> **Assessment ideas:** Learners can be asked to relate the change in temperature to the change in particle movement in the water and what is causing this change.

3 Energy for temperature change (10–20 minutes depending on number of examples)

Learning intention: To consider the difference between thermal energy and temperature in familiar contexts.

Resources: Pictures relating to examples (optional).

Description: Learners can be asked for reasons why for example, on a warm sunny day, the water in an outdoor swimming pool (or the sea) does not

increase in temperature as much as a smaller volume of water in the same location.

> **Differentiation ideas:** Learners that need more challenge could be asked to suggest why the land around the swimming pool increases in temperature faster than the water. Here, it is sufficient for them to recognise that different types of substances need different quantities of heat to increase in termperature.

Learners that need more support can be prompted to consider the number of particles that need to be provided with more energy.

> **Assessment ideas:** Learners can discuss and assess their answers in pairs.

Plenary ideas

1 Methods of heating (3–5 minutes)

Resources: Small, rectangular pieces of paper, approximately 10 cm by 5 cm.

Description: Learners write as many methods of heating as possible. In each case they also write the energy change or transfer that is used. For example, a spirit burner changes chemical energy to thermal energy and the thermal energy is transferred to heat the substance.

> **Assessment ideas:** The activity can be carried out in groups and the pieces of paper can be swapped for discussion and assessment.

2 What did my partner learn? (5 minutes)

Resources: Small pieces of paper.

Description: Learners work in pairs. Each learner asks their partner to say what they learned in the lesson. The other learner summarises this into bullet points.

> **Assessment ideas:** The teacher can ask for volunteers to share their questions (not the answers) for class discussion.

Homework ideas

1 Questions from the Learner's Book

2 Workbook Exercises 3.2A–C

3 Worksheet 3.2

Topic worksheet

- Worksheet 3.2, Heat and temperature

Topic 3.3 Conservation of energy

LEARNING PLAN

Learning Objectives	Learning intentions	Success criteria
9Pf.03 Know that energy is conserved, meaning it cannot be created or destroyed. 9TWSc.07 Collect, record and summarise sufficient observations and measurements, in an appropriate form. 9TSWa.05 Present and interpret results, and predict results between the data points collected.	• Learn that energy cannot be created or destroyed. • Understand that when energy is conserved, there is no increase or decrease in energy. • Understand that thermal energy is dissipated from hotter places to colder places.	• State the law of conservation of energy. • Describe energy changes using energy flow diagrams to show that no energy is destroyed or created. • Describe how heat is dissipated from hotter objects to colder surroundings.

LANGUAGE SUPPORT

Learners will use the following words:

conserved: in this context, conserved means the total quantity of something is kept the same

system: in this context, a system is a place where an energy change or transfer occurs and where no energy enters or leaves that place

created: to be made from nothing or from something different

destroyed: to stop existing

Common misconceptions

Misconception	How to identify	How to overcome
Energy can be made or can cease to exist.	Ask if there are any examples where energy can be made or destroyed.	Use the learner's answer. For example, if they think an electrical cell makes electrical energy, then ask what might be inside a cell. If they think the Sun makes energy, then ask why stars (including the Sun) will eventually stop transferring energy. Both the electrical cell and the Sun change energy and eventually all of that energy will be changed.
The word conserve always means to use sparingly.	After learning about conservation of energy, ask what 'energy is conserved' means.	Learners should know of other examples where one word is used to mean more than one thing. For example, cell or nucleus. The word conserve also has more than one meaning.

Starter ideas

1 Getting started (5 minutes)

Learning intention: To remind learners about the topic of energy.

Resources: Paper and pens, Learner's Book.

Description: Learners work individually or in pairs to answer the questions.

2 Where do you get energy from? (5–10 minutes, depending on structure of activity)

Learning intention: To think about where the human body gets energy from.

Description: Ask learners where they get energy from. Can they make energy? Can they control the quantity of energy they use? Can they destroy energy?

Main teaching ideas

1 Activity: Conservation of energy (10–20 minutes, depending on whether teacher demonstration or class practical)

Learning intention: To observe how energy is transferred from one object to another.

Resources: See Learner's Book

Description: See Learner's Book. The activity can be done by the teacher as a demonstration or by learners working in groups.

⟩ **Differentiation ideas:** Learners needing more support could be asked what energy store the moving bottle has. How does this energy get to the other bottle?

Learners needing more challenge could be reminded of the maximum distance that the first bottle swings. Then ask why both bottles cannot swing by this maximum distance at the same time.

⟩ **Assessment ideas:** Ask learners to explain how the activity shows that energy is conserved.

2 Activity: Bottle racers (20–30 minutes)

Learning intention: To show how energy is changed from one store to another.

Resources: See Learner's Book.

Description: See Learner's Book for instructions. It is preferable if the bottles are supplied with holes already drilled. Learners can bring in their own bottles a few days before the activity.

⟩ **Differentiation ideas:** Learners needing more support can be asked what happens to the energy stored in the elastic band when it is twisted more times.

Learners needing more challenge can be asked where the energy that was stored in the elastic band has gone after the bottle has stopped moving. (The energy has been changed to kinetic, which has moved the bottle to a different place. Some of the energy is dissipated as thermal and sound.)

⟩ **Assessment ideas:** Besides the questions in the Learner's Book, learners can be asked where the energy comes from to twist the elastic band (kinetic energy from muscles in the arm/hand, which in turn comes from chemical energy in our food).

3 Pendulum swing (5–10 minutes)

Learning intention: To show that more energy cannot be made within a system.

Resources: A large pendulum, such as a 1 kg mass hanging on a strong 2–3 metre-long string and a fragile object such as a drinking glass.

Safety: Ensure the string and point of support are strong enough to hold the mass; do not climb on tables or chairs to attach the string to the support.

Description: The mass is displaced to one side in order to make the pendulum swing. The mass can be held just in contact with a fragile object, such as a drinking glass, with the string under tension from the weight of the mass. The learners can be asked to predict whether the mass will swing and return to hit the glass and break it.

Provided the mass is only released and **not pushed** then the pendulum cannot gain energy, so the mass will not hit the glass.

⟩ **Differentiation ideas:** Learners who need more challenge can be asked where the energy goes because the pendulum does not fully return to its original height (used to overcome air resistance).

Learners needing more support can be asked whether the pendulum will continue to swing for ever. It can then be explained that energy is used to overcome friction at the point of support and air resistance as the mass moves.

⟩ **Assessment ideas:** Learners can be asked what energy changes occur in the pendulum as it swings from one side to the other (gravitational potential to kinetic and back to gravitational potential).

Plenary ideas

1 Agreement line (2–5 minutes, depending on number of statements)

Description: Learners to gather at one side or the back of the room where there is clear space for the length or width of the room, which will be the imaginary line. One side represents strongly agree and the other represents strongly disagree. The teacher will make true/false statements about conservation of energy and the learners position themselves along the agreement line according to what each individual thinks. The teacher will then ask some individuals why they are at that position.

> **Assessment ideas:** Assessment is part of the activity.

> **Reflection ideas:** Reflection statements can be used in the activity. For example, 'I feel I really understand the idea of conservation of energy.'

2 Use alternative words (1–2 minutes)

Description: Learners to work in pairs and write the law of conservation of energy without the use of the words 'created' or 'destroyed'.

> **Assessment ideas:** Learners can compare their statement with that of others and discuss which works best.

Homework ideas

1 Questions from the Learner's Book

2 Workbook Exercises 3.3A–C

3 Worksheet 3.3

Topic worksheet

• Worksheet 3.3, Conservation of energy

Topic 3.4 Moving from hot to cold

LEARNING PLAN

Learning Objectives	Learning intentions	Success criteria
9Pf.04 Know that thermal energy will always transfer from hotter regions or objects to colder ones, and this is known as heat dissipation. 9TWSp.01 Suggest a testable hypothesis based on scientific understanding. 9TWSp.03 Make predictions of likely outcomes for a scientific enquiry based on scientific knowledge and understanding. 9TWSp.04 Plan a range of investigations of different types to obtain appropriate evidence when testing hypotheses.	• Discover that thermal energy always transfers from hotter places to colder places. • Understand what is meant by heat dissipation.	• Show the direction of thermal energy transfer between two objects at different temperatures. • Describe what is meant by dissipation of heat.

Learners will use the following words:

hotter: used to describe an object at a higher temperature than another

colder: used to describe an object at a lower temperature than another

Common misconceptions

Misconception	How to identify	How to overcome
'Cold' can move.	After learning about the direction of thermal energy transfer, give true/false statements. Some of these should include the idea of cold moving to a hotter place.	Ask learners to recall some stores and transfers of energy. Prompt for thermal if it is not recalled. Ask whether cold is an energy store (cold is lack of thermal energy). Remind learners that thermal energy will tend to spread out into colder areas, so 'cold' itself does not move. Learners find this confusing because cold substances can move. For example, an air conditioner blows cold air. The cold air moves, but thermal energy from the warm air in the room moves into the cold air. An example like this can be used to illustrate this point.

Starter ideas

1 Getting started (5 minutes)

Learning intention: To allow learners to begin to think about the transfer of thermal energy.

Description: Thermal energy escapes through the window and dissipates to the outside. While cold air may move into the room, thermal energy from the warm air in the room dissipates into this colder air. Either of these will cause the temperature of the air in the room to decrease.

2 Getting warmer (5 minutes)

Learning intention: To experience the transfer of thermal energy.

Resources: A beaker or cup of warm water and a thermometer.

Description: Learners can be asked to measure the temperature of their hand by holding a thermometer; then measure the temperature of the water in the beaker to show it is hotter. Learners can then be asked to hold the beaker or cup of warm water.

Safety: The temperature of the water should be 40–45 °C to prevent burns.

Learners can be asked in what direction the heat moves.

What would happen if the water was at the same temperature as the hand?

What would happen if the water was at a lower temperature than the hand?

Main teaching ideas

1 Activity: Hot coffee (10–15 minutes)

Learning intention: To recognise the rate of thermal energy transfer (cooling) depends on temperature difference.

Description: See Learner's Book.

> **Differentiation ideas:** Learners who need more support can be reminded, before answering the questions, that thermal energy moves faster when the temperature difference is larger.

Learners who need challenge can be asked in what direction the thermal energy will move when two objects in contact are at the same temperature. (The movement is equal and opposite in both directions, so there is no overall movement.)

› **Assessment ideas:** Learners can answer the questions orally, in the form of a discussion or in written form for handing in or swapping with peers.

2 Think like a scientist: Temperature change from heat dissipation (20–30 minutes)

Learning intention: To measure the temperature change in the surroundings caused by heat dissipation.

Resources: See Learner's Book.

Description: See Learner's Book for instructions.

Safety: Only the glass part of the lamp should be in the water. Learners should be reminded not to attempt such an investigation at home.

› **Differentiation ideas:** Learners who need more challenge could be asked whether all the thermal energy from the lamp is dissipated into the water. (Some is dissipated into the air, some used to evaporate water, some through the sides of the beaker and some though the parts of the lamp that are not in water.)

Learners who need more support could be asked where the thermal energy dissipated from a lamp normally goes.

› **Assessment ideas:** Learners can answer the questions in the Learner's Book.

3 Only heat moves – cold cannot move (10–15 minutes)

Learning intention: To show that thermal energy moves and that cold itself cannot move.

Resources: Beakers, water, ice and thermometers.

Description: Learners fill beakers with water and ice. Allow the temperature of the water to fall below 10 °C and measure this temperature. Learners then measure the temperature of their hand by holding the thermometer. Record both temperatures. Learners then hold the beaker. They will probably say the beaker feels cold, but they should be reminded that thermal energy is moving from their hand into the colder beaker.

Immediately after holding the beaker, learners should measure the temperature of their hand again.

› **Differentiation ideas:** Learners who need more support could be asked what will happen to the temperature of the water in the beaker if it is held for long enough.

Learners who need more challenge could be asked from where else thermal energy can enter the beaker.

› **Assessment ideas:** Ask learners to write a short summary of the activity using a labelled diagram with arrows to show the direction of energy transfer.

Plenary ideas

1 Everyday examples (3–5 minutes)

Resources: Paper and pen or pencil.

Description: Learners work in pairs. Make lists of everyday examples of thermal energy moving from hotter places to colder places, for example, hot food cooling. Which pair can list the most examples in the time allocated?

› **Assessment ideas:** Learners can volunteer to share their examples with the class for discussion.

2 Back to the board (5 minutes)

Resources: White/black board or flipchart and pens.

Description: Learners divide into two teams. One learner from each team sits with their back to the board. The teacher writes a word associated with the topic on the board, such as 'temperature', 'cooling', 'dissipates'. Each team tries to explain the word, without saying or spelling the word, to their team member who is seated with their back to the board.

› **Assessment ideas:** The teacher can assess the activity by listening to the explanations offered by each team.

Homework ideas

1 Questions from the Learner's Book

2 Workbook Exercises 3.4A–C

3 Ask learners to provide everyday examples of situations where thermal energy moves.

Topic worksheets

- There are no worksheets for this topic.

Topic 3.5 Ways of transferring thermal energy

LEARNING PLAN

Learning Objectives	Learning intentions	Success criteria
9Pf.05 Describe thermal transfer by the processes of conduction, convection and radiation. 9TWSp.01 Suggest a testable hypothesis based on scientific understanding. 9TWSp.03 Make predictions of likely outcomes for a scientific enquiry based on scientific knowledge and understanding. 9TWSp.04 Plan a range of investigations of different types to obtain appropriate evidence when testing hypotheses. 9TWSp.05 Make risk assessments for practical work to identify and control risks. 9TWSc.01 Sort, group and classify phenomena, objects, materials and organisms through testing, observation, using secondary information, and making and using keys. 9TWSc.02 Decide what equipment is required to carry out an investigation or experiment and use it appropriately. 9TWSc.03 Decide when to increase the range of observations and measurements, and increase the extent of repetition, to give sufficiently reliable data. 9TWSc.04 Take appropriately accurate and precise measurements, explaining why accuracy and precision are important. 9TWSc.05 Carry out practical work safely, supported by risk assessments where appropriate.	• How thermal energy can be transferred by conduction. • How thermal energy can be transferred by convection. • How thermal energy can be transferred by radiation.	• Explain how thermal energy travels through solids and liquids by conduction, using ideas about particles. • Explain how thermal energy travels through liquids and gases by convection, using ideas about expanding and density. • Recall that radiation can transfer thermal energy through substances without the need for particles. • Explain how certain materials and structures, called thermal insulators, are used to reduce the rate of transfer of thermal energy.

CONTINUED

Learning Objectives	Learning intentions	Success criteria
9TWSc.07 Collect, record and summarise sufficient observations and measurements, in an appropriate form.		
9TWSa.01 Evaluate the strength of the evidence collected and how it supports, or refutes, the prediction.		
9TWSa.02 Describe trends and patterns in results, identifying any anomalous results and suggesting why results are anomalous.		
9TWSa.03 Make conclusions by interpreting results, explain the limitations of the conclusions and describe how the conclusions can be further investigated.		
9TSWa.05 Present and interpret results, and predict results between the data points collected.		

LANGUAGE SUPPORT

Learners will use the following words:

vigorously: with a lot of movement and a lot of energy

expand: become larger

conduction: method of thermal energy transfer where more vigorously vibrating particles cause neighbouring particles to vibrate by colliding; conduction works best where particles are close together: in solids and liquids

convection: method of thermal energy transfer where more vigorously vibrating particles cause expansion and decrease in density in a liquid or gas; the less dense material then rises because it floats, setting up a convection current

convection current: method by which all of a liquid or gas becomes heated through convection; particles flow through the material due to differences in density

radiation: method of thermal energy transfer that uses waves and does not depend on particles; occurs through a vacuum, through gases and through transparent liquids and solids

Common misconceptions

Misconception	How to identify	How to overcome
When a substance is heated, the particles expand.	After learning about either conduction or convection, ask specifically about how a substance expands when heated. Ask learners to use ideas about particles.	Model particles using beads or marbles in a tray. Shake these gently so the particles vibrate. Shake more vigorously. Do the particles themselves get bigger? What happens to the space required for each particle to vibrate as the movement gets more vigorous?

Starter ideas

1 Getting started (5 minutes)

Learning intention: Learners recall the arrangements of particles in solids, liquids and gases and consider how particle movement is affected by temperature.

Description: Learners can draw diagrams for question 1 and draw annotated diagrams for question 2 rather than answer in writing.

Many learners draw the particles in a liquid as if it were a gas at high pressure. All the particles must be in contact with at least one other particle in a liquid, but they are randomly arranged.

2 Candle power (5 minutes)

Learning intention: To demonstrate convection in air.

Resources: A candle carousel (if one of these is not available, then instructions on how to make a simple candle carousel are available on many websites) and one or more candles.

Description: The candle carousel is demonstrated before the candle is lit. The candle is then lit and the carousel observed to rotate. It can be explained that air, heated by the candle flame, rises through the fan, causing it to move.

Main teaching ideas

1 Think like a scientist: Conduction of thermal energy in different materials (20+ minutes)

Learning intention: To compare how well different materials conduct thermal energy.

Resources: See Learner's Book.

Description: See Learner's Book. Learners should write a risk assessment for this activity, even if the activity is done as a teacher demonstration. The risk assessment should include not touching the rods, even for some time after the heat source has been removed, and keeping paper and other flammable materials away from the area.

> **Differentiation ideas:** Learners who need more support could be asked what happens to the particles in the rod when the rod is heated.

Learners who need more challenge can be asked to describe the process of thermal conduction.

> **Assessment ideas:** Aside from answering the questions in the Learner's Book, learners could draw a series of particle diagrams showing how conduction occurs in a rod.

2 Activity: Observing convection (10–15 minutes)

Learning intention: To visualise a convection current in water.

Resources: See Learner's Book

Description: See Learner's Book. The activity works best with a large beaker, so the largest possible glass beaker should be used. No gauze should be placed between the beaker and the flame.

> **Differentiation ideas:** Learners who need a challenge can be asked why the convection current moves down after it has crossed the surface of the water. (The water cools at the surface and becomes more dense, so sinks. Also, particles must move towards the heat source to replace those particles that have risen away from the heat source.)

Learners who need support can be asked what everyday methods of heating water would generate convection currents. (Any method that uses a heat source under a container.)

> **Assessment ideas:** Learners can answer the questions in the Learner's Book that involve drawing a series of diagrams to show how a convection current forms. These can be peer-assessed if the teacher shares the criteria with the learners.

3   Think like a scientist: Emitting thermal energy by radiation (20–30 minutes, excluding time taken to paint the cans)

Learning intention: To compare the rate at which thermal energy is emitted by different colours.

Resources: See Learner's Book.

Description: See Learner's Book. In addition to black, white and silver, learners can paint the cans any other colour they choose.

> **Differentiation ideas:** Learners who need support can be asked to make predictions for the next temperatures of each can once the experiment has started and the trend is apparent.

Learners who need a challenge could be asked to make predictions for other colours and textures, such as shiny black or dull white.

> **Assessment ideas:** Learners can be asked, in advance of the activity, how to make this investigation a fair test. What are the independent and dependent variables?

Plenary ideas

1   Hands up to ask questions (3–5 minutes)

Description: Learners think of questions they would like to ask the class about conduction, convection or radiation. They raise their hands to ask a question, which other learners raise their hands to answer. Those answering a question must then ask another, different question to the class.

> **Assessment ideas:** Assessment is the main part of the activity.

2   60-second hot seat (5 minutes)

Resources: Stopwatch and a small prize.

Description: A learner volunteers to sit at the front of the class and talk about conduction, convection and radiation for 60 seconds. A timer is started to measure the elapsed time. Other learners can challenge at any time by clapping their hands once if they hear incorrect science, repetition of any key word, pausing or going off-subject. The timer is stopped on any challenge showing the elapsed time up to that point. A learner making a correct challenge, which they must explain, takes over the hot seat and speaks for the remaining time in a similar way. The learner speaking when 60 seconds elapses is the winner.

> **Assessment ideas:** Assessment is the main part of the activity.

Homework ideas

1   Questions from the Learner's Book

2   Workbook Exercises 3.5A–C

3   Ask learners to describe some everyday examples that (a) use conduction, convection or radiation, and/or (b) attempt to reduce thermal energy transfer.

Topic 3.6 Cooling by evaporation

Learning Objectives	Learning intentions	Success criteria
9Pf.06 Explain cooling by evaporation. 9TWSc.01 Sort, group and classify phenomena, objects, materials and organisms through testing, observation, using secondary information and making and using keys. 9TWSc.04 Take appropriately accurate and precise measurements, explaining why accuracy and precision are important. 9TWSc.05 Carry out practical work safely, supported by risk assessments where appropriate. 9TWSc.07 Collect, record and summarise sufficient observations and measurements, in an appropriate form. 9TWSa.03 Make conclusions by interpreting results, explain the limitations of the conclusions and describe how the conclusions can be further investigated.	• Understand how evaporation causes cooling.	• Explain the process of evaporation in terms of particles. • Explain that evaporation lowers the average energy of the particles that remain in the liquid. • Link this lowering of average energy of particles to a decrease in temperature of the liquid.

LANGUAGE SUPPORT

Learners will use the following words:

random: not predictable or not following any pattern

porous: a solid that has tiny holes allowing water to soak through

Common misconceptions

Misconception	How to identify	How to overcome
Sweat causes cooling because it is a cool liquid coming onto the skin.	After learning about cooling by evaporation, ask learners to explain how sweat causes cooling of the skin.	*Activity: Feeling the effects of evaporation* contains a part where learners blow on the liquid. Blowing increases the rate of evaporation, so this should help to link cooling to evaporation. Also, using liquids with different evaporation rates should illustrate this. Learners could be asked where sweat comes from (the skin) so how will the temperature of the sweat compare with that of the skin (it will be the same). So what else can be causing the cooling effect, and why is this increased in windy conditions?

Starter ideas

1 **Getting started (5 minutes)**

Learning intention: To consider the process of evaporation in terms of particles.

Resources: Paper and pencil, Learner's Book.

Description: Learners often confuse evaporation and boiling, so it is useful to clarify the difference. Learners may need support answering this question.

2 **Rate of evaporation (5–10 minutes)**

Learning intention: To show liquids evaporating at temperatures lower than their boiling points.

Resources: A tile or metal plate, heat source, dropper pipette, paper towel, water and ethanol or isopropanol (if *Activity: Feeling the effects of evaporation* is to be carried out).

Description: Warm the tile or metal plate so it is warmer than room temperature. Allow learners to touch the surface to demonstrate that it is cooler than the boiling point of water. Use the dropper pipette to put some water on the paper towel. Transfer this water to the surface by wiping a thin film of water onto the surface. Watch as the water evaporates.

If perfume is to be used, then the two liquids should be transferred onto the surface at approximately the same time to compare the evaporation rate.

Safety: If a naked flame is used as the heat source, then perfume which contains ethanol or alcohol should not be used.

Main teaching ideas

1 **Think like a scientist: Making an air cooler (10–15 minutes)**

Learning intention: To show that evaporation causes cooling.

Resources: See Learner's Book.

Description: See Learner's Book.

> **Differentiation ideas:** Learners who need support could be asked to suggest why we use a thermometer and do not just put our hand into the air to feel if cooling has happened. (So that a measurement can be made or a value can be recorded.)

Learners who need more challenge could be asked why, when measuring the temperature of the air from the fan, the thermometer must be dry. (The moving air will increase the speed of evaporation of water on the thermometer bulb, lowering its temperature and so giving an artificially lower reading.)

> **Assessment ideas:** Ask learners to explain, in terms of particles, how the wet towel causes the air to become cooler.

2 **Activity: Feeling the effects of evaporation (10–15 minutes)**

Learning intention: To show the cooling effect of evaporation and link this to the rate of evaporation.

Resources: See Learner's Book.

Description: See Learner's Book. If the starter activity on evaporation rates has not been done with alcohol, then a comparison of the evaporation rates of the alcohol and water could be done before this activity.

> **Differentiation ideas:** Learners who need more support could be asked for ways in which this activity is made a fair comparison.

Learners who need more challenge could be asked to suggest reasons for the differences in evaporation rates of water and the alcohol in terms of particles. (Suggestions need only be reasonable, for example, 'alcohol particles are smaller than water particles', which is not correct but reasonable from the learner's point of view. Answers such as this should be credited with responses such as 'Yes, that's a good suggestion', rather than saying it is correct.)

> **Assessment ideas:** Learners can be asked to explain the cooling effects using ideas about particles. They can also be asked what effect blowing has (increases the speed of the evaporation).

3   **How does sweating work? (10–15 minutes)**

Learning intention: To demonstrate the effect of sweat on cooling.

Resources: Two thermometers, cotton wool, adhesive tape, water, fan and clamp stands.

Description: Use the adhesive tape to fix a small, similar-sized piece of cotton wool around the bulb of each thermometer. Allow the water to come to room temperature. Water that is colder than room temperature must not be used. Add water to the cotton wool around one of the thermometer bulbs. Clamp both thermometers the same distance from the fan and switch on the fan.

Readings on the thermometers should be taken at regular intervals.

> **Practical guidance:** The cotton wool surrounding the thermometer bulbs should form quite a thin layer. The one that has water must have a sufficient quantity of water so that the liquid is in contact with the thermometer bulb.

> **Assessment ideas:** Ask learners to explain any differences between the thermometer readings. This activity is a model. Ask: What do each of the parts represent? (The thermometer is the body, cotton wool is the skin, water is the sweat, fan is the wind.)

How does this observation link to sweating? Why, when you are sweating, does wind make you feel cooler?

Plenary ideas

1   **Suggestions for learning (5–10 minutes)**

Description: Learners work in pairs to think of suggestions to help others learn this topic.

> **Assessment ideas:** Learners can be asked to volunteer their suggestions to the class for discussion.

2   **You write the questions! (5 – 10 minutes)**

Resources: Prepared answers that can be given on a handout or written on the board. Examples could include 'When a liquid changes to a gas.' or 'This will increase the cooling effect.'

Description: Learners work in pairs to write their questions for each answer.

> **Assessment ideas:** Learners can volunteer to share their questions to the class. A variety of different questions may be offered for one particular answer. Do all of these different questions work?

Homework ideas

1   Questions from the Learner's Book

2   Workbook Exercises 3.6A–C

PROJECT GUIDANCE

This project addresses the following learning objectives:

9Pf.01 Use density to explain why objects float or sink in water.

9SIC.02 Describe how science is applied across societies and industries, and in research.

9SIC.03 Evaluate issues which involve and/or require scientific understanding.

Learners have the opportunity to do some independent research using secondary sources of information, then to carry out an investigation using their findings.

Load lines can be accompanied by various letters according to the national organisation that has approved the load line. However, the letters shown in the picture in the Learner's Book are:

- TF – tropical fresh water
- F – fresh water
- T – tropical seawater
- S – summer temperate seawater
- W – winter temperate seawater
- WNA – winter North Atlantic.

Tap water can be used for fresh water.

Sea water is approximately 3.5% (mass to volume) salt. Therefore 3.5 g of sodium chloride dissolved in water and made up to a volume of 100 cm^3 will make a solution similar to sea water.

The difference between the level at which the model floats in tap water and the salt solution is quite small. The difference is more easily detected in a larger model. If this is not possible, then the percentage of salt in the water can be increased to make the difference more noticeable.

The density of water will change when heated or cooled. Again, these differences will be small, but learners can explain any differences theoretically in their presentation.

The model would be expected to float higher in water that is more dense.

> 4 Maintaining life

Unit plan

Topic	Learning hours	Learning content	Resources
4.1 Plants and water	3-4	How plants absorb and transport water	**Learner's Book:** Questions 1 and 2 Activity: Annotating a diagram Think like a scientist: Investigating transport in a celery stalk Think like a scientist: Planning an experiment **Workbook:** Exercise 4.1A, Water uptake by orange plant seedlings Exercise 4.1B, Celery experiment Exercise 4.1C, Interpreting data about water uptake **Teacher's Resource:** Worksheets 4.1A–C, Water uptake in plants Template 1: Outline for *Activity: Annotating a diagram*
4.2 Transpiration	2.5-3	Water loss from plant leaves	**Learner's Book:** Questions 1 and 2 Think like a scientist: Investigating transpiration Think like a scientist: Which side of a leaf loses most water? Activity: Conserving water in the desert **Workbook:** Exercise 4.2, How temperature affects water loss **Teacher's Resource:** Worksheets 4.2A–C, Water movement through a leaf Template 2: Graph for *Think like a scientist: Investigating transpiration* Template 3: Results chart for *Think like a scientist: Which side of a leaf loses most water?*
4.3 Excretion in humans	1.5-2	Structure and function of the excretory system	**Learner's Book:** Questions 1–3 Activity: Excretory system words and meanings **Workbook:** Exercise 4.3, Structure and function of the excretory system **Teacher's Resource:** Worksheets 4.3A–C, Crossword

Topic	Learning hours	Learning content	Resources
4.4 Keeping a fetus healthy	2–2.5	Maintaining a healthy pregnancy	**Learner's Book:** Questions 1–4 Activity: Display about diet during pregnancy **Workbook:** Exercise 4.4A, Length of pregnancy Exercise 4.4B, Does caffeine affect birthweight? Exercise 4.4C, Smoking and birthweight **Teacher's Resource:** Worksheet 4.4: Stopping smoking during pregnancy
Cross-unit resources			**Learner's Book:** Check your Progress **Project:** How scientists linked smoking to health **Teacher's Resource:** Language development worksheets 4.1 Linking words to their meanings 4.2 Unscrambling words to complete sentences

BACKGROUND/PRIOR KNOWLEDGE

Learners found out about root hair cells in Stage 7, and should remember that they take up water from the soil, and how they are adapted for this. They learnt about photosynthesis earlier in Topic 1.1, and should recall that water is needed for this process, and that it is transported from the soil to the leaves. They have looked at the structure of leaves in Unit 1. They may also remember some of the adaptations of desert plants, which they looked at in Stage 8, Unit 4. They should understand the process of evaporation, in which a liquid changes to a gas, and also diffusion; understanding of these processes is needed to explain how water is lost from plant leaves in transpiration.

Excretion has only been briefly touched on in earlier units, where it is one of the characteristics of living things that is covered at Stage 7.

Health during pregnancy links to previous work on balanced diets, covered in Stage 8. There is further coverage of human reproduction – limited to gametes and fertilisation – in Unit 7 of this book. Learners who have followed a science curriculum in earlier years may have learnt the names of the parts of the human reproductive system at Primary level, but no detail of how reproduction takes place in humans is required at this level.

TEACHING SKILLS FOCUS

Setting achievable targets

In Assessment for Learning, teachers and learners think carefully about where the learner is in respect of their learning, and then decide where they want to move on to next. This involves setting clear targets for the learner to aim for.

Ideally, targets are set through consultation between the teacher and the learner, so that the learner is fully involved in thinking about what they need to do next and in agreeing on a manageable target. If time is short, however, it may be that

the teacher takes a leading role in this process, perhaps by suggesting a target in the feedback on a piece of written work.

Targets must be **SMART**: Specific, Measurable, Achievable, Relevant and Timed.

Specific targets are specific both to the learner and the task. Generic targets addressed to the whole class or a group of learners rarely have any effect at all, whereas a personalised target is much more likely to be accepted and attempted. Targets also

CONTINUED

need to be specific in terms of what is to be achieved. For example, an exhortation to 'work harder' or to 'draw graphs more carefully' is difficult for a learner to engage with. An agreement to 'put up my hand at least three times when questions are being asked in class' or to 'use a ruler to draw graph axes' is much more specific, and far more likely to be accepted by the learner as a worthwhile target. Small steps work better than giant ones.

Measurable targets enable the learner (and also the teacher) to know when they have been achieved. The two examples above illustrate this; both the teacher and the learner can easily know whether a hand has been put up three times, or whether the graph axes have been drawn with a ruler.

Achievable targets are important. The target set must not be so challenging that the learner feels they have no hope of achieving it within, at most, a few weeks. Again, it is important to think in small steps. If graph drawing is very poor, deal with one part of this at a time. If behaviour and concentration are poor, set a small and achievable aim, such as getting one mark more for behaviour this week than last week. Once that has been achieved, then a further step can be taken towards where you and the learner agree they should be.

Relevant targets are seen by the learner as genuinely useful and able to help them to do better in science. This can best be achieved by discussing the target with the learner, helping them to see how the change can help them to move forward.

Timed targets have a defined period within which they are to be achieved. This must not be too far ahead. It could be in the next lesson, or in the next piece of homework, or by next week.

Here are some examples of poor and good target setting:

Poor target	Good target
I will work harder to learn science vocabulary.	I will practise science vocabulary with my family every weekend until the end of term.
I will improve my behaviour in class.	I will get a B rather than a C for my behaviour in science classes in the next three weeks.
I will try harder to draw good graphs.	I will practise choosing scales for graph axes using the guidance my teacher has given me; I aim to be really confident at this within two weeks.
I will take more responsibility in my group when we do practical work.	I will take on the role of handling the apparatus in every science experiment that we do this week.

In this unit, for example, you could try using the experiment plans that learners write in Topic 4.1 to assess how well they are able to do this, and then set a target with each learner about what they will try to do better when they next plan an experiment.

Topic 4.1 Plants and water

LEARNING PLAN

Learning Objectives	Learning intentions	Success criteria
9Bs.01 Describe the pathway of water and mineral salts from the roots to the leaves in flowering plants, including absorption in root hair cells, transport through xylem and transpiration from the surface of leaves (part; See Topic 4.2 for the second part of this learning objective). 9TWSc.05 Carry out practical work safely, supported by risk assessments where appropriate.	• To describe how water is absorbed into root hairs, and transported upwards through xylem vessels. • Plan a fair test experiment to investigate the relationship between two variables.	• Make an annotated diagram showing how water is absorbed through root hairs and transported upwards through a root. • Plan (and if possible carry out) a workable experiment that provides data relating changes in temperature to changes in the rate of water transport.

LANGUAGE SUPPORT

Learners will use the following words:

root hairs: specialised cells in the outer layer of a plant root that increase the surface area through which water and minerals can be absorbed from the soil

xylem vessels: specialised cells in which all cell contents and end walls have disappeared, leaving an empty tube through which water is transported

Common misconceptions

Misconception	How to identify	How to overcome
Learners may think that the plant does something active to take up and transport water. In fact, all of this involves no energy input from the plant.	This should become apparent while talking with the class about water uptake and movement up through xylem, and also when learners write annotations on the diagram in the activity.	Take care to use appropriate language when talking about water uptake and transport, and encourage learners to do so as well. For example, do not say that 'plants move water up through their xylem', but rather 'water moves up through the xylem'.

Starter ideas

1 Getting started (10–15 minutes, including sharing ideas)

Description: Ask learners to work with a partner to write sentences as described in the Learner's Book. Allow 5 minutes and then ask pairs to give you their sentences, or to write them on the board. Use all of their ideas to make a list of reasons why living things need water.

2 Functions of roots (5–10 minutes)

Resources: A young bean (or other) seedling, with visible root hairs; hand lenses or magnifying glasses for students to use when looking at the root hairs.

Description: Show learners the seedling and ask questions appropriate to what can be seen, which will help to lead into the topic of water uptake. For example, you could ask:

- Why do you think seeds always grow a root before they grow a shoot?

- What are these tiny hairs you can see here?

- Why do you think they are in this part of the root, and not right at the very tip?

- What do these hairs do?

Main teaching ideas

1 Activity: Annotating a diagram (20–30 minutes)

Learning intention: To consolidate understanding of the relationship between the structure of a root and the uptake of water.

Resources: Per group:

- diagram of a cross section of a root from Topic 4.1 in the Learner's Book

- a large sheet of paper

- pens, rulers and other materials for labelling and annotating the diagram.

Optional: Template 1.

Description: Ask learners to follow the instructions in *Activity: Annotating a diagram*. When everyone has finished, and you are happy that they have completed the task appropriately, ask them to put their diagram onto the wall as part of a display.

> **Differentiation ideas:** Learners who would benefit from more structure and support can be given Template 1 with the outline diagram already in place.

Learners who need a further challenge could include information about how each part is adapted to carry out the function they describe in their annotations.

> **Assessment ideas:** This is a good opportunity for self assessment, where learners can compare their own annotated diagram with those produced by other groups, and use this to make suggestions about how they could improve their annotations.

2 Think like a scientist: Investigating transport in a celery stalk (approximately 30 minutes, but the rate at which the dye moves up the stalk is rather unpredictable; you may like to try this out first to enable you to plan the timings of the lesson)

Learning intention: To see at first hand how water moves through xylem vessels in a plant stem.

Resources:

- a stalk of celery, pak choi or another plant that has a thick stalk – it works best if there are leaves at the top of the stalk

- a small container, such as a beaker or Petri dish

- some water mixed with a coloured dye, such as blue ink or methylene blue stain

- a sharp knife and a safe cutting surface, such as a cork board.

Description: Ask learners to follow the instructions in the Learner's Book. You may like to demonstrate first, and then ask each group to set up their own apparatus. You could consider using different plant material with different groups.

> **Practical guidance:** This normally works reliably, although timing can vary considerably. This is affected by how much leaf is present on the stalk, and by temperature.

> **Differentiation ideas:** Learners who would benefit from a challenge could compare the rate of uptake of the dye in celery stalks with and without leaves.

> **Assessment ideas:** You can mark the answers to the questions to determine how well learners understand what happened in their experiment.

3 Think like a scientist: Planning an experiment (20 minutes if only the plan is done; another 30–40 minutes if groups actually do their planned experiment)

Learning intention: To practise designing a fair test experiment by building on and modifying a technique already experienced at first hand.

Resources: None if the experiment is only planned.

If learners carry out their experiment, they should include a list of apparatus and materials that they require. These are likely to be the same as those for *Think like a scientist: Investigating transport in a celery stalk*, with the addition of a timer. They will also need access to areas that provide at least two different temperatures, for example, a fridge and the classroom.

Description: Ask learners to follow the instructions in the Learner's Book. They could either work alone or in pairs to write their plan.

Check learners' plans before you allow them to do their experiment. However, only correct anything that is potentially hazardous, or where learners ask for equipment that you cannot provide. For other mistakes or shortcomings, it is suggested that you simply mention to learners that there are a few things they may want to change as they do their experiment, and encourage them to do this. Very often they will do this themselves, which is a far better learning experience than following your instructions.

⟩ **Practical guidance:** See the previous experiment. Learners may be able to see the position of the dye through the semi-transparent tissues of the leaf stalk. If not, they will need to cut sections across the stem to find out where the dye has reached. They will therefore need to set up several stems and cut each one at successive time intervals.

⟩ **Differentiation ideas:** Some learners may benefit from being provided with questions 1 to 4 on a worksheet, with spaces provided for them to write their answers.

All learners would benefit from being allowed to carry out their experiment. Learners requiring a further challenge could not only record and display their results, but also discuss the strength of the evidence that they have collected.

Plenary ideas

1 Sharing experiment plans or descriptions (20–30 minutes)

Resources: Plans or experimental write-ups from *Think like a scientist: Planning an experiment.*

Description: Put a selection of the plans or write-ups onto the wall and ask everyone to bring a chair and sit round where they can see them.

You could then ask one or two groups to describe their plan or their experiment, inviting comments and questions from other groups.

Alternatively, you can start with the first step of the plan – identifying the independent variable and how it is changed – and discuss how the different groups have dealt with this. Then move on to the next step, and so on. Give different group members the opportunity to explain their decisions, actions and results, and encourage questions and comments from the other groups.

⟩ **Assessment ideas:** The discussion described above is effectively peer assessment.

2 Reflection discussion (10 minutes)

Description: Ask learners to think about the issues raised in the Reflection section in Topic 4.1 in the Learner's Book. Allow a couple of minutes for thinking and then ask some learners to give their responses to the questions. Involve as many different people in the class as possible.

⟩ **Assessment ideas:** The points raised in the discussion may help to give you information about how well the class has understood the topics covered in this unit.

Homework ideas

1 Workbook Exercises 4.1A–C

2 Worksheets 4.1A–C

Topic worksheets

• Worksheets 4.1A–C, Water uptake in plants

Topic 4.2 Transpiration

LEARNING PLAN

Learning Objectives	Learning intentions	Success criteria
9Bs.01 Describe the pathway of water and mineral salts from the roots to the leaves in flowering plants, including absorption in root hair cells, transport through xylem and transpiration from the surface of leaves part: See Topic 4.1 also. 9TWSc.03 Decide when to increase the range of observations and measurements, and increase the extent of repetition, to give sufficiently reliable data. 9TWSc.04 Take appropriately accurate and precise measurements, explaining why accuracy and precision are important. 9TWSc.05 Carry out practical work safely, supported by risk assessments where appropriate. 9TWSc.07 Collect, record and summarise sufficient observations and measurements, in an appropriate form. 9TWSa.01 Evaluate the strength of the evidence collected and how it supports, or refutes, the prediction. 9TWSa.02 Describe trends and patterns in results, identifying any anomalous results and suggesting why results are anomalous. 9TWSa.03 Make conclusions by interpreting results, explain the limitations of the conclusions and describe how the conclusions can be further investigated. 9TWSa.04 Evaluate experiments and investigations, including those done by others, and suggest improvements, explaining any proposed changes.	• Describe how water moves through leaves, including evaporation and transpiration. • Carry out fair test experiments about transpiration. • Use knowledge and understanding of transpiration to explain results.	• Give correct answers to questions 1 and 2. • Explain the changes in mass between two pot plants (question 4 in *Think like a scientist: Investigating transpiration*) • Collect, record and display results for *Think like a scientist: Which side of a leaf loses most water?* • Correctly answer the questions associated with *Think like a scientist: Which side of a leaf loses most water?*

Learners will use the following words:

transpiration: the loss of water vapour from the leaves of a plant

wilted: of a plant: having lost so much water that the soft tissues (especially leaves) lose their firmness and flop over

Common misconceptions

Misconception	How to identify	How to overcome
Learners may think that liquid water is lost from plant leaves.	Ask learners to list the form in which water is absorbed into a plant, travels through the xylem, moves into a leaf cell and diffuses out of the leaf.	Take care always to use the term 'water vapour' when describing transpiration.

Starter ideas

1 Getting started activity (10–15 minutes, including sharing ideas)

Description: Ask learners to make drawings and descriptions, as described in the Learner's Book, to elicit how well they understand the process of evaporation.

2 Wilted plant (5 minutes)

Resources: If possible, two plants in pots, one that has plenty of water and looks healthy, and one that is short of water and is wilting. If these are not available, use the photographs in the Learner's Book instead.

Description: Ask learners to describe the differences between the two plants and suggest what has happened to them.

Main teaching ideas

1 Think like a scientist: Investigating transpiration (15 minutes on the first day, a few minutes on each of the following few days to measure the mass of the plants)

Learning intention: To gain first-hand experience of how plants lose water vapour; to practise collecting, recording and interpreting results.

Resources: Per group:
- two very similar plants, both growing in the same size pots
- two big, transparent polythene bags
- access to a balance for measuring the mass of the plants in their pots.

Description: Ask learners to follow the instructions in the Learner's Book.

> **Practical guidance:** The types of plant used are not critical, but those with broad leaves are likely to lose water more quickly than xerophytic plants (ones that are adapted to grow in dry conditions).

Ideally, the masses should be measured at approximately the same time each day. You may like to allocate this task to one or two learners, rather than expecting the whole class to return to the lab each day. You may also like to ask them to record any changes in the conditions each day, for example, more sunshine falling onto the plants or the ceiling fans being put on in the lab.

> **Differentiation ideas:** Template 2 provides an outline graph for learners who need more support.

Learners who would benefit from a challenge could be asked to suggest how they could modify this experiment to investigate whether the number of leaves on the potted plant affects the rate at which it loses mass.

> **Assessment ideas:** Ability to construct results charts and graphs could be assessed.

2 Think like a scientist: Which side of a leaf loses most water? (20–25 minutes to set up the experiment, another 20 minutes the next day to measure and record masses)

Learning intention: To appreciate how the loss of water vapour from leaves is affected by surface covering; to practise carrying out a fair test experiment and interpreting the results.

Resources: Per group:
- eight leaves, all from the same kind of plant, and all roughly the same size
- some petroleum jelly
- at least eight paperclips or another way of fixing the leaves to your 'washing line'
- a 'washing line' that learners can hang their leaves from; you may be able to hang some string across the whole room for the whole class to share, or each group can set up their own personal washing line with some string held between two retort stands
- a balance to measure the mass of the leaves (it needs to be quite sensitive, because leaves have only a small mass)
- some filter paper or other paper to put on the balance when learners find the mass of the leaves, so that they do not get petroleum jelly on the balance.

Description: Provide each group with a set of similar leaves. Different groups could use different leaf types.

Show them how they will construct their 'washing line', either using one for the whole class or one per group.

Ask the groups to follow the instructions in the Learner's Book.

> **Practical guidance:** Some learners may find it difficult to handle the petroleum jelly without getting it on themselves, on leaves it is not supposed to be on, or on various other surfaces too. Discuss this with them beforehand and decide on techniques they can use to avoid this problem.

> **Differentiation ideas:** Template 3 would be beneficial for students who need support in designing a suitable results chart.

Learners who require a further challenge could calculate the percentage loss in mass for each leaf, and then explain why this is more informative than simply recording the loss in mass.

> **Assessment ideas:** You can assess ability to handle apparatus and materials carefully and effectively, as well as using the answers to the questions to assess understanding of experimental methods.

3 Activity: Conserving water in the desert (10–15 minutes)

Learning intention: To relate new learning about water transport and transpiration to earlier work on desert ecosystems and plant adaptations.

Resources: None are essential, but you may like to provide some pictures of plants, or live plants, that grow in dry conditions.

Description: Ask learners to follow the instructions in the Learner's Book. Allow 3 to 5 minutes for the pairs to discuss their ideas, then settle the class and ask for suggestions. Use these to discuss some of the adaptations of desert plants and relate them to water absorption and/or transpiration.

> **Differentiation ideas:** This is an activity that all can do, and in which differentiation will be by outcome. Most learners will be able to suggest at least one adaptation for the roots and for the upper parts of the plant, while some will be able to think of up to four adaptations. A few learners will be able to give clear and scientifically correct explanations of how these adaptations help the plant to conserve water.

Plenary ideas

1 Email explanation (10 minutes)

Description: In pairs, learners write an email to a learner who has missed today's lesson, explaining what has been learnt. You may like to put a word limit on the email.

Ask some pairs to read out their email.

> **Assessment ideas:** Use the emails to determine how well learners have understood the facts and concepts covered in this topic.

2 Question and answer (15 minutes)

Description: Organise learners into groups of three. Ask each group to write two questions relating to Topic 4.1 or Topic 4.2, which they will ask other groups to answer.

Choose one group to ask their question. They should choose a group to answer it. If that group answers it correctly then they ask their first question. If the group gets the answer wrong then the question is passed to another group.

> **Assessment ideas:** Both questions and answers will provide information about understanding of the facts and concepts covered in these two topics.

Homework ideas

1 Workbook Exercise 4.2

2 Worksheets 4.2A–C

Topic worksheets

• Worksheets 4.2A–C, Water movement through a leaf

Topic 4.3 Excretion in humans

LEARNING PLAN

Learning Objectives	Learning intentions	Success criteria
9Bs.02 Describe the structure of the human excretory (renal) system and its function (limited to kidneys filtering blood to remove urea, which is excreted in urine).	• Label the parts of the excretory system and outline their functions. • Describe how the kidneys excrete urea.	• Contribute to writing functions of parts of the excretory system in *Activity: Excretory system words and meanings.*

LANGUAGE SUPPORT

Learners will use the following words:

excretion: getting rid of waste materials from the body; specifically, these waste materials have been inside the body (so do not include the egestion of faeces)

renal: to do with the kidneys

kidneys: a pair of organs in the upper abdomen, which filter the blood and produce urine

urea: an excretory product made in the liver from excess amino acids

urine: a liquid produced by the kidneys which contains urea and other waste substances dissolved in water

ureter: a tube that carries urine from the kidneys to the bladder

bladder: an organ in which urine is stored before removal from the body

urethra: a tube that carries urine from the bladder to the outside of the body

Common misconceptions

Misconception	How to identify	How to overcome
It is very common for learners to think that urea is made in the kidneys not the liver.	This will become apparent when answering questions or discussing the roles of the kidneys.	*Activity: Excretory system words and meanings* involves learners writing descriptions of the functions of each part; writing the function of the kidney should help to consolidate understanding of this concept.

Starter ideas

1   Getting started (10–15 minutes, including sharing ideas)

Description: Ask learners to discuss the questions in the Learner's Book with a partner, and then share their ideas with the rest of the class.

2   Looking at a model of the excretory system (10 minutes)

Resources: A three-dimensional plastic model of the human body that includes the kidneys, ureters, bladder and urethra.

Description: Bring learners to sit together while you show and describe the different organs of the excretory system. Use questioning to determine whether learners already have any ideas about the names of the organs or what each of them does.

Main teaching ideas

1   The excretion of urea (15 to 20 minutes)

Learning intention: To understand what is meant by excretion and to name the main excretory products of humans; to learn where urea is made and how it is excreted.

Resources: Text and illustrations in the Learner's Book.

Description: Use the material in the Learner's Book to discuss with the class what excretion is (and is not) and where urea is made and excreted.

> **Differentiation ideas:** This is a class discussion, so everyone can take part. Make sure that even less-confident learners attempt to answer questions.

2   Structure of the human excretory system (15 to 20 minutes)

Learning intention: To learn the names, positions and functions of the organs of the excretory system.

Resources: If available, a model of the excretory system; diagram of the excretory system in the Learner's Book; if required, outline diagrams for learners to label for themselves.

Description: Using the model (if available) and the diagram in the Learner's Book, explain the relationship between the different organs of the excretory system. Pay particular attention to the difference between urine and urea, and between the ureter and the urethra. Ask learners for ideas about how to remember these words and not mix them up (as described in the Reflection section in the Learner's Book).

Learners could be provided with outline diagrams of the excretory system to label themselves and stick into their notebooks.

> **Differentiation ideas:** Learners of all abilities should be able to take part in this discussion, and should be able to label the outline diagrams. Some learners are more likely to have interesting ideas about how to remember the meanings of the similar-sounding words.

3   Activity: Excretory system words and meanings (20 minutes; less if the cards have already been produced by another class)

Learning intention: To consolidate understanding of the meanings of the terms describing the structure and function of the human excretory system.

Resources: Sixteen identical pieces of card, large enough to contain descriptions of up to fifteen words. (If another class has already done this activity, learners could reuse their cards, but it is a valuable learning experience for them to construct the cards themselves.)

Description: Ask learners to follow the instructions in the Learner's Book.

> **Differentiation ideas:** All learners can be successful in this activity. Some learners are likely to take the lead in suggesting meanings for each word; it would be helpful for you to move between the groups and encourage more reticent learners to take part in suggesting or writing down the meanings.

Plenary ideas

1   Naming the parts of the excretory system (5 minutes)

Description: Draw or project an unlabelled image of the excretory system on the board. Ask a learner to name a part of the system. Ask another learner to come and label this part on the board. Repeat with each part.

> **Assessment ideas:** Use answers to check ability to recognise and name the parts of the excretory system.

Check that learners can pronounce and spell the names correctly.

2 Mastermind (5 minutes)

Resources: A card for each learner, with a tick on one side and a cross on the other side.

Description: Choose a learner (or ask for a volunteer) to be Mastermind.

You ask the Mastermind a question about the excretory system, based on the work done in this lesson. The Mastermind gives an answer – they can purposefully give a wrong answer if they like. The other members of the class hold up their cards to show whether the answer is correct or incorrect. You can then question the rest of the class to find the correct answer if necessary, or to find out why a learner has identified a correct answer as a wrong one.

Repeat with more questions to the same Mastermind.

> **Assessment ideas:** Use responses of the class to indicate any misunderstandings.

> **Reflection ideas:** See the Reflection activity in the Learner's Book. Learners have been presented with a lot of new words in this lesson; what tactics might work best for them to try to learn these words?

Homework ideas

1 Workbook Exercise 4.3

2 Worksheets 4.3A–C

Topic worksheets

- Worksheets 4.3A–C, Crossword

Topic 4.4 Keeping a fetus healthy

LEARNING PLAN

Learning Objectives	Learning intentions	Success criteria
9Bp.08 Discuss how fetal development is affected by the health of the mother, including the effect of diet, smoking and drugs.	• Explain how diet, smoking and drugs affect fetal development.	• Answer questions 1 to 4 correctly. • Contribute to a display as part of *Activity: Display about diet during pregnancy*.

LANGUAGE SUPPORT

Learners will use the following words:

fetus: a developing child while still within the uterus; specifically, the term embryo is used for the first few weeks, and fetus from about 11 weeks onwards

fetal: to do with the fetus

Common misconceptions

Misconception	How to identify	How to overcome
Learners may have heard that a pregnant woman needs to 'eat for two' and think this means that she must double the quantity of food she eats.	This may become evident during general class discussion or during the construction of the display about diet during pregnancy.	This is best addressed while learners are looking at other learners' displays and discussing what they show.

Starter ideas

1 **Getting started activity (10–15 minutes, including sharing ideas)**

   Description: Ask learners to discuss the questions in the Learner's Book with a partner and then share their ideas with the rest of the class.

2 **Diet during pregnancy (10–15 minutes)**

   Resources: A variety of foods, or pictures of foods, that a pregnant woman might enjoy eating; include vegetables, fruit and some good protein sources, as well as some very sweet foods and very fatty foods.

   Description: Get the learners to help you to set out a display of the foods on a desk, and then all sit around. Ask them: 'Which of these foods would be good for a pregnant woman to eat?' 'Why do you think that?' Start to build up some ideas about why diet is important during pregnancy.

Main teaching ideas

1 **A healthy pregnancy (15–20 minutes)**

   Learning intention: To understand how diet can affect the health of a pregnant woman and her fetus.

   Resources: Text and photographs in the Learner's Book.

   Description: Use the material in the Learner's Book to discuss with the class how a good diet can help a mother and her fetus to stay healthy. You could use questions 1 to 4 as part of the discussion by putting them to the class at suitable intervals.

   > **Differentiation ideas:** This is a class discussion in which everyone can take part. Some learners will need encouragement to put forward ideas or to answer questions. Some learners, on the other hand, may have challenging questions that they want answered. Be prepared to research answers for them on the internet, if necessary.

   > **Assessment ideas:** Questioning can help to determine how well learners understand the concepts covered.

2 **Activity: Display about diet during pregnancy (collecting information and ideas could be done out of class time; putting together the display is likely to take at least 30 minutes)**

   Learning intention: To consolidate understanding of the importance of diet during pregnancy.

   Resources: Access to the internet, large sheets of paper (at least A3), scissors, glue and coloured pens.

   Description: Ask learners to work in groups of three or four, following the instructions in the Learner's Book.

   > **Differentiation ideas:** Within a group, some learners are likely to take a lead, while others will need encouragement to contribute. Try to make sure that everyone has a role and helps to construct the final product.

   > **Assessment ideas:** Listen to the discussions within groups to check understanding. Ask questions about how they have decided on the most reliable and useful sources of information. Use the final displays to check understanding of the topic.

3 **Smoking and drugs during pregnancy (15–20 minutes)**

   Learning intention: To appreciate the importance of not smoking during pregnancy and avoiding non-prescription drugs.

   Resources: Text and photographs in the Learner's Book.

   Description: Ask learners to quietly read the paragraphs under the heading 'Smoking cigarettes'. Then ask a learner to explain, in their own words, why a pregnant woman should not smoke. Then ask others: 'Do you agree?'

   You could then move on to the list of bullet points providing recommendations during pregnancy, and ask learners to explain each one in turn. This could be done as a big chart on the board with the bullet point on the left and an explanation – produced in discussion with the class – on the right.

   > **Differentiation ideas:** The starting point is a very open-ended question, which more confident learners will be more willing to answer. As the discussion continues you could gradually move to more closed questions (e.g., 'What is the name of the addictive drug in cigarettes?' 'How does carbon monoxide affect the transport of oxygen in the blood?') to which less confident learners could be asked to respond

Plenary ideas

1 Mind map (20–30 minutes)

Resources: Large sheets of paper

Description: Ask learners to make a mind map of everything they have learnt in this unit. They could do this individually or work in pairs.

When each learner or pair has finished, display the mind maps on the wall. Learners can move along the wall and look at other people's mind maps. Which one do they think is best? Why?

〉 **Assessment ideas:** The mind maps can be used to indicate any misconceptions or misunderstandings in this unit.

2 Video voice-overs (20–30 minutes)

Resources: Video of pregnant woman/women shopping for food and cooking.

Description: Organise learners into pairs or groups of three. Show the video and then ask learners to write a commentary to go over the clips, referring to a balanced diet during pregnancy.

〉 **Assessment ideas:** The commentaries will provide insight into learners' understanding of this topic.

Homework ideas

1 Workbook Exercises 4.4A–C

2 Worksheet 4.4

Topic Worksheet

- Worksheet 4.4, Stopping smoking during pregnancy

PROJECT GUIDANCE

This project addresses the following learning objectives:

9SIC.01 Discuss how scientific knowledge is developed through collective understanding and scrutiny over time.

9SIC.04 Describe how people develop and use scientific understanding as individuals and through collaboration, e.g. through peer review.

9SIC.05 Discuss how the uses of science can have a global environmental impact.

The story of how we came to understand that smoking is damaging to health is an excellent illustration of the way in which scientific knowledge is developed through collective understanding and scrutiny over time. It also involves the difficulty of challenging strong institutions, such as the tobacco industry, and of carrying out research into the effects of environmental factors on human health.

It would be good to allocate one question to each group. However, if your class is very small you may ask each group to research more than one of the questions.

By Stage 9, many learners should be reasonably proficient in doing their own research. This is a good opportunity for them to practise their skills of finding reliable sources of information on the internet. However, it would be useful for you to support them in this, either by checking their sources or by suggesting search terms or even specific web sites that they could use. It would, therefore, be very useful for you to prepare by doing your own research: looking for suitable sites that are easily accessible from your country, and that, where possible, refer to data or stories from the country in which your school is situated or your students have their homes.

Often, one of the biggest challenges for learners is how to reduce the large quantity of information that they find to something that is manageable and that they genuinely understand. Again, depending on their past experience of this type of research, you can either expect them to do this themselves or help them out. One way of helping is to take some early ideas from a group and show how this can be reduced to something simpler, more striking and easier for everyone to understand.

The final product could be a presentation made by the whole class (perhaps to another class) or a display that is put up onto the wall.

> 5 Reactivity

Unit plan

Topic	Learning hours	Learning content	Resources
5.1 Reactivity and displacement reactions	2-3	The reactivity series; using the reactivity series to predict which metals will displace others form their salts; some displacement reactions	**Learner's Book:** Questions 1–9 Activity: Learning the order Think like a scientist: Displacing metals **Workbook:** Exercise 5.1A, Using the reactivity series Exercise 5.1B, Displacement reactions Exercise 5.1C, Displacing metals **Teacher's Resource:** Worksheet 5.1, Is there a reaction? Template 1: Reactivity series cards Template 2: Peer assessment: Practical planning exercise
5.2 Using the reactivity series and displacement reactions	2-4	An investigation to identify an unknown metal using displacement reactions; the use of some useful displacement reactions	**Learner's Book:** Questions 1–3 Think like a scientist: Identifying a mystery metal – planning the investigation Think like a scientist: Identifying a mystery metal – carrying out the investigation Think like a scientist: Extracting metals using carbon **Workbook:** Exercise 5.2, Using displacement reactions **Teacher's Resource:** Template 3: Using the reactivity series and displacement reactions: Investigation help sheet
5.3 Salts	2-4	What a salt is with examples and uses of salts; prepare a salt by reacting a metal with an acid; prepare a salt by heating a metal oxide with an acid	**Learner's Book:** Questions 1–9 Activity: Researching a salt Think like a scientist: Making the salt zinc sulfate Think like a scientist: Making the salt copper sulfate **Workbook:** Exercise 5.3A, Which acid is used to make which salt? Exercise 5.3B, Making salts Exercise 5.3C, Practical steps for making salts

Topic	Learning hours	Learning content	Resources
5.4 Other ways of making salts	3-4	Preparation of salts by reacting a carbonate with an acid and by neutralisation; carry out practical work safely, use of risk assessments; using word and symbol equations	**Learner's Book:** Questions 1–10 Think like a scientist: Preparing a salt from acid and a carbonate Think like a scientist: Preparing a salt by neutralisation **Workbook:** Exercise 5.4A, Preparing copper chloride Exercise 5.4B, Preparing potassium chloride Exercise 5.4C, Mystery substances **Teacher's Resource:** Worksheets 5.4A–C, Salts, alkalis, formulae and equations Template 4: Risk assessments
5.5 Rearranging atoms	2-3	Rearrangement of atoms in chemical reactions; conservation of mass; conservation of energy	**Learner's Book:** Questions 1–6 Think like a scientist: The law of conservation of mass Think like a scientist: Burning magnesium in air **Workbook:** Exercise 5.5A, What happens to the atoms and mass when chemicals react? Exercise 5.5B, Before and after the reaction Exercise 5.5C, Investigating burning magnesium **Teacher's Resource:** Worksheet 5.5, How much more mass?
Cross-unit resources			**Learner's Book** Check your Progress **Project:** Where is the evidence? **Teacher's Resource:** Language development worksheets 5.1 Sorting chemicals 5.2 Correcting statements

BACKGROUND/PRIOR KNOWLEDGE

This unit brings together a lot of knowledge that the learners will have acquired in Stages 7 and 8. For example, they know that some elements are more reactive than others from learning about the Group 1 metals, so this forms a basis for the reactivity of metals and displacement reactions at the start of this unit. They will build on their knowledge of equations using the different methods, for example, drawing the atoms, word equations and they will begin to use symbol equations. The section on the formation of salts brings together some reactions they have met before, but gives an opportunity to think about the formation of one type of compound and to improve the writing of equations. There is also an opportunity to link the ideas of pure substances to the formation of crystals of various salts and what must be done to ensure they are pure substances.

The ideas about conservation of mass and energy have their foundations in the work already covered in Stages 7 and 8, so the concepts should present no major problems.

TEACHING SKILLS FOCUS

Moving towards peer- and self-assessment

One of the barriers to successful peer- and self-assessment can be that learners do not give good feedback and merely say that the work was OK. If this becomes normal for the class then even self-assessment will be superficial. The learners may say 'What is the point of us doing this – we aren't teachers – we do not know if it's good or not?'

You need to model the type of feedback for peer assessment either with a prepared and cooperative learner or by providing groups with the same piece of work (perhaps manufactured by you) and asking small groups of learners to critique it amongst themselves and then feed back to the class. You would need to lead a class discussion on how helpful or otherwise the feedback is. You could provide the learners with key statements such as: 'To improve you need to…', 'This part of the work did not have enough detail…', or 'You need to explain why this happened.'

To help the learners give their assessment, you need to break down the points they should be looking for into simple language and ideas. You could suggest some probing questions, such as:

- Has the person shown they understand this?
- How could they make it clear that they have understood?
- If you see a mistake in understanding, can you see why that person made that mistake, and can you suggest a way to help them overcome the misunderstanding?

In this way you can help them to think up questions of their own and to think about the assessment of their own work.

Encourage peers to talk to one another, especially about their mistakes, as many learners may find it less intimidating to discuss this with another learner rather than the teacher.

Aim to provide at least one session about how to assess someone else's work during this unit. You could use a number of different areas, such as in Topic 5.1 *Learning the order of the reactivity of*

metals or risk assessments for practical work in various topics.

You could do an assessment and make comments about why you have suggested improvements and how you have suggested them, or you could ask the class to suggest why you did it that way.

You could do an assessment yourself, do it badly and then ask the class to improve on your feedback.

You could give each group of two or three learners the same piece of work, which has a number of areas that are incorrect or need improvement and ask them to assess it; give them a fixed time to do this. Then bring the class together and ask different groups to provide feedback. You could use this to ask questions such as: 'Why did you think that?' 'How could you say that in a way that is more helpful?' 'Can you help explain where and/or why they have made that mistake?' 'Would your feedback help them do a better job next time?' 'How would you feel if you had received that feedback?'

You could ask the learners to think about what the point of the assessment is. It is not done to give a grade but to help the person improve their work. Do they want to give themselves or their classmate an easy time or help them make progress? Make the link between the questions you need to ask for peer assessment and those you would ask yourself when you look at your own work.

Ask learners to say what type of assessment they found helpful. You could write these comments on sticky notes and place them on a board to remind learners whenever they do peer- or self-assessment.

Ask yourself: Do learners really give useful feedback to one another? How can I ensure all learners are engaged with this? How can I improve their feedback and engagement? How can I use the discussion of the assessment to focus on the improvement of work? Can I use this session to get learners to think more carefully about their own work?

Topic 5.1 Reactivity and displacement reactions

LEARNING PLAN

Learning Objectives	Learning intentions	Success criteria
9Cc.01 Use word equations and symbol equations to describe reactions (balancing symbol equations is not required). 9Cc.02 Identify examples of displacement reactions and predict products (limited to reactions involving calcium, magnesium, zinc, iron, copper, gold and silver salts). 9TWSm.03 Use symbols and formulae to represent scientific ideas. 9TWSp.03 Make predictions of likely outcomes for a scientific enquiry based on scientific knowledge and understanding.	• Use the reactivity series to predict which metals will displace others from solutions of their salts. • Carry out some displacement reactions. • Practise writing word equations.	• Use the reactivity series to predict the metals that will displace others from a solution of their salts. • Carry out some displacement reactions safely. • Write word equations.

LANGUAGE SUPPORT

Learners will use the following words:

reactivity: how quickly or slowly a chemical reacts compared with another

reactivity series: a list of metals in order of how reactive they are; the most reactive are at the top of the list and the least reactive at the bottom

displacement reaction: a reaction in which a more reactive metal 'pushes out' a less reactive one from a compound

Common misconceptions

Misconception	How to identify	How to overcome
Some learners do not see any pattern in which metal can displace another.	The mistakes the learners make when asked direct questions about which metal will displace another will reveal this misconception.	You could try acting out the reactions using learners as the particles of copper sulfate and iron.

Starter ideas

1 Getting started (10 minutes)

Learning intention: To assess how much learners have understood about how to tell that a chemical reaction has taken place.

Description: Ask learners to discuss with a partner how you can tell if a chemical reaction has taken place. Ask them to share their ideas with another pair. Share ideas with the class and spend some time reinforcing the ways to tell if a chemical reaction has taken place.

2 Words that begin with... (10 minutes)

Learning intention: To improve scientific vocabulary.

Resources: Learner's Book

Description: Write the word 'reactivity' vertically on the board. Challenge learners to find scientific words starting with those letters. You could restrict learners to words connected with this particular topic or give them a wider choice of vocabulary. You could allow access to the Learner's Book or not.

Allow a fixed time (5 minutes or less) and ask for ideas from the learners. Check that they have an idea what the word means. You can award points for a correct word and extra points if no one else has this word.

Make sure learners do not choose difficult words they do not know the meaning of, although some learners love to find the hardest words they can. This can be a real boost to their scientific vocabulary, especially if this technique is used regularly.

Main teaching ideas

1 Activity: Learning the order (at least 40 minutes)

Learning intention: To learn the order of the reactivity series using different methods and to decide which method is most effective for the learners.

Resources: Learner's Book, poster-making resources (e.g., paper and/or card, glue, coloured pencils or pens), Template 1: Reactivity series cards.

Description: Suggest to the learners that, working with a partner, they should try the methods described in the Learner's Book to learn the order of the reactivity series: making up a mnemonic and making it into a poster to share with the class; using the cards made from the template to place them in

the correct order in the fastest time; taking a card and the partner having to name the metal above or below the metal selected.

You could encourage them to use any other methods that they choose.

> **Differentiation ideas:** The use of different methods of learning is a way of differentiating.

> **Assessment ideas:** You could ask the learners to list the reactivity series metals in the correct order as an individual test or by going around the room and asking learners to name the next one. You could use the posters of the mnemonics to assess their work.

2 Introducing the idea of displacement reactions (30 minutes)

Learning intention: To demonstrate a displacement reaction.

Resources: A beaker of copper sulfate solution, an iron nail.

Description: Introduce the idea of displacement reactions using the copper sulfate and iron nail experiment, as in the Learner's Book. It can be useful to introduce the experiment as a 'trick' and ask the learners, 'What is going on here?'

Make sure you draw learners' attention to the change in the copper sulfate solution and take time to go over the word equation. You could use this as an illustration of the reactivity series and the displacement reactions. Ask questions such as: 'You have seen iron displace copper from copper sulfate. What would happen if you used iron sulfate and a copper nail? Why would this be?' You could suggest a variety of metals and ask whether there would be a displacement reaction.

> **Differentiation ideas:** For learners requiring support, questions such as those examples given above could be used to support understanding and elicit further ideas.

You could ask the learners who need a challenge to write a word equation for the reaction they have seen demonstrated.

> **Assessment ideas:** You could use questions 1–9 to assess progress and understanding.

3 Think like a scientist: Displacing metals (40 minutes)

Learning intention: To carry out some displacement reactions and to understand which metals will displace others.

Resources:

- solutions of copper sulfate, magnesium sulfate, iron sulfate and zinc sulfate
- small pieces of the metals iron, zinc, copper and magnesium
- test tubes
- test tube rack
- forceps
- safety glasses.

Description: Ask the learners to read through the method in the Learner's Book and to prepare a results table before they start to do the practical task. You may need to demonstrate good laboratory practice and logical, careful working with particular emphasis on safety.

> **Practical guidance:** Learners should work in pairs. Make sure that the solutions and metals are clearly labelled and that the learners have a way of ensuring they do not mix up the solutions and metals. Copper sulfate solution is an irritant.

Make sure that there is a sieve in each sink so that the small pieces of metal do not block the waste pipes when the learners clear up.

> **Differentiation ideas:** As you circulate while the learners carry out the practical work, ask questions such as: 'Has this metal reacted or not? How can you tell?' You may need to provide support to groups who find it difficult to tell if a reaction has taken place. Some groups may need help with recording their results.

For those groups that need a challenge, ask them to write the word equation for each reaction that takes place.

> **Assessment ideas:** You could use *Think like a scientist* questions 1–3 to assess the work done in this practical.

Plenary ideas

1 Speed listing (10 minutes)

Description: Ask learners to list the metals in the reactivity series in order without the help of the Learner's Book. Then ask them to compare their list with a partner and to correct their list if necessary. Ask them to leave the corrected lists when they leave the lesson.

> **Reflection ideas:** How well have I done learning the list?

2 Word equations (10 minutes)

Resources: Pre-prepared equations.

Description: Put some incomplete word equations on the board. Ask learners to complete those in which a reaction would take place. Compare answers with a partner.

> **Reflection ideas:** Have I understood when a displacement reaction takes place? Can I explain it?

Homework ideas

1 Workbook Exercises 5.1A–C

Topic worksheet

- Worksheet 5.1, Is there a reaction? (with support and extension sheets)

Topic 5.2 Using the reactivity series and displacement reactions

LEARNING PLAN		
Learning Objectives	**Learning intentions**	**Success criteria**
9Cc.02 Identify examples of displacement reactions and predict products (limited to reactions involving calcium, magnesium, zinc, iron, copper, gold and silver salts).	• Use displacement reactions to identify an unknown metal.	• Be able to identify an unknown metal using displacement reactions.

CONTINUED

Learning Objectives	Learning intentions	Success criteria
9TWSm.03 Use symbols and formulae to represent scientific ideas. 9TWSp.03 Make predictions of likely outcomes for a scientific enquiry based on scientific knowledge and understanding.	• Learn about some useful displacement reactions.	• Describe some useful displacement reactions.

LANGUAGE SUPPORT

Learners will use the following words:

molten: in a liquid state

ores: rocks or minerals that contain a metal compound

Common misconceptions

Misconception	How to identify	How to overcome
Some learners think all metals can be extracted using carbon.	Ask direct questions about which metals could be extracted by using carbon	Reinforcement of the reactivity series, placing carbon in the list in an appropriate place.

Starter ideas

1 **Getting started (10 minutes)**

Learning intention: To reinforce the reactivity series.

Description: Ask learners to work with a partner. One of the pair writes down the name of a metal in the reactivity series in the middle of a piece of paper. The paper is then passed to the partner and they add the name of the metal that is just above or just below the first metal. The paper is passed back and the first person adds the name of the metal that is just above or below the metals on the paper. Do this until the reactivity series is complete. Share your list with the class.

2 **Will A displace B? (10 minutes)**

Learning intention: To reinforce the idea of the reactivity series and which is the more or less reactive metal.

Resources: You could use the cards of the metals from the reactivity series from Template 1.

Description: Working in pairs, one learner takes a card from those placed face down on the desk: this is metal A. The other learner takes a card: this is metal B. The question is, will A displace B?

Learners should list their choices and answers and share these with the class.

Main teaching ideas

1 **Think like a scientist: Identifying a mystery metal – planning the investigation (40 minutes)**

Learning intention: To plan an investigation.

Resources: Template 3 Planning outline could be used for some learners.

Description: Explain to learners that their task is to identify a mystery metal. It is one of the metals listed on the reactivity series. They are going to investigate which metal it could be and can make observations of the metal, for example, its appearance and its reactions with water, oxygen and dilute acid. They must also use displacement reactions.

Ask them to plan the investigation to identify the mystery metal.

Remind learners that they should remember their safety and include in their plan anything they need to consider. They should identify the equipment and chemicals they need to use. Explain that they need to give full details of what they will do and indicate what information they will get from that part of the investigation, and explain how it will help them to identify the mystery metal. You could allow learners to work in pairs or alone for this task. If they work in pairs, ensure both partners are involved equally.

〉 **Differentiation ideas:** Template 3 could be given to those learners who find organising the planning of an investigation challenging and need to have a more structured approach. As you circulate, keep a close eye on what learners have written and, to see which learners need support, ask questions such as: 'What will that tell you about the metal?' 'Which solutions will you use?'

〉 **Assessment ideas:** You could use the plans to assess learners' progress in planning an investigation.

2 Think like a scientist: Identifying a mystery metal – carrying out the investigation (50 minutes)

Learning intention: To use knowledge of the reactivity series, displacement reactions and observations of the properties to identify an unknown metal.

Resources: This will depend on what the learners have planned for, but is likely to include: test tubes, test tube rack, forceps, eye protection, dilute acid, water, heating equipment, a selection of common solutions of salts (such as copper sulfate, silver nitrate, zinc chloride), small pieces of an unknown metal (choose one that is in the middle of the reactivity series).

Description: Since you will have approved the plans for the investigation and their risk assessments, allow the learners to select their equipment and start their investigations. Ensure that safety is being considered as you circulate. Encourage the learners to do the observations that do not involve displacement reactions first, so they will have an idea of how reactive their metal is. Encourage them to use the information they get about the metal to change their plan if necessary, but insist that any changes need to be approved first.

You may choose to give the class an outline of what you want them to do and the order in which to do it, rather than to use their plans.

〉 **Practical guidance:** You will need to be vigilant and circulate throughout the room to ensure safe working and to make sure learners know what each investigation has told them about the mystery metal.

〉 **Differentiation ideas:** You could use different metals and offer more help to those learners who find a complex set of investigations confusing. Offer suggestions and ask: 'What does that observation/ reaction tell you about the metal?'

This task can be used as a real challenge to those learners who need one. As long as you are able to ensure they are working safely, give these learners little or no technical guidance and allow them to work it out for themselves.

〉 **Assessment ideas:** You could use the answers to *Think like a scientist* questions 1–3 to assess the outcomes.

3 Think like a scientist: Extracting metals using carbon (20 minutes)

Learning intention: To show a practical application of a displacement reaction using carbon.

Resources: Safety glasses, copper oxide powder, charcoal powder, spatula, test tube or boiling tube, heatproof mat, Bunsen burner. (Other forms of heating are unlikely to generate enough direct heat for this activity.)

Description: The learners should place a spatula of copper oxide in a test tube. A spatula of charcoal powder should be added on top of the copper oxide. The two powders should not be mixed. This will enable you to spot the changes when the copper oxide and charcoal react. The two layers should be heated strongly in a Bunsen flame for five minutes. The tube must be allowed to cool. Once the contents have cooled the students should look carefully at the area where the two layers meet. The students should record their detailed observations. It should be possible to see the copper formed at the junction of the two powders.

〉 **Practical guidance:** Safety glasses should be worn. Care should be taken as the tube will get very hot. You may choose to do this as a demonstration.

〉 **Differentiation ideas:** You may need to give differing levels of practical support to those who are less dexterous.

〉 **Assessment ideas:** You could use this task as an opportunity to assess the learners' ability to carry out an adequate risk assessment.

4 Using displacement reactions in industry (40 minutes)

Learning intention: To understand some industrial uses of displacement reactions. The details of the thermite reaction and blast furnace are extension material. However, they provide useful examples of the use of displacement reactions. Note that this is extension material.

Resources: Learner's Book. For thermite reaction:

- large filter papers
- pipeclay triangle
- tripod
- Bunsen burner (it is unlikely that alternative heating arrangements will be able to generate enough heat safely in the laboratory for this activity)
- a thick-walled beaker (1 litre)
- dry sand
- heatproof mats – enough to protect the work surface
- safety screens – enough to surround the apparatus
- a face shield for you
- safety glasses for observers
- a bar magnet
- thermite mixture: iron(III) oxide and aluminium powder (This mixture should be in the ratio of three parts iron oxide to one part aluminium powder; use no more than 9 g of iron oxide and 3 g of aluminium powder)
- ignition mixture: magnesium powder and barium sulfate in the ratio 1 : 10 (0.2 g magnesium powder is enough)
- magnesium ribbon (about 10 cm).

Description: Introduce the idea of using displacement reactions in industry by explaining the reactions given in the Learner's Book.

You may want to demonstrate the thermite reaction. If so, check local health and safety requirements. You should carry this out after practicing without learners present and in suitable conditions, possibly outside. The thermite reaction is a spectacular reaction and learners enjoy seeing it. There are a number of ways of carrying out this reaction; all methods require a great deal of preparation and care. There are a number of safety issues. The learners should be encouraged to observe the reaction and explain what happens. The use of the term 'exothermic' would be a useful reminder of a previous topic. It is worth discussing the melting point of iron and thus giving an idea of how much energy is released in this reaction. The reaction could be shown via a video clip from the internet.

You could then go on to discuss the role of carbon in the displacement of iron from iron ore and the use of the blast furnace.

⟩ **Practical guidance:** There are a number of ways in which this reaction can be carried out and a search of the internet will provide ideas. It is important that you practise this before carrying out the reaction with a class. The reaction is very vigorous and you need to be prepared. The basic idea is that the thermite mixture, composed of iron oxide and aluminium powder, reacts to form aluminium oxide and iron.

The reaction is started by the use of an ignition mixture. This ignition mixture is composed of barium nitrate and magnesium powder, which is placed into the thermite mixture. The ignition reaction is started by lighting a magnesium ribbon fuse, which is stuck into the ignition mixture so that it stands clear of the mixture. The ignition reaction proceeds, producing enough heat energy to start the thermite reaction. Safety is an issue, as there is a great deal of heat energy released.

The method given here can be carried out on a laboratory bench. The mixtures must be prepared in advance. The iron oxide must be dry, the iron oxide and aluminium powder should be well mixed and the quantities used must be in the exact ratio specified.

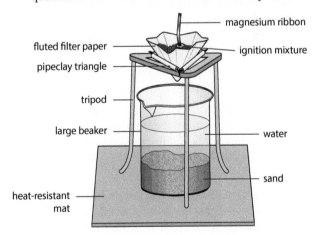

Fold two filter papers into a fluted shape. Place dry sand in the large beaker (about a third full) then add water (about two-thirds full). Clear the bench and cover with heatproof mats. Assemble the apparatus as shown above. Add the thermite mixture to the filter paper. Make a dent in the surface of the mixture (this can be done with the closed end of a boiling tube) and add the ignition mixture. Place the magnesium ribbon into the ignition mixture so that the ribbon stands clear above the filter paper. Ensure the safety screens are in place and that the students are standing well away from the reaction.

Heat the magnesium ribbon with a Bunsen burner and move quickly to the other side of the safety screen. The reaction will be very vigorous; there will be flying sparks. The residue, which will include the hot molten iron, will fall through the filter paper into the beaker. The iron can be recovered once the reaction has stopped and cooled by pouring away the water and using a magnet.

A laboratory coat should be worn as there is a lot of mess while clearing up the reaction.

Other ways of carrying out this reaction involve placing the thermite mixture on top of some dry sand in a large tin. The ignition mixture is added as above into a depression in the thermite mixture. The ignition mixture is ignited via a magnesium ribbon fuse as in the method above. It takes a long time to cool the residue and then the iron can be found in the sand by the use of a magnet. An internet search of chemistry sites will provide alternative methods.

Learners should wear safety glasses and be placed as far away as possible behind safety screens. The demonstrator should wear a face shield and a laboratory coat.

Aluminium powder and magnesium powder are both highly flammable and should not be left in the area while the reaction is taking place. Barium nitrate is harmful and oxidising.

⟩ **Differentiation ideas:** This demonstration cannot involve learners, so differentiation will be in the explanations and questions asked to the learners as you demonstrate the reaction or explore the ideas from the Learner's Book.

For learners who need support, helpful questions to find out what they have understood include: 'What do we mean by an exothermic reaction?' 'Why do we need to use the magnesium ribbon?' 'What did you see happening?'

Examples of questions that could be used to challenge learners include: 'What reaction happens when the magnesium ribbon is lit?' 'What is the

word equation for this?' 'The heat given off from the burning magnesium reaction is used to do what?' 'What happens in the ignition mixture?' 'What is the word equation for the reaction between the iron oxide and aluminium powder?'

Workbook Exercises 5.2 could be used to help with understanding.

⟩ **Assessment ideas:** You could use questions 1–3 from the Learner's Book.

Plenary ideas

1   Pyramid ideas (10 minutes)
Description:

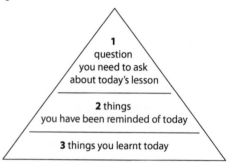

Ask learners to complete the pyramid as above and use it as an exit card so that you have a chance to see what, if anything, they need to have explained to them in the next session.

⟩ **Reflection ideas:** Does stopping and thinking about the lesson or parts of the lesson help me to learn more easily?

2   What did I learn today? (10 minutes)
Description: Ask learners to work in pairs and to share one new thing they learnt today and one new word they learnt today. Share these with the class.

⟩ **Reflection ideas:** Does doing a practical task help me to remember facts more easily?

Homework idea

1   Workbook Exercise 5.2

Topic 5.3 Salts

LEARNING PLAN

Learning Objectives	Learning intentions	Success criteria
9Cc.01 Use word equations and symbol equations to describe reactions (balancing symbol equations is not required). 9Cc.03 Describe how to prepare some common salts by the reactions of metals with acids and metal carbonates with acids, and purify them using filtration, evaporation and crystallisation. 9TWSm.03 Use symbols and formulae to represent scientific ideas. 9TWSp.05 Make risk assessments for practical work to identify and control risks.	• Learn what a salt is and some examples of salts and their uses. • Carry out a practical to prepare a salt by reacting a metal with an acid. • Carry out a practical to prepare a salt by heating a metal oxide with an acid. • Practise writing word equations.	• Be able to explain what a salt is. • List some examples of salts and state their uses. • Prepare a salt safely by reacting a metal with an acid. • Prepare a salt safely by heating a metal oxide with and acid. • Write word equations.

LANGUAGE SUPPORT

Learners will use the following words:

salt: a compound formed when a metal reacts with an acid, for example, magnesium chloride

formula: uses chemical symbols to show how many atoms of different elements are present in a particle of an element or compound (the plural is formulae)

chloride: a salt that is made from hydrochloric acid

sulfate: a salt that is made from sulfuric acid

nitrate: a salt that is made from nitric acid

carbonate: a salt that is made from carbonic acid

citrate: a salt that is made from citric acid

crystallisation: the process of turning into crystals

Common misconceptions

Misconception	How to identify	How to overcome
Some learners do not believe they need to organise themselves to carry out a multi-step practical.	Watch carefully as they carry out the practical.	Offer support and help with organisation.
All acids are strong and corrosive.	Ask learners direct questions as to what the risks of acids are.	Give learners examples of weak acids that are not corrosive.
Alkalis (the opposite of acids) are not dangerous.	Directly ask learners whether alkalis can be dangerous.	Describe examples of reactions involving alkalis that show how they can be dangerous if safety precautions are not taken.

Misconception	How to identify	How to overcome
All salts are the same as table salt (sodium chloride).	Ask learners to provide examples of salts.	Explain what a salt is and give other examples of salts, and explain that they will learn how they are formed.
When a metal reacts with an acid, it vanishes.	It should be obvious from their comments, otherwise keep asking.	If you spend time ensuring they understand which elements are present in the reactants and products, particularly in the compounds, it really helps them to understand.

Starter ideas

1   Getting started (10 minutes)

Learning intention: To ensure ideas about reactivity and displacement reactions are fully understood.

Resources: Learner's Book.

Description: Ask learners to write word equations for three displacement reactions with a partner. Ask learners to name the compounds, the elements they are made from and the number of atoms of each element present in the formula. Write all five equations on a piece of paper and swap them with another pair of learners. Can each pair identify the reactions that would not take place?

2   What elements are present? (10 minutes)

Learning intention: To remind learners about the use of formulae

Description: Write five formulae on the board, such as $NaCl$, $NaOH$, MgO, KCl and H_2SO_4. Ask learners to name the compounds, the elements they are made from and the number of each element present. Ask them to work in pairs and then share answers with the class.

Main teaching ideas

1   What is a salt and Activity: Researching a salt (50 minutes)

Learning intention: To introduce the idea of what a salt is, to give examples and uses of some salts; to research a salt and how it is produced and used.

Resources: Learner's Book, internet access, examples of common salts found in the laboratory.

Description: Introduce the idea of what a salt is and familiarise learners with terms, such as carbonates and chlorides. You could use the examples given in

the Learner's Book or other examples from salts you have available in the laboratory. Use the table of formulae of acids and salts in the Learner's Book to reinforce these facts.

Lead learners towards the research task, making it clear that you only want a brief account of the way in which the salt is obtained or made and what it is used for. This task could be done in pairs or individually. It would be helpful if you allocated salts rather than allowed learners to pick one. You could use the salts mentioned in the Learner's Book.

〉 **Differentiation ideas:** You could be selective in the salts you allocate to pairs of learners (or individuals). Some of the most obscure could be given to pairs or individuals that need a challenge.

〉 **Assessment ideas:** You could use questions 1–5 to assess knowledge and understanding.

You could also use learners' presentations on the salts to assess.

2   Think like a scientist: Making the salt zinc sulfate (40 minutes plus time to allow evaporation to take place and then look at the crystals)

Learning intention: To carry out a practical task safely and to make a salt using a metal and acid.

Resources: 250 cm³ beaker, dilute sulfuric acid, measuring cylinder, zinc metal, evaporating basin, pipeclay triangle, tripod, Bunsen burner (or other suitable risk assessed means of heating, such as a hot plate), tongs, heatproof mat, safety glasses.

Description: Remind learners of the reaction between some metals and acids. You may want to demonstrate the reaction of acid and zinc in a test tube and work through the general equation, the word equation and the symbol equation. A reminder about the exothermic reaction might be useful revision.

Talk learners thorough the practical task, reminding them of the risks. You could demonstrate using some learners as assistants and ask them to comment on the risks. Another idea is to demonstrate badly and ask learners to identify what you did in an unsafe or inaccurate manner. Ask the learners to stop you if they see you do anything wrong or inaccurate. Perhaps wear your safety glasses on your head at the start of the demonstration or be a little careless about measuring or transferring liquids.

> **Practical guidance:** Circulate while the learners are carrying out the practical and keep asking them what they are doing to stay safe.

> **Differentiation ideas:** Keep a watch on those who find the organisation of practical work a challenge and offer them more help and support.

You could give the groups who need a challenge the same mass of zinc metal and challenge them to find the mass of the salt produced and compare the results obtained. Which groups produced the greatest mass of salt? Why were the masses obtained different? What should they do to ensure they produced the greatest possible mass of salt?

> **Assessment ideas:** You could use *Think like a scientist* questions 1–4 to assess the learners' understanding.

3   Think like a scientist: Making the salt copper sulfate (40 minutes)

Learning intention: To carry out a practical safely and use another method for producing a salt.

Resources: Safety glasses, 250 cm^3 beaker, glass stirring rod, copper oxide powder, dilute sulfuric acid, measuring cylinder, filter funnel, filter paper, conical flask, evaporating basin, tripod, gauze, pipeclay triangle, heatproof mat, Bunsen burner, tongs.

Description: Talk learners through the steps for the practical. You may decide to demonstrate each step. You could demonstrate using some learners as assistants and ask them to comment on the risks. Another idea is to demonstrate badly and ask learners to identify what you did in an unsafe or inaccurate manner. Perhaps use an inappropriately sized measuring cylinder or be a little careless about transferring liquids. You could use whichever idea you did not use in the previous practical.

Make sure that before they start the practical task the learners answer *Think like a scientist* questions 1 and 2. These ask learners to decide what equipment

they will need and to do a risk assessment.

> **Practical guidance:** Circulate while they are carrying out the practical and offer additional help to those who find the organisation of a multi-step practical a challenge.

> **Differentiation ideas:** See above and offer additional help to those who find the organisation of a multi-step practical a challenge. You could help some groups with ideas about what equipment they will need by asking questions such as: 'How will you measure the volume of acid?' 'How will you move the hot evaporating basin?'

The learners who need a challenge could be asked to write word and chemical equations for the reaction. You could try the same idea as in the formation of the zinc salt. You could give the groups who need a challenge the same mass of copper oxide and challenge them to find the mass of the copper sulfate produced and compare the results obtained. Which groups produced the greatest mass of copper sulfate? Why were the masses obtained different? What should they have done to ensure they produced the greatest possible mass of copper sulfate? Where are the sources of error in the practical steps taken?

> **Assessment ideas:** You could use *Think like a scientist* questions 1–6 to assess learners. You could also watch them carefully and assess their practical skills.

Plenary ideas

1   Five fingers (10 minutes)

Description: Learners draw around their hand on a scrap of paper or in their book and write the answers to the following questions along each finger.

- Thumb: What have you learnt? What do you understand?
- Index finger: What skills have you used today?
- Middle finger: Which skills did you find difficult today?
- Ring finger: Who did you help today?
- Little finger: What will you make sure that you remember from today's lesson?

It will be useful to collect these in and use them to help you decide what you need to concentrate on in the next lesson.

> **Reflection ideas:** This type of plenary is a way of structuring learners' reflection time. It allows the learners who need most support to celebrate what they have done well and encourages those who need a challenge to think about the next steps in learning.

2 Exit ticket emoji (10 minutes)

Resources: Sticky notes or paper.

Description: Ask learners to draw an emoji for how they feel they did in the lesson and to answer the following.

* How well did you understand today's material?

* What did you learn today?

* What did you find difficult today?

Homework ideas

1 Workbook Exercises 5.3A–C

Topic worksheets

* There are no worksheets for this topic

Topic 5.4 Other ways of making salts

LEARNING PLAN

Learning Objectives	Learning intentions	Success criteria
9Cc.03 Describe how to prepare some common salts by the reactions of metals with acids and metal carbonates with acids, and purify them using filtration, evaporation and crystallisation. 9TWSm.03 Use symbols and formulae to represent scientific ideas.	• Learn how to safely prepare a salt by action of an acid on a carbonate. • Learn how to safely prepare a salt by neutralisation. • Carry out risk assessments for practical work. • Use word and symbol equations.	• To safely prepare a salt by action of an acid on a carbonate. • To prepare a salt by neutralisation. • Write risk assessments for practical tasks. • Use word and symbol equations.

LANGUAGE SUPPORT

Learners will use the following words:

crystallise: to form crystals

limestone: a sedimentary rock made from calcium carbonate

erodes: wears away

neutralisation: to change an acid or alkaline solution to one that has a pH of 7

bases: metal oxides are known as bases

Common misconceptions

Misconception	How to identify	How to overcome
Some learners may have difficulty with the practical tasks.	Watch carefully as they attempt the tasks.	Demonstrate the tasks carefully before the class undertake them. You could use learners to help in the demonstration. Offer help and support during the practical work.

Starter ideas

1 Getting started (10 minutes)

Learning intention: To revise the properties of acids and alkalis.

Description: Ask the learners to make a list of the properties of acids and alkalis, such as their pH values, what element they all contain, the colour they turn universal indicator solution. Ask them to write the properties down but mix together the properties of acids and alkali. Learners should exchange their list with a partner and sort the properties into those of acids and alkalis. Ask them how well they did and feedback to the class.

2 Name that salt (10 minutes)

Learning intention: to familiarise the learners with the names and formulae of salts.

Resources: Prepared list of formulae for salts on the board.

Description: Write a list of common salt formulae on the board and ask the learners to name them. You could allow them to work individually or in pairs.

Main teaching ideas

1 Metal carbonates and acids (15 minutes, or 40 minutes if learners do the practical task)

Learning intention: To revise the reactions and focus on the word and symbol equations.

Resources: Learner's Book, various metal carbonates and common acids, test tubes, delivery tube arrangement suitable for testing the gas given off, limewater, safety glasses.

Description: You could do this as a demonstration to remind learners of this reaction, which they will have met in stage 8, or you could allow the learners to do it themselves. Remind them of the reaction. Discuss the word equations and ensure they are happy with what happens if you change the acid and/or change the carbonate. You could spend some time looking at the symbol equations. At this level learners are not expected to balance the equations.

⟩ **Practical guidance:** Remind learners of safety issues if they are carrying out the practical.

⟩ **Differentiation ideas:** Use the learners who have the most difficulty with practical skills to help you with the demonstration. Ask them, 'What do I do next?'

'What should I be careful with here?' 'How can I keep myself safe?' You could ask others to suggest the next steps and just allow your demonstrating learner to follow instructions.

⟩ **Assessment ideas:** You could use questions 1–3.

2 Think like a scientist: Preparing a salt from acid and a carbonate (50 minutes plus time for crystallisation)

Learning intention: To prepare a salt by action of an acid on a carbonate, to improve practical skills and to write a risk assessment.

Resources: Safety glasses, copper carbonate, dilute hydrochloric acid, beaker, measuring cylinder, spatula, filter funnel, filter paper, conical flask, evaporating basin, pipeclay triangle, tripod, Bunsen burner or other suitable heating arrangement, such as a hot plate or spirit burner, heatproof mat, tongs.

Description: Talk learners through the method as in the Learner's Book. You could do a demonstration of the various steps using some class members to help. Allow learners to work in groups of two or three. Make sure that they understand that they have to answer the first two questions before they do the practical task; these involve writing the equipment list and carrying out the risk assessment.

⟩ **Practical guidance:** Circulate as they carry out the task, asking about the risks and what they are doing to overcome them. You could also stress what they should do to make sure that they get pure crystals of the salt.

⟩ **Differentiation ideas:** You could use learners to help with the demonstration and have them guided by the class as to what they should do next and how they should do it. This can be done using the least practically skilled learners to undertake the practical at the direction of the class. Or you could give the least practically skilled the task of directing the most skilled at practical tasks.

You could provide the learners who have difficulty thinking of the equipment they will need with a list of equipment with some obvious missing items to help them produce a list more easily.

You could use Template 4 to help those who find a longer written task a challenge.

When you circulate during the practical, you could offer help and advice about the task to those who need it. You could ask: 'Why are you doing that?' 'How will that ensure you produce a pure product?'

> **Assessment ideas:** You could use *Think like a scientist* questions 1–9 to assess understanding and progress. You could also use the crystals obtained to assess how careful the learners were in carrying out the task.

3 Think like a scientist: Preparing a salt by neutralisation (50 minutes plus time for crystallisation)

Learning intention: To prepare a salt by neutralisation, to improve practical skills and to write a risk assessment.

Resources: Safety glasses, dilute hydrochloric acid, dilute sodium hydroxide solution, universal indicator solution, charcoal powder, burette, burette stand, small funnel (to fill burette), measuring cylinder, two conical flasks, beaker, glass stirring rod, filter funnel, filter paper, tripod, pipeclay triangle, evaporating basin, tongs, heatproof mat.

Description: You could revise the ideas about neutralisation before you attempt the practical task.

Talk learners through the method as in the Learner's Book. You could do a demonstration of the various steps using some class members to help. Allow learners to work in groups of two or three. Make sure that they understand that they have to answer the first two questions before they do the practical task; these involve writing the equipment list and carrying out the risk assessment.

> **Practical guidance:** There are safety issues here from the very start with filling the burette; make sure learners are aware how this should be done.

> **Differentiation ideas:** You could use learners to help with the demonstration and have them guided by the class as to what they should do next and how they should do it. This can be done using the least practically skilled learners to undertake the practical at the direction of the class. Or you could give the least practically skilled the task of directing the most skilled at practical tasks.

You could provide the learners who have difficulty thinking of the equipment they will need with a list of equipment with some obvious missing items to help them produce a list more easily.

You could use Template 4 to help those who find a longer written task a challenge.

When you circulate during the practical, you could offer help and advice about the task to those who need it. You could ask: 'Why are you doing that?' 'How will that ensure you produce a pure product?'

> **Assessment ideas:** You could use *Think like a scientist* questions 1–9 to assess the understanding of this task. You could also use the crystals obtained to assess how careful the learners were in carrying out the task.

Plenary ideas

1 Match the formula and the name (10 minutes)

Resources: List of names of salts and a list with formulae of salts.

Description: Learners to work in pairs to match the names of the salts to the formulae. When they have completed them, share with the class.

> **Reflection ideas:** How does writing a risk assessment help me to think about what I can do to avoid any safety problems?

2 Pyramid ideas (10 minutes)

Description: Ask learners to complete the statements on the pyramid and to leave them behind at the end of the lesson. Use these to assess what the learners need to do next in terms of improving their practical work.

> **Reflection ideas:** How does writing an equipment list help me to think about what I need to do in a practical task?

Homework ideas

1 Workbook Exercises 5.4A–C

Topic worksheets

• Worksheets 5.4A–C, Salts, alkalis, formulae and equations

Topic 5.5 Rearranging atoms

LEARNING PLAN

Learning Objectives	Learning intentions	Success criteria
9Cc.01 Use word equations and symbol equations to describe reactions. **9Cc.05** Understand that in chemical reactions mass and energy are conserved. **9TWS Sm.3** Use symbols and formulae to represent scientific ideas. **9TWS Sp.02** Describe examples where scientists' unexpected results from enquiries have led to improved scientific understanding. **9TWS Sp.03** Make predictions of likely outcomes for a scientific enquiry based on scientific knowledge and understanding. **9TWS Sp.05** Make risk assessments for practical work to identify and control risk.	• Look at the rearrangement of atoms in chemical reactions. • Understand what happens to the mass of reactants and products in a reaction. • Understand what happens to the energy involved in chemical reactions. • Carry out practical work safely.	• Use word and symbol equations to describe chemical reactions. • Explain what is meant by the law of conservation of mass. • Explain what is meant by the law of conservation of energy. • Carry out practical work safely.

LANGUAGE SUPPORT

Learners will use the following words:

the law of conservation of mass: the principle that there is no loss or gain of mass in a chemical reaction

crucible: a piece of laboratory equipment; a container that is heated directly at high temperatures

exothermic reaction: a chemical reaction in which energy is transferred to the environment

endothermic reaction: chemical reaction in which energy is transferred from the environment

the law of conservation of energy: the principle that energy cannot be created or destroyed, only changed or transferred

Common misconceptions

Misconception	How to identify	How to overcome
Some learners believe that, if there is a chemical reaction, the mass also changes.	It should be obvious from their comments, otherwise keep asking.	If you spend time ensuring they understand which elements are present in the reactants and products, particularly in the compounds, it really helps them to understand.
Some learners find symbol equations confusing.	They will make errors and not understand what to do with the equations.	Use the layout as in the Learner's Book and show the word equation, the equation showing the atoms and the symbol equations under one another. It helps them to see that the same reaction is being described in different ways.

Starter ideas

1   Getting started (10 minutes)

Learning intention: To revise formulae and names of compounds.

Resources: Piece of paper.

Description: Ask learners to write on a piece of paper the formulae for five compounds, each one on a new line. Then they write the names of an acid, a salt, an alkali and a metal oxide. They swap their paper with a partner and ask them to try to write the name of the compound against each formula and write the formula against each name. How well did they do? Were all the formulae that were written correct? You could ask them to write some on the board for the whole class to share and check.

2   Find a word beginning the letter... (10 minutes)

Learning intention: Improve vocabulary.

Resources: Learner's Book.

Description: Write the word 'formula' vertically on the board. Ask learners to find scientific words beginning with those letters. Feed back to the class. You could award one point for each correct word and two points if no one else has that word.

Main teaching ideas

1   Equations (10–15 minutes)

Learning intention: To look at different ways of representing chemical reactions and to focus on symbol equations.

Resources: Learner's Book.

Description: Look at the first equation for the reaction between iron and sulfur; go through the various ways of representing this reaction by drawing the atoms, writing the word equation and then the symbol equation. Ask the learners what they think of each method. What does the symbol equation tell them that the word equation does not?

Look at the equation for the reaction between magnesium and hydrochloric acid. Ask them to write the equations for the reaction between magnesium and the other common acids. The aim here is to make learners familiar with symbol equations. There is no requirement for them to be able to balance equations. This is a chance to stop and think about writing equations.

⟩ **Differentiation ideas:** For those who need a challenge, you could ask them to go back thorough the Learner's Book and attempt to write symbol equations for each word equation they find.

Those learners who need support would benefit from doing more examples in small groups with teacher support step-by-step. This will give them confidence to try some on their own.

⟩ **Assessment ideas:** You could use questions 1–2.

2 Think like a scientist: The law of conservation of mass (60 minutes)

Learning intention: To introduce the idea of conservation of mass and to demonstrate it by carrying out a practical test.

Resources: Learner's Book, Safety glasses, top pan balance, flask with stopper, calcium carbonate, dilute hydrochloric acid.

Description: There are several ways you could introduce this: either by working through the content in the Learner's Book and then doing the practical or by carrying out a demonstration, without giving away what will happen. You could use learners as assistants and ask them to observe closely as it will help them when it is their turn to undertake this practical work. You could ask for suggestions as to what would happen rather in the manner of the children in the text. For the practical task, learners should work in pairs if possible.

Some learners are confused by the lack of change in the mass, as they think the gas should somehow make it lighter. So, discussion of the results obtained is essential. Referring back to the equations and the fact that the atoms have not been lost or created just re-arranged into new products will help.

You may be restricted as far as a class practical is concerned by a lack of top pan balances. You could overcome this by preparing small amounts of the calcium carbonate in advance for each group (perhaps on filter paper) and recording the mass for them on the filter paper. Then all learners need to do is find the mass of the flask and acid (which they can do at any time before adding the carbonate) and add the mass of the calcium carbonate to find the total mass at the start. Each group can then find the total mass again when the reaction has stopped. This may need some careful organisation on your part.

> **Practical guidance:** You will need to make it clear that the stopper needs to be placed in the neck of the flask as soon as possible once the calcium carbonate has been added. Circulate as the groups are waiting for the reaction to finish and ask questions such as: 'What are the products of this reaction?' 'What is the equation?' 'Can you write it out?' 'Are there any safety concerns with this experiment?' 'Are there any sources of error?'

You could follow up the practical task with a look at the experiment with the same chemical reaction in the flask but with no stopper. You could do this as a demonstration in class or organise for one group to do the practical without a stopper (keep it hidden from the rest of the class if possible.) This is a good time to make the general point about how results may appear to be unexpected and need to be investigated further.

> **Differentiation ideas:** Choose to use some less confident learners to be your assistants. Make positive comments about how quickly they got the stopper in the flask or how carefully they added the carbonate so it did not splash; this may help to give these learners more confidence.

Think about the groups you will use for the practical work and ensure that the least confident cannot shelter behind more confident learners. Plan the use of the top pan balance(s) if sharing is necessary, making allowances for those who will be slower getting set up.

You could use one of the groups that need to be challenged to be the group without the stopper. They should be able to deflect any other group who notice what they have done and to cope with any criticism.

> **Assessment ideas:** You could use *Think like a scientist* questions 1–4 and questions 3–5 to assess understanding.

3 Think like a scientist: Burning magnesium in air (40 minutes)

Learning intention: To look closely at the conservation of mass when the results are not what were expected.

Resources: Safety glasses, piece of magnesium ribbon, crucible with lid, pipeclay triangle, tripod, Bunsen burner (alternatives for heating such as a spirit burner may not generate enough heat for this task and the use of a hot plate would need to be carefully risk assessed) heatproof mat, tongs, spatula, access to a top pan balance.

Description: Doing a demonstration, working through the text or just directing the learners to carry out the practical task to see what will happen, all qualify as ways to introduce this idea. Whichever way you choose, you will need to have a full discussion of what the results show and what they mean in terms of the law of conservation of mass.

If you chose to demonstrate, use learners as assistants and stress the safety issues. Ask questions such as: 'What is happening in this reaction?' 'What will happen to the mass?' 'How can we ensure the magnesium has enough oxygen to react with?'

This is another example of what you should do if the results are not what you expect. A look at the story of Lavoisier would be helpful at this point. Ask the class whether they would have the confidence to say something that is different from that which is expected? Or would they just hide the results and think they did the experiment wrong in some way?

> **Practical guidance:** There are some risks associated with this practical as the crucible gets very hot. You could ask the learners to do a risk assessment using Template 4. Circulate as the learners carry out this practical work and keep an eye out for safety concerns. It is very important that the crucible is allowed to cool before placing it on the top pan balance to avoid damage.

> **Differentiation ideas:** Some learners may have difficulty with organising their readings so you could put a layout on the board for them to follow. If you are doing a demonstration, use the least confident learners and support them by giving clear instructions and asking the rest of the class why a particular step is being done. Ask the more confident learners what they think would happen if the lid of the crucible was not raised at intervals during the process of heating.

> **Assessment ideas:** You could use *Think like a scientist* questions 1–6.

Plenary ideas

1 Pyramid points from the lesson (10 minutes)

Resources: Pyramid outlines: a triangle divided into three by two horizontal lines so that the pyramid is divided into three parts.

Description: Ask learners to write one sentence to summarise the lesson in the base of the pyramid, one phrase to sum up the lesson in the middle section of the pyramid and a single word to be the point of the lesson in the top part of the pyramid. Share some with the class.

> **Reflection ideas:** What have I learnt in this lesson? How does it fit in with the whole unit?

2 Practical points (10 minutes)

Description: Ask learners to state one practical step they made to ensure their experimental work was done safely, one practical step they made to ensure their experimental work was accurate and one practical step they made to ensure their experimental work was well organised. Share some of these with the class.

> **Reflection ideas:** Early scientists got accurate results using very simple equipment: Lavoisier did not have an electronic balance, for example. How can I make sure my practical work is done as carefully and accurately as theirs?

Homework ideas

1 Workbook Exercises 5.5A–C

Topic worksheet

• Worksheet 5.5, How much more mass? (with support and extension sheets)

PROJECT GUIDANCE

This project addresses the following learning objectives:

9SIC.02 Describe how science is applied across societies and industries, and in research.

9SIC.03 Evaluate issues which involve and/or require scientific understanding.

This project is designed to get learners thinking about everyday occasions when the scientific method would be useful.

The project could be introduced by using some advertisements from newspapers, magazines, TV, posters, leaflets or flyers from shops and other businesses; you could also use online advertisements. You will also need to know what the rules about advertising claims are in your area, if there are any, and to be able to suggest where learners can find out what the rules are.

You could introduce the project with the local material or even by using global brand advertising. Try to find examples that fit the two main groups that the project suggests you look at, namely the 50% more or extra free and the ones making claims such as eight out of ten people with headaches recover more quickly if they take this brand of headache cure.

The first group will enable learners to exercise some logic and maths skills and work out how much they are paying for a fixed mass or volume of the product. They can then compare prices and find the better deal. It may be necessary for you to find prices from local supermarkets for the product in various sizes. You might find it easier to purchase the items and allow the learners to find the information given on the packages.

You could approach the second group, where various claims are made, by asking learners to look at TV advertisements and choose the one they would like to investigate or you could allocate appropriate ones, depending on their complexity and the groups of learners.

After a general introduction and class discussion of what the task is about and exactly what you want them to do, split learners into groups of no more than three. Think about how you will group them – a spread of ability or similar abilities. Also think about how you want them to divide the work – all working on each task or on separate tasks and feeding back to the others in the group. Encourage short, focused presentations for each task. You could ask different groups to present different tasks; you could use a peer-assessment template to help them assess one another's work.

Bear in mind that the idea is to get them to question what they are being told and to think about the information and be able to assess how true the statements are.

❯6 Sound and space

Unit plan

Topic	Learning hours	Learning content	Resources
6.1 Loudness and pitch of sound	3-4	The amplitude of a sound wave; the frequency of a sound wave; how amplitude is linked to loudness; how frequency is related to pitch; how to recognise amplitude and frequency from a diagram of a sound wave	**Learner's Book:** Questions 1–4 Activity: Pitch and frequency in music Think like a scientist: Vibrations in a ruler **Workbook:** Exercise 6.1A, Comparing sound waves Exercise 6.1B, Drawing sound waves Exercise 6.1C, Understanding sound waves **Teacher's Resource:** Worksheets 6.1A–C, Amplitude and frequency Template 1: Table of results and graph for *Think like a scientist: vibrations in a ruler*
6.2 Interference of sound	1.5-3	How sound waves can reinforce each other to make louder sounds; how sound waves can cancel each other out to make no sound	**Learner's Book:** Questions 1 – 5 Activity: Reinforcing and cancelling waves Think like a scientist: Listening to sound waves reinforcing **Workbook:** Exercise 6.2A, Reinforcing sound Exercise 6.2B, Cancelling and reinforcing Exercise 6.2C, Interfering sound waves **Teacher's Resource:** Worksheet 6.2, Sound waves reinforcing or cancelling Template 2: Results table for *Think like a scientist: Listening to sound waves reinforcing*
6.3 Formation of the Moon	1.5-2	Evidence for the collision theory for the formation of the Moon	**Learner's Book:** Questions 1–4 Activity: Evidence for the collision theory **Workbook:** Exercise 6.3A, How was the Moon formed? Exercise 6.3B, Describing the collision theory Exercise 6.3C, Evidence for the collision theory
6.4 Nebulae	1.5-2	Nebulae are clouds of dust and gas in space; how stars can form in nebulae.	**Learner's Book:** Questions 1–5 Activity: Virtual tour of nebulae **Workbook:** Exercise 6.4A, What are nebulae? Exercise 6.4B, Types of nebulae Exercise 6.4C, Stellar nurseries

Topic	Learning hours	Learning content	Resources
6.5 Tectonics	1.5-2	How convection currents cause movement of tectonic plates; the evidence we have for tectonic plates.	**Learner's Book:** Questions 1–6 Activity: Pangaea **Workbook:** Exercise 6.5A, Movement of tectonic plates Exercise 6.5B, Tectonic plates Exercise 6.5C, Evidence for tectonic plates
Cross-unit resources			**Learner's Book:** Check your Progress **Project:** Impact craters **Teacher's Resource:** Template 3: Results table for *Project: Impact craters* Language development worksheets 6.1 Forces and energy vocabulary 6.2 Correcting the statements

BACKGROUND/PRIOR KNOWLEDGE

Learners will recall some information about sound and sound waves from Stage 7. The movement of particles in a sound wave and the terms pitch and loudness should be understood before beginning Topics 6.1 and 6.2. Any familiarity with musical instruments of any kind will be beneficial for Topic 6.1.

Although vector addition of particle displacements in waves is beyond the scope of the curriculum, the concept of adding positive and negative numbers can help some learners understand how sound waves can reinforce or cancel in Topic 6.2. For example, the addition of a positive and negative number of equal magnitude gives a result of zero.

The formation of the Solar System was covered in Stage 7. Understanding the way in which planets form from dust and gas will be helpful for learners understanding the collision theory of the formation of the Moon (Topic 6.5); note, this theory is also known as the giant impact hypothesis. The formation of the Solar System will also be helpful for describing what happens in stellar nurseries in Topic 6.4.

Recalling the descriptions of galaxies given in Stage 8 will be helpful for learners understanding what nebulae are in Topic 6.4.

For Topic 6.5, learners will find it helpful to recall the internal structure of the Earth and the model of plate tectonics from Stage 7, together with the concept of convection currents from Stage 9, Unit 3.

TEACHING SKILLS FOCUS

Giving feedback

Keeping feedback simple but effective is helpful for both the teacher and the learner. During a lesson the teacher is preoccupied with many things at once and remembering how to give effective feedback can be a challenge. Learners are also under pressure to remember the content of the topic and to perform well in tasks, so complex feedback will not be effective.

Two simple but effective feedback strategies are two stars and a wish, and the sandwich. As a challenge, try both of these approaches with the same learners during different lessons and see which appears to be more effective.

Two stars and a wish

This approach involves the teacher selecting two things that the learner has done well and giving

CONTINUED

specific praise for these. These could be outcomes that have been achieved or even a good effort applied if the outcome has not been successful.

These are the two stars. The wish is an area for improvement that should always be phrased in a positive way. For example, 'This would be even better if…' The two stars and a wish approach is sometimes also referred to as WWW-EBI (What Went Well, and Even Better If).

The sandwich

Here, the 'bread' at the top and bottom are two things that the learner has done well or two areas of positive praise. The 'filling' in the middle is the area for improvement. Many who use the sandwich approach often forget the second piece of 'bread', but this is important because it leaves the learner with a positive comment.

Topic 6.1 Loudness and pitch of sound

LEARNING PLAN

Learning Objectives	Learning intentions	Success criteria
9Ps.01 Draw and interpret waveforms, and recognise the link between loudness and amplitude, pitch and frequency. 9TWSm.02 Describe some important models, including analogies, and discuss their strengths and weaknesses. 9TWSp.03 Make predictions of likely outcomes for a scientific enquiry based on scientific knowledge and understanding. 9TWSp.04 Plan a range of investigations of different types to obtain appropriate evidence when testing hypotheses. 9TWSc.05 Carry out practical work safely, supported by risk assessments where appropriate. 9TWSc.06 Make an informed decision whether to use evidence from first-hand experience or secondary sources. 9TWSc.07 Collect, record and summarise sufficient observations and measurements, in an appropriate form.	• Find out about the amplitude of a sound wave. • Find out about the frequency of a sound wave. • Learn how amplitude is linked to loudness. • Learn how frequency is related to pitch. • Learn how to recognise amplitude and frequency from a diagram of a sound wave.	• Identify the amplitude from a wave as displayed on an oscilloscope. • Describe how a wave as displayed on an oscilloscope would change if the frequency changed. • Describe how amplitude of a sound wave changes as the loudness of the sound changes. • Describe how the frequency of a sound wave changes as the pitch of the sound changes. • Match different wave forms as displayed on an oscilloscope to different sounds that are described in terms of loudness and pitch.

CONTINUED

Learning Objectives	Learning intentions	Success criteria
9TWSa.01 Evaluate the strength of the evidence collected and how it supports, or refutes, the prediction. 9TWSa.02 Describe trends and patterns in results, identifying any anomalous results and suggesting why results are anomalous. 9TWSa.03 Make conclusions by interpreting results, explain the limitations of the conclusions and describe how the conclusions can be further investigated.		

LANGUAGE SUPPORT

Learners will use the following words:

loudness: the intensity of a sound; very quiet sounds are difficult to hear, whereas very loud sounds can be painful and damaging to the ears

amplitude: the maximum distance moved by a particle in a wave as measured from the position of the particle when there is no wave; the height of a wave, or graph of a wave, from the mid-point to the top

peak: the top of a wave graph where the line is at its highest; also known as a crest

trough: the bottom of a wave graph where the line is at its lowest

oscilloscope: electronic equipment used to display a waveform on a screen

pitch: the highness or lowness of a musical note

frequency: the number of complete vibrations of an object in 1 second

Common misconceptions

Misconception	How to identify	How to overcome
Amplitude is measured from the trough to the peak of a wave.	After learning about amplitude, ask learners to point out amplitude on a wave graph.	Amplitude is a definition that should be learned. Practice at pointing out amplitude correctly is required. The amplitude on a wave graph is from the middle of the graph (x-axis) to the highest (or lowest) point on the graph. Of a vibrating particle or object, the amplitude is the maximum distance moved away from the position where there is no vibration.

Common misconceptions continued

Misconception	How to identify	How to overcome
Frequency can be seen directly from a diagram or graph of a wave.	n/a	Learners should not be asked to label or to point out frequency on a diagram of a wave or on a graph. How to determine frequency from a diagram of a wave or from a graph is beyond the scope of the curriculum. Learners need only know that the distance between the peaks will change if the frequency changes. The peaks will get closer if the frequency increases.

Starter ideas

1 Getting started (5 minutes)

Learning intention: To recall information about sound waves from Stage 7.

Description: Learners can answer the questions individually or by discussing the answers in pairs.

Misconceptions are possible here as some learners think that a sound wave resembles a water wave in terms of particle movement.

2 Slinky spring 'sound' wave (5–10 minutes)

Learning intention: To remind learners how particles vibrate in a sound wave.

Resources: Slinky spring.

Description: Hold one end of the slinky spring and allow a learner to hold the other end. Stretch the spring across a flat surface.

Tell learners that you are the sound source. What way should you move the spring to model a sound wave?

Tell learners to look at the movement of the hand at the source. Ask what ways the movement could change and still keep the coils of the spring vibrating like particles in a sound wave. (The distance of each push and pull; the time between each push and pull.)

Explain that the topic will explain how these changes affect the sound that we hear.

Some learners may think that the spring should be moved from side to side as this resembles what they think of as a wave.

Main teaching ideas

1 Activity: Pitch and frequency in music (15–20 minutes)

Learning intention: To explore the relationship between frequency and pitch.

Resources: The activity can be done without resources, but access to a piano or even another musical instrument such as a guitar would be helpful.

Description: Learners who study music or who play an instrument could be asked to explain the musical scale to the class. This should be restricted to a scale being comprised of seven 'major' notes called A–G, then the next scale starts from A again.

The purpose of the activity is to allow learners to see the mathematical relationship between the frequencies of musical notes.

It could also be explained that the difference between music and noise is that noise has no such mathematical relationship between the frequencies. Composers of music such as J. S. Bach (1685–1750) were among the first to understand these relationships and used them in their music.

⟩ **Differentiation ideas:** Learners needing more support could be helped to reach the conclusion that the frequency of each A note is double the frequency of the A in the octave below. They could then be given the frequency of any other note, such as B, and asked for the frequency of the note one octave higher.

Learners needing more challenge could research the frequencies of other notes in the scale for themselves and look for relationships between these.

> **Assessment ideas:** Learners can swap the answers to the questions for discussion. If peer-marking, then the teacher should provide the criteria.

2 Think like a scientist: Vibrations in a ruler (20–30 minutes, to include recording results)

Learning intention: To investigate one (or more) of the factors affecting frequency of a vibrating object.

Resources: As listed in the Learner's Book.

Description: Instructions and suggestions are in Learner's Book.

The investigation should be introduced as being based on the familiar activity of flicking the end of a ruler at the edge of a desk.

As an extension, the mass could be kept constant and the length of the ruler that is free to vibrate could be changed.

> **Practical guidance:** Learners must be reminded to count a complete oscillation of the ruler and not half oscillations. It is easier for them to count the number of times the ruler reaches the top or bottom of its oscillation rather than the middle, as the end of the ruler will pass the middle twice per oscillation.

> **Differentiation ideas:** Learners needing more support could be asked to predict the trend. A prompt could be given such as 'As the mass increases, what will happen to the time taken for the ruler to move up and down?'

Learners needing more challenge could be asked about the point about counting made in the practical guidance above.

> **Assessment ideas:** Answers to the *Think like a scientist* question 3 could be used for class discussion.

3 Oscilloscope simulation (10+ minutes)

Learning intention: To relate the graph of a sound wave as seen on an oscilloscope screen to amplitude and frequency, if an oscilloscope is not available.

Resources: Computers or mobile devices and internet access, oscilloscope and sound simulator, headphones (optional).

Description: Some websites have very good oscilloscope simulations. A search term could be 'oscilloscope and sound simulation'. Some of these allow the oscilloscope settings (vertical sensitivity and time base) to be changed, but the teacher

should (initially) provide settings for learners to use. These must stay the same if fair comparisons between waves are to be made.

Learners can vary the pitch and loudness of the sound and observe how the oscilloscope display changes.

> **Differentiation ideas:** Learners needing support can be asked to predict what would change if, for example, the pitch stays the same and the loudness increases.

Learners who need more challenge could be asked to summarise the trends that link pitch to the appearance of the wave on the display and loudness to the appearance of the wave on the display.

> **Assessment ideas:** After the activity, learners can be shown a wave drawn on the board to represent a sound as seen on an oscilloscope. Learners can be asked to come up to the board and draw the wave when, for example, the loudness stays the same and the pitch increases.

Plenary ideas

1 Sketch what you hear (3–5 minutes)

Resources: One musical instrument, paper and pencils.

Description: The teacher, or a learner who has access to their own musical instrument, plays a note of medium pitch (with respect to the instrument's range) and medium loudness. Sketch a wave, as it would appear on an oscilloscope screen, for learners to copy approximately. Leave space for the amplitude and wave spacing to be changed in further sketches. This is the 'reference' note for comparison.

Then play single notes of varying pitch and loudness, allowing time in between for learners to sketch the wave for each.

> **Assessment ideas:** Learners can work in pairs to compare their sketches after each note is played and sketched.

2 What I learned today (1–5 minutes, depending on number of statements)

Resources: Paper, pens.

Description: Learners to list a minimum of four things they have learned in the lesson.

> **Assessment ideas:** This activity can be done in notebooks for assessment at the same time as the next homework or as exit slips.

Homework ideas

1 Questions from the Learner's Book

2 Workbook Exercises 6.1A–C

3 Worksheets 6.1A–C

Topic worksheets

• Worksheets 6.1A–C, Amplitude and frequency

Topic 6.2 Interference of sound

LEARNING PLAN

Learning Objectives	Learning intentions	Success criteria
9Ps.02 Use waveforms to show how sound waves interact to reinforce or cancel each other. **9TWSp.01** Suggest a testable hypothesis based on scientific understanding. **9TWSp.03** Make predictions of likely outcomes for a scientific enquiry based on scientific knowledge and understanding. **9TWSp.05** Make risk assessments for practical work to identify and control risks. **9TWSc.01** Sort, group and classify phenomena, objects, materials and organisms through testing, observation, using secondary information and making and using keys. **9TWSc.03** Decide when to increase the range of observations and measurements, and increase the extent of repetition, to give sufficiently reliable data. **9TWSc.04** Take appropriately accurate and precise measurements, explaining why accuracy and precision are important. **9TWSc.05** Carry out practical work safely, supported by risk assessments where appropriate.	• Find out how sound waves can reinforce each other to make louder sounds. • Find out how sound waves can cancel each other out to make no sound.	• Draw waveforms that would reinforce. • Draw waveforms that would cancel. • Describe the effects of sound waves reinforcing or cancelling.

CONTINUED

Learning Objectives	Learning intentions	Success criteria
9TWSc.07 Collect, record and summarise sufficient observations and measurements, in an appropriate form.		
9TWSa.01 Evaluate the strength of the evidence collected and how it supports, or refutes, the prediction.		
9TWSa.02 Describe trends and patterns in results, identifying any anomalous results and suggesting why results are anomalous.		
9TWSa.03 Make conclusions by interpreting results, explain the limitations of the conclusions and describe how the conclusions can be further investigated.		
9TWSa.04 Evaluate experiments and investigations, including those done by others, and suggest improvements, explaining any proposed changes.		
9TSWa.05 Present and interpret results, and predict results between the data points collected.		

LANGUAGE SUPPORT

Learners will use the following words:

concentric: circles or arcs with a different radius but having the same centre

interference: the effect produced when two or more waves meet

reinforce: in this context, where interference results in an increase in amplitude

Common misconceptions

Misconception	How to identify	How to overcome
Two sounds meeting each other could only ever make a louder sound.	After learning about reinforcing and cancelling, ask what possible effects could occur if two sound waves of the same amplitude and same frequency were to meet.	Show the effects of waves meeting. A result of zero amplitude means no sound.

Starter ideas

1 Getting started (5 minutes)

Learning intention: To allow learners to recall how to compare the amplitudes and frequencies of waves from diagrams.

Resources: Paper and pens.

Description: Learners work in groups, but each learner draws a wave individually without looking at what others are drawing. Squared paper is not needed as these are rough sketches. Learners then sort the waves according to amplitude and again according to frequency.

Learners often mistakenly think the amplitude is the total distance from peak to trough in a wave, so learners could be asked to point out the amplitude on their waves.

2 Showing interference (3–10 minutes, depending on what resources are used)

Learning intention: To show how waves can reinforce or cancel.

Resources: Either an online video clip of a ripple tank with two dippers or a real ripple tank with two dippers.

Description: Explain to learners that all types of wave share some of the same behaviours. Explain that the ripple tank allows water waves to be seen.

The two dippers are used to model two sound sources.

The pattern produced shows waves spreading out from each source, and where the waves meet a pattern can be seen.

The pattern results from alternate positions where waves add together to reinforce each other, or cancel each other out completely. Sound waves can do the same.

The pattern produced by the ripple tank can be difficult for learners to interpret, so it is important that they understand what is being shown. This can be limited to the pattern showing alternate areas of light and dark.

Main teaching ideas

1 Activity: Reinforcing and cancelling waves (10+ minutes)

Learning intention: To use water waves as a model for sound waves and show reinforcing and cancelling.

Description: See Learner's Book.

⟩ **Differentiation ideas:** Learners needing support can be asked for examples where there are two sound sources producing the same sound. (It is acceptable that they say music systems with two speakers; although most of these are stereo, so the sound from each speaker is not exactly the same, this can be overlooked.)

Learners needing a challenge can be asked what each of the parts is modelling.

⟩ **Assessment ideas:** Learners can be asked to draw waves that would meet to reinforce and waves that would meet to cancel.

2 Think like a scientist: Listening to sound waves reinforcing (20 minutes)

Learning intention: To show the effect on loudness of two sound waves reinforcing.

Description: See Learner's Book.

The demonstration of sound wave interference is sometimes done with two loudspeakers connected to the same signal generator. Learners walk around the room and locate areas of louder and quieter sounds. This activity rarely works in a convincing way for learners because there are so many sound reflections in the room.

The activity described in the Learner's Book is similar to one done at a higher level to show stationary waves. Stationary waves should not be mentioned here. All learners need to know in this activity is that the sound from the tuning fork is reflected at the water surface and returns back up the pipe.

If a signal generator and small loudspeaker are available, then this can replace the tuning fork to make the effect even more convincing.

Care should be taken to only hear the first harmonic (shortest possible length of tube to hear an increase in loudness), otherwise there will be no clear trend in the results.

> **Differentiation ideas:** Learners who need support can be asked whether the sound waves are reinforcing or cancelling when the louder sound is heard.

Learners who need a challenge can be asked how the amplitude of the sound wave after reinforcing compares with the amplitude of the sound waves that meet. (It is the sum of the two amplitudes.)

> **Assessment ideas:** Learners can be asked questions to assess their recall of sound wave reflections from Stage 7.

3 Drawing wave forms (15–20 minutes)

Learning intention: To show learners how to draw wave forms and how to align these wave forms to show how they would reinforce or cancel.

Resources: Squared paper, pencil, ruler.

Description: Ask learners to draw a horizontal line across their lined paper with space above and below. This line represents the position of particles when there is no wave.

Ask learners to place dots along their line at regular intervals, for example every four squares. These will be the points where their wave form will cross the line.

Then, at every alternate mid-point between these dots, place another dot at a height above the line that will be the amplitude. For example, if their dots on the line are every four squares then the upper dots should be in a line, say, three squares above the horizontal line. These upper dots should be eight squares apart and positioned mid-way between the dots on the line.

Then form another row of dots three squares below the line, again every eight squares apart, but alternate with the upper row. The curved wave form can then be drawn by joining the dots.

Waves that will meet to reinforce will be identical and aligned vertically peak to peak. Waves that will meet to cancel will also be identical, but aligned vertically peak to trough.

> **Differentiation ideas:** Learners who need support can be helped by the teacher or other learners to draw their wave.

Learners who need a challenge can be asked to draw a wave form with, for example, double the frequency of the first.

> **Assessment ideas:** Ask learners to label the amplitude on their wave. The frequency cannot be labelled, but learners could mark the distance on the diagram (for example, one peak to the next) that would change when the frequency changed.

Plenary ideas

1 What did my partner learn? (2–5 minutes)

Resources: Small, rectangular pieces of paper, approximately 10 cm by 5 cm.

Description: Learners work in pairs and each tells the other what they learned in the lesson or topic. Each learner then summarises, in bullet points, what their partner told them.

> **Assessment ideas:** Read the statements to see what has been learned. If anything is missing, recap next lesson.

2 Interference questions (5 minutes)

Resources: Small pieces of paper.

Description: Each learner writes a question of their choice about waves that cancel or reinforce on their piece of paper. The questions are swapped and learners write the answers to other learners' questions on the reverse of the paper. The question is returned to the person who wrote it for the pair to discuss.

> **Assessment ideas:** The teacher can ask for volunteers to share their questions (not the answers) for class discussion.

Homework ideas

1 Questions from the Learner's Book

2 Workbook Exercises 6.2A–C

3 Worksheet 6.2

Topic worksheet

• Worksheet 6.2, Sound waves reinforcing or cancelling (with support and extension sheets)

Topic 6.3 Formation of the Moon

LEARNING PLAN

Learning Objectives	Learning intentions	Success criteria
9ESs.02 Describe the evidence for the collision theory for the formation of the Moon. 9TWSc.06 Make an informed decision whether to use evidence from first-hand experience or secondary sources. 9TWSm.01 Understand that models and analogies reflect current scientific evidence and understanding, and can change. 9TWSm.02 Describe some important models, including analogies, and discuss their strengths and weaknesses.	• Describe evidence for the collision theory for the formation of the Moon.	• Describe events that comprise the collision theory. • Describe evidence that supports the collision theory. • Describe evidence that contradicts the collision theory.

LANGUAGE SUPPORT

Learners will use the following words:

collision theory: one of the theories for the formation of the Moon; sometimes called the giant impact hypothesis

Starter ideas

1   Getting started (5 minutes)

Learning intention: To start learners thinking about objects, such as the Moon, that can form from dust and gas.

Description: Learners discuss the formation of planets and the Sun in groups.

Dust and gas particles are attracted to each other by gravity. Small objects begin to form that have more gravity and so attract more dust and gas. In this way the object continues to grow and increase in mass.

The activity could show gaps in learning from the formation of the Solar System.

2   Giant impact animation (5 minutes)

Learning intention: To introduce the collision theory.

Resources: Internet access, animation of the giant impact hypothesis.

Description: Internet video sites have animation videos showing what possibly happened to cause the formation of the Moon. Use a search engine to look for 'giant impact hypothesis animation'. One of these can be shown to learners at the start of the lesson to introduce the topic.

Main teaching ideas

1   Activity: Evidence for the collision theory (20–30 minutes)

Learning intention: For learners to research information on the collision theory and find evidence that supports, and evidence that contradicts, the hypothesis.

Resources: Internet access.

Description: See Learner's Book for instructions.

> **Differentiation ideas:** The activity will differentiate by outcome. Learners needing support may find

fewer pieces of evidence and may quote directly from secondary sources, rather than putting the information into their own words.

Learners needing a challenge will find more information and will write this in their own words.

› **Assessment ideas:** Groups can volunteer to present their findings to the class for discussion. Ensure that all members of the group have an active role in the presentation.

2 Explaining the evidence (10–20 minutes, depending on structure)

Learning intention: For learners to consider how the evidence given in the Learner's Book relates to the collision theory.

Description: Each piece of evidence should be discussed by learners in groups. For example, why might the Moon having a lower density than Earth be evidence for this theory? Learners consider the events in the collision theory and realise that the Moon formed from a disc of rocks and dust brought together by gravity. The mass of the Moon is less than Earth, so the rocks and dust would have been pulled together with a smaller force, making it less dense.

› **Differentiation ideas:** This activity is challenging. Learners needing support can be guided through the steps of considering each piece of evidence. This can be done by other learners or by the teacher.

› **Assessment ideas:** Learners can work in groups and present their evidence and reasons why the evidence supports the collision theory. This can be done as if they are scientists presenting a theory for the first time.

3 Other theories (20–30 minutes)

Learning intention: To compare the collision theory with other theories for the formation of the Moon.

Resources: Internet access.

Description: Learners work in groups to do their own research into other theories for the formation of the Moon.

What evidence is there for each of these theories? Is there any evidence for these theories that also supports the collision theory? Why is the collision theory generally accepted over the other theories today?

Learners should, as far as possible, write this up in their own words and avoid copying whole passages from websites.

Learners should reference their findings with the website uniform resource locator (url) and the date it was accessed.

› **Differentiation ideas:** This activity will differentiate by outcome. Learners can be divided into mixed-ability groups, but ensure all members of a group have a role assigned to them.

› **Assessment ideas:** Learner groups can each choose a different theory and a class debate can be held where each group tries to defend their chosen theory.

Plenary ideas

1 Agreement line (2–5 minutes, depending on number of statements)

Description: Learners to gather at one side or the back of the room, where there is clear space for the length or width of the room, which is the imaginary line. One side represents strongly agree and the other represents strongly disagree. The teacher or learner volunteers will make true/false statements about the formation of the Moon and the learners position themselves along the agreement line according to what each individual thinks. The teacher will then ask some individuals why they are at that position.

› **Assessment ideas:** Assessment is part of the activity.

2 Was it easy or difficult? (2–3 minutes)

Resources: Paper and pens.

Description: Learners recall three ideas or concepts from the lesson and rank each as easy, medium or difficult to understand or remember.

› **Assessment ideas:** Learners can compare each other's output from this activity and discuss.

Homework ideas

1   Questions from the Learner's Book

2   Workbook Exercises 6.3A–C

Topic 6.4 Nebulae

LEARNING PLAN

Learning Objectives	Learning intentions	Success criteria
9ESs.03 Know that nebulae are clouds of dust and gas, and can act as stellar nurseries.	• Discover that nebulae are clouds of dust and gas in space. • Learn how stars can form in nebulae.	• Describe what is meant by the word nebula. • Recall that some nebulae contain, or act as, stellar nurseries. • Recall that stellar nurseries are where stars are formed.

LANGUAGE SUPPORT

Learners will use the following words:

nebulae: clouds of dust and gas in space

northern hemisphere: the part of the Earth that is north of the equator

southern hemisphere: the part of the Earth that is south of the equator

stellar nurseries: places within some nebulae where stars are formed

Common misconceptions

Misconception	How to identify	How to overcome
Stars have always existed.	Ask learners whether new stars are coming into existence today, or whether all stars were formed at the same time. This question can be asked before or after learning about stellar nurseries, as the formation of the Sun in the Solar System was described in Stage 7.	Remind learners about the formation of the Solar System. Were there other stars in existence before the Solar System? If yes, then there are other star systems and planet systems forming today. Show images of these.

Starter ideas

1 Getting started (5 minutes)

Learning intention: To allow learners to recall how the Sun and planets were formed.

Description: Learners can work individually, in pairs or in groups.

2 Brainstorm on space (5–10 minutes)

Learning intention: To allow learners to organise their ideas about space.

Resources: Paper and pens.

Description: Learners work in pairs to create a mind map (spider diagram) about space. This should include the types of objects found in space and any other facts learners can recall about these objects.

Some learners may only recall stars and planets but forget about other objects, such as galaxies and asteroids.

Main teaching ideas

1 Activity: Virtual tour of nebulae (20+ minutes)

Learning intention: To research information about nebulae.

Resources: Internet access.

Description: See Learner's Book.

> **Differentiation ideas:** The activity will differentiate by outcome. Learners needing support can extract relevant information, but this can be copied directly from secondary sources. Learners needing a challenge will find more information and will present this in their own words.

> **Assessment ideas:** Learners can volunteer to present their findings to the class for discussion.

2 Explaining nebulae (10–20 minutes)

Learning intention: To explain some facts about different types of nebula.

Description: Different types of nebula are presented to learners, for example, emission, reflection and dark nebulae. Learners can be asked to suggest reasons for the differences. Why might some nebulae emit their own light while others do not?

> **Differentiation ideas:** Learners needing support can be prompted or assisted with making their suggestions. Learners needing challenge can be asked to offer more suggestions for the differences.

> **Assessment ideas:** Pairs of learners can be asked to take it in turns to explain different types of nebula to each other.

3 Stellar nurseries (10 minutes)

Learning intention: To outline the process of star formation.

Description: The life cycle of a star is beyond the scope of the curriculum at this stage, so minimal details of star formation are required. Learners can be reminded about the formation of the Solar System from Stage 7. Star formation can be covered to the same level of depth, explaining that the difference between a star and a planet is size and

mass. The greater pressure inside a more massive object can be large enough to start the reactions that produce heat and light. It could be added that many scientists consider Jupiter to be a 'failed star' in that it did not become quite massive enough to start these reactions.

> **Differentiation ideas:** Learners needing support could think of their own mnemonic to help them remember the stages in star formation. Learners needing a challenge could research information about star formation by themselves and write this up in their own words.

> **Assessment ideas:** Learners could create a storyboard outlining the events in star formation.

Plenary ideas

1 Move around and pair up (3–5 minutes)

Description: Learners, when instructed, will move around the room randomly so they are passing as many different people as possible. When the teacher calls 'stop', learners pair up with the person closest to them. The teacher then asks one member of each pair to explain something about nebulae to their partner; they have 20 seconds. Then they swap roles. The teacher then asks for volunteers to share what their partner told them. Always confirm with the partner that this was correct.

> **Assessment ideas:** Assessment is part of the activity.

2 What did your partner learn? (5 minutes)

Resources: Paper and pens.

Description: Learners work in pairs. One learner describes three things that they learned in the lesson. Then their partner does the same. This can be scaffolded with statements such as: 'Today we used the word ... which means ...'

> **Assessment ideas:** Learners can ask each other questions on what the other has learned, or individuals can volunteer to ask the whole class questions about what they have learned.

Homework ideas

1   Questions from the Learner's Book

2   Workbook Exercises 6.4A–C

Topic 6.5 Tectonics

LEARNING PLAN

Learning Objectives	Learning intentions	Success criteria
9ESp.01 Explain the movement of tectonic plates in terms of convection currents. 9ESp.02 Explain why the jigsaw appearance of continental coasts, location of volcanoes and earthquakes, fossil record and alignment of magnetic materials in the Earth's crust are all evidence for tectonic plates. 9TWSm.01 Understand that models and analogies reflect current scientific evidence and understanding, and can change. 9TWSa.01 Evaluate the strength of the evidence collected and how it supports, or refutes, the prediction. 9TWSa.02 Describe trends and patterns in results, identifying any anomalous results and suggesting why results are anomalous.	• Discover how convection currents cause movement of tectonic plates. • Learn about the evidence we have for tectonic plates.	• Describe how convection currents happen in the mantle and draw diagrams of these. • Recognise the jigsaw appearance of the continents. • Describe how the locations of volcanoes and earthquakes are evidence for tectonic plates. • Describe how the distribution of fossils and the alignment of magnetic parts of rocks are also evidence for tectonic plates.

LANGUAGE SUPPORT

Learners will use the following words:

jigsaw: a type of puzzle where a complete picture is made by fitting smaller interlocking pieces of the picture together

continental coasts: the outlines of the continents that form the boundary between land and sea or ocean

fossil record: the collection of remains of dead animals and plants from millions of years ago that provide evidence of what conditions were like in those times

alignment: the orientation of objects or the way things are lined up according to some external influence

Common misconceptions

Misconception	How to identify	How to overcome
The continents are either in fixed positions and have never moved, or they have moved in the past and are now in fixed positions.	Ask learners whether the continents are moving, or have ever moved in the past.	Learners may not consider that continents are moving because the movement is so slow and they will realise that world maps do not have to be dramatically changed every few months. Show some evidence of continental positions in the past, and also give some speeds of continental movements today (in the range 1–10 cm per year).

Starter ideas

1 Getting started (5 minutes)

Learning intention: To allow learners to draw on prior understanding of the model of tectonic plates that was discussed in Stage 7.

Description: Learners should work in groups of three or four.

2 Naming the continents (5–10 minutes)

Learning intention: To allow learners to think about present-day continents.

Description: Learners work in pairs to make a list of continent names. These should include: North America, South America (or just the Americas), Europe, Asia (or Eurasia), Africa, Oceania (or Australasia) and Antarctica. Learners can be helped with this, if needed.

Next, provide a list of previous continents, such as Pangaea, Laurentia, Baltica and Gondwana. Where could these have been? Where are they now? The object is not to elicit the correct answers, but to start learners thinking of the concept of continents not being fixed or constant throughout Earth's history.

Some learners may consider that the current arrangement of continents has been and always will be constant.

Main teaching ideas

1 Activity: Pangaea (20 minutes)

Learning intention: To investigate the jigsaw appearance of present-day continents.

Resources: See Learner's Book.

Description: See Learner's Book, internet access (optional).

> **Differentiation ideas:** Learners needing support should be able to see that South America and Africa fit together but may need assistance with the others.

Learners needing a challenge could be asked to think about the possible future arrangement of the continents. Could they all come back together to form another Pangaea or super-continent? Some scientists think this has happened in the past and that the formation and break-up of a super-continent is a cyclical process.

> **Assessment ideas:** Learners can make drawings of the outlines of their larger continents and compare these.

2 Presenting the evidence (20–30 minutes)

Learning intention: Learners give presentations about evidence for tectonic plates and their movement.

Resources: To be decided by learners or allocated by teachers, internet access.

Description: In 1912, Alfred Wagener suggested that the continents could move. His theory was not accepted because of a lack of evidence and because he could not suggest a mechanism for this movement.

Learners should work in groups of two or three and each should have an active role in giving the presentation. Learners have access to today's evidence for making their presentation but will be presenting to an audience that is opposed to the ideas. This roleplay is intended to encourage critical thinking, evaluation of evidence and discussion.

> **Differentiation ideas:** The activity will differentiate by outcome. Learners that need more of a challenge should be expected to present more evidence in a more sophisticated argument.

> **Assessment ideas:** Learners can be involved in the development of criteria to assess each other's presentations.

3 Explaining evidence from the fossil record (10–20 minutes)

Learning intention: To understand the fossil record and how it can be used to gain evidence about past conditions on Earth.

Resources: Internet access (optional).

Description: Fossils and the process of fossilisation are not covered in Lower Secondary, but learners may be aware of fossils from previous courses or from knowledge of organisms such as dinosaurs.

Learners should be aware that:

- different animals and plants lived on Earth at different times

- many of these animals and plants are now extinct

- some of these animals and plants died but did not decay

- their remains have turned to stone over millions of years

- the collection of these remains, together with where they are found, is called the fossil record.

The *Mesosaurus* mentioned in the Learner's Book was a fresh-water reptile similar to a present-day crocodile or alligator. This animal lived on the continent (Gondwana) that is now Africa and South America. When the continent split the animal was found on both parts. This animal could not survive in salt water, so would not have been able to cross the ocean, which provides evidence for tectonic plate movement. The animal and plant names appear in italics because they are Latin, scientific names.

> **Differentiation ideas:** Learners needing support could think of present-day animals or plants that are found naturally on only one continent (e.g. grizzly bears in North America, tigers in Asia). Learners needing a challenge could research

information about other evidence from fossils that support tectonic plate theory.

> **Assessment ideas:** Learners could work in groups to produce outline world maps, colour-coded according to where similar fossils have been found.

Plenary ideas

1 60-second hot seat (3–5 minutes)

Resources: Stopwatch.

Description: A learner volunteers to sit in the hot seat and talk for 60 seconds about tectonic plates. A timer is started to measure the elapsed time. Other learners can challenge at any time by clapping their hands once if they hear repetition of any key word, pausing or going off-subject. The timer is stopped on any challenge showing the elapsed time up to that point. A learner making a correct challenge takes over the hot seat and speaks for the remaining time in a similar way. The learner speaking when 60 seconds elapses is the winner.

Assessment ideas: Assessment is part of the activity.

2 True/false flash cards (2–3 minutes)

Resources: Green and red cards for each learner.

Description: The teacher makes a series of statements about tectonic plates, some of which are true and some of which are false. Learners individually hold up the appropriate card.

> **Assessment ideas:** The teacher can quickly assess understanding from the colours of the cards that are shown.

Homework ideas

1 Questions from the Learner's Book

2 Workbook Exercises 6.5A–C

PROJECT GUIDANCE

This project addresses the following learning objectives:

9ESs.01 Describe the consequences of asteroid collision with the Earth, including climate change and mass extinctions.

9SIC.01 Discuss how scientific knowledge is developed through collective understanding and scrutiny over time.

9SIC.02 Describe how science is applied across societies and industries, and in research.

9SIC.03 Evaluate issues which involve and/or require scientific understanding.

See health and safety information in the Learner's Book. Learners can do an extended investigation with many different variables, and research using secondary sources can also be incorporated.

Impact craters are found on many planets, including Earth, and impact craters can clearly be seen on the Moon.

The suggested starting point for the investigation is to use dry sand in a tray to model the planet or moon surface and a marble or small rock to model the impacting object. The height of the drop is used to vary the impact speed, which is the first suggested independent variable. Other independent variables that could be investigated are:

- mass of impacting object
- diameter of impacting object
- material in the tray (wet sand or mud with varying consistency).

The suggestion for the first dependent variable is crater diameter, measured across the rim. The diagram shows some different measurements which could constitute other dependent variables.

In this investigation, learners should be given the opportunity to think of variables for themselves and only be provided with them when necessary.

Strengths of the analogy include:

- a real object impacts on a real surface
- a crater is formed
- the crater has many similarities with real impact craters.

Weaknesses include:

- planet/moon surfaces are not always made from sand
- the real objects making the craters have much greater masses
- the real objects making the craters have much higher impact speeds
- heat and melting are not part of this model.

Improvements could include:

- making changes to the surface to make it more like a planet or moon, using wet cement or wet clay, for example
- greatly increasing the speed of the impact, for example, by increasing the height or using a catapult. If this is done, then a revised risk assessment should be made.

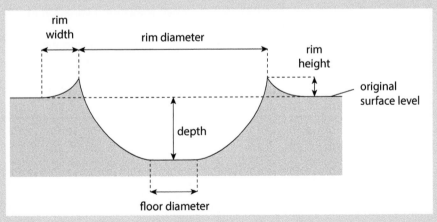

>7 Genes and inheritance

Unit plan

Topic	Learning hours	Learning content	Resources
7.1 Chromosomes, genes and DNA	2-2.5	Chromosomes contain genes, which are made of DNA	**Learner's Book:** Questions 1–4 Activity: Making models of chromosomes in a cell **Workbook:** Exercise 7.1, Chromosomes, genes and DNA
7.2 Gametes and inheritance	2-2.5	Egg cells, sperm cells and sex inheritance	**Learner's Book:** Questions 1–4 Activity: Modelling sex inheritance **Workbook:** Exercise 7.2, Egg cells and sperm cells **Teacher's Resource:** Worksheets 7.2A–C, Swimming speed of sperm cells Template 1: Recording results for *Activity: Modelling sex inheritance*
7.3 Variation	3-4	Measuring and recording variation within a species	**Learner's Book:** Questions 1–6 Activity: Looking at variation in humans Think like a scientist: Investigating variation in leaves Think like a scientist: Measuring variation in humans **Workbook:** Exercise 7.3A, Recording variation Exercise 7.3B, Variation in holly leaves Exercise 7.3C, Variation in pea pods **Teacher's Resource:** Worksheets 7.3A–C, Variation in finger length

Topic	Learning hours	Learning content	Resources
7.4 Natural selection	2	How natural variation and environmental pressures can lead to natural selection	**Learner's Book:** Questions 1–4 Activity: Does natural selection always produce change? **Workbook:** Exercise 7.4A, Blue-tailed lizards Exercise 7.4B, Camouflaged caterpillars Exercise 7.4C, Woolly mammoths **Teacher's Resource:** Worksheets 7.4A–C, Development of antibiotic resistance in bacteria
Cross-unit resources			**Learner's Book:** Check your Progress **Project:** How did we discover DNA? **Teacher's Resource:** Language development worksheets 7.1 Constructing sentences 7.2 Matching terms and descriptions

BACKGROUND/PRIOR KNOWLEDGE

This is the first time that most learners will learn about chromosomes, genes and DNA. They learnt in Stage 7, Unit 1 that the nucleus controls the activities of a cell, but they did not find out anything about how this happens. Note that only an outline is required at this stage, and it would be confusing for learners to be given too much detail. This topic is covered much more fully at O Level and Cambridge IGCSE™.

Topic 7.2, Gametes and inheritance, concentrates on considering gametes as specialised cells, adapted for a particular function. Some learners may have used gametes as examples when thinking about the structure of specialised cells in Unit 1. Sex inheritance has not been dealt with at all before, so

this is likely to be new to everyone. Note that it is not recommended that learners try to draw genetic diagrams at this stage, as they do not yet have the knowledge or tools to fully understand them.

Variation and natural selection are also, essentially, entirely new topics. Learners will, however, have previously met the idea that species are adapted to survive in their environment, so it will not be a very big step to appreciate that some individuals may be better adapted than others. The variation topic develops the ability to collect, organise and display measurements to show variation within a species. This uses mathematical tools that learners will have covered in Mathematics at Stages 5 and 6.

TEACHING SKILLS FOCUS

Reflection

Reflection is a tool that can help learners to think about their learning – not only what they have learnt, but how they learn. It can help them and you to better understand their strengths and weaknesses. This can provide considerable benefits, as the learner becomes more confident in taking charge of their own learning and in

developing techniques that help them to learn better in future.

Throughout the three stages of this science course, suggestions for reflection are provided in the Learner's Book. These are mostly quite narrowly focused, often linked to a particular task that is covered in a particular topic. This is helpful

CONTINUED

because it can make it easier for learners to think clearly about a particular process as they reflect. You may need to encourage them to see how they can apply the results of this reflection to other tasks that they may be faced with in the future. Reflection can also happen as the result of feedback that you give following an activity or a piece of written work; the learner can be encouraged to respond to any suggestions you have made for improvement, and think about how they can take a step forward from where they are now.

Reflection can also be useful when it is considered on a larger scale, looking more generally at an approach to learning over time. For example, at the start or end of a topic that involves the introduction of a new concept, you can ask learners to consider whether they feel that they do better when they just try to memorise the concept, or when they work at truly understanding it. Many teachers like to ask learners to reflect on their mindset at the start of the year, with questions such as: 'How do you feel about starting this course?' 'Do you have any worries about it?' 'What are you looking forward to?' At the end of the year, learners could review their responses: 'Were your worries appropriate?' 'Did you enjoy the things you thought you would, or were there unexpected things that you found really interesting?' 'Are there any concepts that you still do not really understand?' 'What are you going to do to try to sort those out?' 'How will your experience this year affect the way you work and learn next year?'

Reflection can be a very personal thing, and it is often a good idea to ask learners to reflect in a way that keeps their thoughts as a private conversation between you and themselves, rather than sharing them with everyone else in the class. If you have good internet access for everyone then an online platform can be used to conduct these 'conversations'.

Reflection can be expressed in different ways. Do not assume that speaking or writing words is the only way. Some students might like to draw pictures of themselves working, showing what is good and what is not so good, what was successful and what was not. While they are working on a group project they could take photographs of different stages and make an annotated record (in print or another medium) of what each person did; they can then reflect on their own role in the group during the activity, and think about what they have learnt from this and what they might do differently in a similar group activity in future.

Many learners will, at least at first, tend to give very basic responses when asked to reflect. For example, they may simply list what they did well or badly. As they become more used to reflecting, you can expect deeper thought. For example, you could encourage them to think about patterns in how they have approached their work, and what was successful and what was not.

In this unit you could try asking students to think about these ideas as you near the end of the final topic:

- Did discussing ideas with a partner in the *Activity: Does natural selection always produce change*? help me to understand the process of natural selection?

- In general, do I find that talking to another learner can help me to understand difficult concepts?

- How well do I feel that I have understood the material in this unit? Are there are any parts of it that I am not confident about? What would I like to happen to help me with that?

- What have I done in my work during this unit that I am really proud of?

- What can I improve about the way that I work when I start my new science courses next year?

Topic 7.1 Chromosomes, genes and DNA

LEARNING PLAN

Learning Objectives	Learning intentions	Success criteria
9Bs.03 Know that chromosomes contain genes, made of DNA, and that genes contribute to the determination of an organism's characteristics.	• Explain that chromosomes contain genes, which are made of DNA.	• Make a model of a cell containing chromosomes. • Contribute to discussions about chromosomes, genes and DNA.

LANGUAGE SUPPORT

Learners will use the following words:

chromosomes: long thread-like structures, found in the nuclei of cells, which are made of DNA and contain genes

genes: lengths of DNA on a chromosome which contain a code that determines which protein a cell makes; this in turn determines some of the characteristics of the cell and of the organism

DNA: the chemical from which genes and chromosomes are made; its structure constitutes a code that determines the proteins made in a cell

Common misconceptions

Misconception	How to identify	How to overcome
It is common for learners to think that all cells have 46 chromosomes.	This may be shown by answers to questions in class, or during class or group discussions.	Learners are asked to research chromosome numbers during the chromosome modelling activity.

Starter ideas

1 Getting started (10–15 minutes, including sharing ideas)

Description: This activity is designed to focus on the word 'nucleus', and ensure that learners not only recall their knowledge of a nucleus in a cell, but also that they are aware that a nucleus in an atom is an entirely different thing.

Ask learners to discuss the questions in the Learner's Book with a partner. Allow about 4 minutes then invite pairs to share their ideas with the rest of the class.

2 Chromosomes in dividing cells (5 minutes)

Resources: A video clip of chromosome movement in a dividing cell (clips can be found on the internet: suggested search terms include 'animal cell undergoing mitosis').

Description: Show learners a video clip of the movement of chromosomes as an animal cell divides. Show the whole clip through first, then return to the start and ask: Does anyone know what is happening here? What are these threads that we can see? What are they doing? Use the answers to develop the idea that cells contain chromosomes, and that these are shared out into daughter cells when a cell divides.

Main teaching ideas

1 Chromosomes (10–15 minutes)

Learning intention: To become familiar with the idea of chromosomes being present in the nucleus of a cell.

Resources: Text and illustrations from the Learner's Book; if not used earlier, you could also use the video clip of a dividing cell.

Description: Use the text and illustrations in the Learner's Book to discuss the concept of chromosomes in cells. Explain why learners were not able to see chromosomes when they looked at cells in Stage 7. Show the video clip (if not previously used) of a dividing cell and look also at the micrographs in the Learner's Book, explaining that chromosomes are long threads.

Discuss the number of chromosomes in a cell. Learners usually remember that human cells have 46 chromosomes, but it is important that they appreciate that different species have different numbers of chromosomes.

> **Differentiation ideas:** Everyone can take part in the discussion. Some learners may think beyond the fairly basic level here and ask challenging questions – be prepared! Other learners may need considerable encouragement to answer or ask questions.

2 Activity: Making models of chromosomes in a cell (20–30 minutes)

Learning intention: To use modelling to help learners to become familiar with chromosomes, bringing them from a microscopic scale to one that they can directly interact with.

Resources: Per group:

- access to the internet to research chromosome numbers
- a large sheet of paper
- materials for making chromosome models, e.g., lengths of string, wool or electrical wires
- glue or double-sided sticky tape
- scissors.

Description: Ask learners to follow the instructions in the Learner's Book. You could provide a range of different materials for them to use so that they have a choice for making their chromosomes.

The models could be put on display when everyone has finished, which will make it easier for learners to compare the success of their model with those of others.

> **Differentiation ideas:** Learners who are not confident with finding information about chromosome numbers could be given help with this. Learners who would benefit from a challenge might like to make their model more complex by showing the chromosomes being shared out into two new cells as their first cell divides. (Note: do not encourage anyone to learn about the details of mitosis; this is too demanding at this level.)

> **Assessment ideas:** The models will help to check that learners understand what chromosomes are, where they are found and that different species have different chromosome numbers.

3 Genes and DNA (15–20 minutes)

Learning intention: To understand that chromosomes contain thousands of genes, and that chromosomes and genes are made of DNA.

Resources: Text, illustrations and questions from the Learner's Book.

Description: Use the text and illustrations in the Learner's Book to discuss the concept of genes. At this level, focus on genes affecting characteristics; later, learners will find out that each gene codes for the production of a protein, but this is much better left until IGCSE or O Level. Similarly, do not go into too much detail about the structure or function of DNA. Some learners may have heard about DNA as a 'double helix' and you could use the illustration to discuss this.

> **Differentiation ideas:** Some learners will already have heard something about DNA, and may have ideas to share and challenging questions to ask. Others may find this very challenging, particularly as genes and DNA are far too small to be seen, and are, therefore, effectively abstract concepts. If learners find questions 3 and 4 difficult, these could be discussed together as a class before they are asked to write their own answers.

Plenary ideas

1 Write a summary (5 minutes)

Description: Ask learners to write a summary of what they have learnt in this topic. This could be done either individually or in small groups. You could make this a challenge – the shortest summary that contains the most information is the winner.

> **Assessment ideas:** Summaries will indicate how well learners have understood what has been covered in this topic.

2   **What would you like to find out more about? (5 minutes)**

Description: Ask learners to tell you what they would like to know more about, building on today's lesson. Do not worry if this goes well beyond a suitable level of coverage, or if you do not know the answers! The idea is to get them to think about questions and ideas that have been raised in their minds as they learnt about chromosomes, genes and DNA.

> **Assessment ideas:** Some of the questions and ideas may give insight into learners' understanding of the concepts covered in this topic.

Homework ideas

1   Workbook Exercise 7.1

2   Use the internet to research this question: Do larger organisms have larger numbers of chromosomes in their cells?

Topic worksheets

* There are no worksheets for this topic

Topic 7.2 Gametes and inheritance

LEARNING PLAN

Learning Objectives	Learning intentions	Success criteria
9Bp.01 Describe the fusion of gametes to produce a fertilised egg with a new combination of DNA. **9Bp.02** Describe the inheritance of sex in humans in terms of XX and XY chromosomes.	• Describe adaptations of male and female gametes in humans. • How X and Y chromosomes are passed from parents to offspring, and how male and female children are produced.	• Construct, or contribute to construction, of a table comparing egg cells and sperm cells. • Use modelling to explain why approximately equal numbers of boys and girls are born.

LANGUAGE SUPPORT

Learners will use the following words:

sperm cell: the male gamete of an animal

egg cell: the female gamete of an animal

gametes: specialised cells that contain only half the normal number of chromosomes (that is, one set rather than the usual two sets) and that join together during sexual reproduction to produce a zygote

fertilisation: the fusion of the nucleus of a male gamete with the nucleus of a female gamete

zygote: the new cell that is formed when a male gamete fuses with a female gamete; it contains one set of chromosomes from the male gamete and one set from the female gamete

inheritance: the passing on of genes (DNA) from parents to offspring

sex inheritance: the way in which the sex of a child is determined by the inheritance of X and Y chromosomes from its parents

Common misconceptions

Misconception	How to identify	How to overcome
Learners often think that sperm cells contain male chromosomes, and egg cells contain female chromosomes.	This may become apparent in *Activity: Modelling sex inheritance*, particularly when learners attempt to answer question 3.	Take learners steadily through the diagram showing how X and Y chromosomes are inherited; discuss answers to question 3 at the end of the activity.

Starter ideas

1 Getting started (10–15 minutes, including sharing ideas)

Description: The purpose of this activity is to remind learners of the concept of specialisation in cells, so that they are ready to apply this concept to the adaptive features of sperm cells and egg cells.

Ask learners to think, individually, about the answers to the questions. Then ask someone to describe the features of one kind of specialised animal cell. They should know, for example, about red blood cells and neurones. They may be able to draw one on the board. Use these examples to discuss the concept of specialised cells.

2 Image of fertilisation (5–10 minutes)

Resources: Image showing sperm cells around an egg cell (images can be found on the internet).

Description: Show learners an image, made using a microscope, of sperm cells clustering around an egg cell. Ask: 'What do you think this is?' Use the image to discuss how much bigger the egg cell is than the sperm cells; that the sperm cells move and the egg cell does not, and that there are many sperm cells for only one egg cell.

Main teaching ideas

1 Gametes (15–20 minutes)

Learning intention: To know that sperm cells and egg cells are male and female gametes and to understand that, at fertilisation, a sperm cell fuses with an egg cell to produce a zygote.

Resources: Text and illustrations in the Learner's Book; video clip(s) of fertilisation, if not used as a starter activity.

Description: Use the diagrams, photographs and text in the Learner's Book as the basis of a discussion with the class about gametes and fertilisation.

Question 2 could then be done individually, in small groups or as a whole-class activity, in which the table is drawn on the board and learners make suggestions about what can be written in the two columns.

⟩ **Differentiation ideas:** If the comparison table is done as a class activity, some learners will need a lot of encouragement to suggest ideas. Accept even poorly expressed suggestions, give praise and then ask others in the class if they can improve on the way the idea is worded.

⟩ **Assessment ideas:** Suggestions for the comparison table will give insight into how well the material about gametes and fertilisation has been understood.

2 Sex inheritance (15–20 minutes)

Learning intention: To understand how the X and Y chromosomes determine whether a child is male or female.

Resources: Text and illustrations in the Learner's Book and karyotypes (pictures of chromosomes arranged in order) for males and females from the internet.

Description: Use the material in the Learner's Book to explain how X and Y chromosomes determine sex and are passed from parents to offspring.

Put question 3 to the class and encourage them to work out how to express their answer in the clearest and simplest way possible.

Show some karyotypes to the class; there is one for a female in Topic 7.1, and you should be able to find a similar one for a male. (If you cannot find a similar one, try to find two similar ones for a male and female on the internet, so that learners can directly compare them and are not distracted by other differences such as their colours. Take care to avoid karyotypes showing unusual chromosome numbers, such as an extra chromosome 23.) Ask learners to suggest why the X and Y chromosomes are shown at the end of the chromosome arrangement, rather than in size order like all the others.

> **Differentiation ideas:** Everyone can take part in this discussion and question answering, but some learners will need more support and encouragement than others.

3 Activity: Modelling sex inheritance (20–25 minutes)

Learning intention: Through modelling, to make sex inheritance a more concrete concept.

Resources: Two identical containers (preferably non-transparent) that a hand can easily fit into; stiff string or electrical wire of two colours, cut into equal lengths. You need 45 pieces of one colour and 15 pieces of another colour.

Description: Ask learners to work either individually or in pairs and follow the instructions in the Learner's Book.

> **Practical guidance:** It is important that both the 'X' and 'Y' chromosomes are the same length, to equalise the chances of a learner picking either one up.

> **Differentiation ideas:** Template 1 is available if any learners need help in recording results. Learners requiring a further challenge could be asked what assumptions we are making when we use this model. (For example, we are assuming that it is equally likely that a sperm carrying a Y chromosome or a sperm containing a X chromosome will be first to reach an egg and fertilise it).

Plenary ideas

1 Vocabulary check (5–10 minutes)

Description: Write descriptions of each of the key words introduced in this topic on the board. Ask the class (hands up, or select a learner to give you the answer) to tell you the word that is being described. Ask a learner to write the word, spelt correctly, on the board.

> **Assessment ideas:** Responses will help to show whether learners have picked up the new words, and whether they can spell them correctly.

2 Spot the mistakes (10 minutes)

Resources: A short descriptive passage, or some sentences, written by you, that covers the work done in this topic but contain some mistakes. These could be:

- spelling mistakes
- misused terms, e.g., gamete instead of zygote
- incorrect statements, e.g., all sperm contain a Y chromosome.

Description: Write or project the passage or sentences onto the board. Ask learners: 'Who can spot the mistakes?' Take their answers and make corrections.

Assessment ideas: Suggestions and answers will show up misconceptions or misunderstandings.

Homework ideas

1 Workbook Exercise 7.2

2 Worksheets 7.2A–C

Topic worksheets

- Worksheets 7.2A–C, Swimming speed of sperm cells

Topic 7.3 Variation

LEARNING PLAN

Learning Objectives	Learning intentions	Success criteria
9Bp.03 Describe variation within a species and relate this to genetic differences between individuals.	• Know the meaning of the term 'variation', and that variation is partly caused by differences in genes. • Describe and measure variation in humans and other organisms. • Use bar charts and frequency diagrams to display data about variation.	• Construct a bar chart to display information about variation in leaves.

LANGUAGE SUPPORT

Learners will use the following words:

variation: differences between individuals belonging to the same species

genetic differences: differences between the genes of different organisms

Common misconceptions

Misconception	How to identify	How to overcome
Learners may use the term 'variation' to mean differences between species, rather than between individuals of the same species.	This can become apparent during discussions or when answering questions.	Take care only to use the term 'variation' when you mean differences within a species. Reinforce this meaning in the activity and the *Think like a scientist* investigations in this topic.

Starter ideas

1 **Getting started (10–15 minutes, including sharing ideas)**

Description: The purpose of this activity is to ensure that everyone knows what a species is before beginning to look at variation between individuals belonging to the same species.

Ask learners, working either individually or in pairs, to think of words to complete the sentence starter.

Ask for suggestions and take all answers, even if they are not particularly helpful. Then work with the class to select the most useful answers and put them together to make one or two sentences that correctly explain what a species is.

2 **Examples of variation (5–10 minutes)**

Resources: Pictures (from the internet) showing variation in a species, for example, different breeds of dog, horse or sheep; you can also use the pictures of goats in the Learner's Book.

Description: Show the pictures to the class. Ask: 'Do all these organisms belong to the same species?' 'What differences can you see between them?' Introduce the idea of variation in the characteristics of organisms that belong to the same species.

Main teaching ideas

1 Activity: Looking at variation in humans (20–25 minutes)

Learning intention: To begin to appreciate the types of variation within a species.

Resources: Rulers or tape measures.

Description: Ask learners to follow the instructions in the Learner's Book. You do not need to use the particular features shown in the outline results chart; ask learners to change these to ones that will work well with your class.

> **Differentiation ideas:** Some learners will need help in selecting suitable features to observe or measure, and may also need support in making measurements. Use questioning to challenge learners who would benefit from it. For example, ask: 'How do you know that really is their shoe size. Can you trust everyone to give you the correct information?' 'What have you done to make sure that you have measured height in exactly the same way for everyone?'

2 Think like a scientist: Investigating variation in leaves (30–40 minutes)

Learning intention: To collect, record and display numerical but discrete variation, using material learners collect themselves.

Resources: Access to one or more trees belonging to the same species, which have leaves divided into several leaflets. If you do not have access to trees with this feature, look for other features that could be used instead: the number of insect galls on a leaf, the number of prickles or the number of flowers on a flower stalk. Take care to use features that can be counted and that do not need to be measured.

Description: Take learners outside and show them the trees from which they can collect their samples. They then collect their samples and take them inside. They can then follow the instructions in the Learner's Book to record and display their results.

> **Practical guidance:** Discuss safety: no one should need to climb in order to reach leaves. You may be able to ask them to collect fallen leaves, rather than pick them from the tree.

You can either explain to learners what they are to do before moving outside, or when they are next to the trees they will be investigating. You may like to provide each group with a small bag or other container into which they can put their leaves.

It is best if they take the leaves back into the classroom to count the numbers of leaflets and to record their results.

> **Differentiation ideas:** All learners can help to collect the leaves. Some will need help in constructing the bar chart. Template 2 can be provided to help with this. Questions 1–3 require learners to recall skills they will have covered in Maths, and again some may need help here. Question 4 is quite challenging, although you could expect some learners to give quite full and insightful answers to this.

> **Assessment ideas:** Use the bar charts to check that learners can successfully display their results in this form.

3 Think like a scientist: Measuring variation in humans (30–45 minutes)

Learning intention: To collect measurements that need to be categorised, and to display them as a frequency diagram.

Resources: Tape measures.

Description: Learners can work individually or in pairs. Ask them to follow the instructions in the Learner's Book.

This is more challenging than earlier investigations, as it involves continuous data that have to be placed in categories. Students have constructed frequency diagrams for continuous data at Stage 5 in maths.

> **Practical guidance:** Rather than everyone making the same measurements, you may prefer to organise things so that only one set of measurements is made, and these are put onto the board or elsewhere for the whole class to share.

> **Differentiation ideas:** Learners who need help in constructing the frequency diagram can be given Template 3 to help them. Learners who require a greater challenge could be asked to make another measurement, such as arm or little finger length, and decide whether or not there is any correlation between the two measurements.

Plenary ideas

1 What did you enjoy? (5 minutes)

Description: Ask learners: 'What was the best part of today's lesson?' Alternatively, or as well, ask: 'Which part of today's lesson do you think you will remember best?'

> **Assessment ideas:** Responses may highlight particular activities that learners found helpful as well as enjoyable; they can also indicate which parts of the lesson they did *not* enjoy or which they think they will find difficult to remember.

2 Comparing frequency diagrams (10 minutes)

Resources: Frequency diagrams drawn by learners in *Think like a scientist: Measuring variation in humans.* (Alternatively, you could use the bar charts produced in *Think like a scientist: Investigating variation in leaves.*)

Description: Display some or all of the frequency diagrams (or bar charts) on the wall and bring learners to sit around them. Use questioning to stimulate thought about how the diagrams have been constructed, and features that make one a little better than another.

> **Assessment ideas:** Use comments and answers to questions to determine how well learners understand how to construct a frequency diagram to display information about variation.

Homework ideas

1   Workbook Exercises 7.3A–C

2   Worksheets 7.3A–C

Topic worksheets

•   Worksheets 7.3A–C, Variation in finger length

Topic 7.4 Natural selection

LEARNING PLAN

Learning Objectives	Learning intentions	Success criteria
9Bp.04 Describe the scientific theory of natural selection and how it relates to genetic changes over time. 9Be.01 Describe what could happen to the population of a species, including extinction, when there is an environmental change.	• Explain how natural variation between individuals in a species can lead to natural selection.. • Explain how natural selection can (but does not always) lead to genetic changes over time.	• Contribute constructively to the discussions about the 'thought experiment' relating to the long necks of giraffes, and whether natural selection always produces change. • Relate results of the caterpillar experiment to ideas about natural selection.

Learners will use the following words:

advantageous feature: a feature of an individual that gives it a better chance of survival than other individuals in the population

natural selection: a process in which only the best-adapted individuals survive and reproduce, passing on the genes that produce their advantageous features to their offspring

resistant: an adjective describing an organism that it is not harmed by a chemical that kills others: for example, bacteria can be resistant to antibiotics and weeds can be resistant to herbicides

Common misconceptions

Misconception	How to identify	How to overcome
It is very common for learners to suggest that organisms purposefully develop particular features in order *to* make them better adapted to their environment.	This may appear in the discussions in *Activity: Does natural selection always produce change?*	Careful explanations and discussions can dispel this misconception. The way that ideas are expressed is very important: avoid saying, for example, that a population changes to become better adapted to its environment. In that expression, the word 'to' suggests intention. You can also ask: 'Imagine the Earth became much colder, and was covered in snow and ice. Could you change yourself to grow fur all over your body to keep warm?' Use learners' answers to explain that no organism can purposefully change itself to become better adapted to its environment.

Starter ideas

1 **Getting started (10–15 minutes, including sharing ideas)**

    Resources: Photograph of leaf frog in the Learner's Book.

    Description: The purpose of this activity is to remind learners about adaptations to the environment, before they begin to think about how small changes in these adaptations might affect the survival chances of individuals in a population.

    Ask learners to make suggestions about adaptations of the frog. Allow two or three minutes thinking time, then ask for suggestions.

2 **Struggle for existence (5–10 minutes)**

    Resources: At least one picture of an animal that is different from the others of its species: for example, an albino kangaroo or tiger, or a zebra with spots instead of stripes.

    Description Ask: 'What do you think has caused this animal to look different?' (Answer: probably its genes.) Ask: 'Do you think this animal will be able to survive?' 'Will it have as good a chance of surviving as the rest of the population?' Use answers to introduce the idea that variations can affect how likely an animal is to survive long enough to be able to reproduce.

Main teaching ideas

1 How the giraffe (possibly) got its long neck (15–20 minutes)

Learning intention: To begin to understand the theory of natural selection.

Resources: Text and illustrations in the Learner's Book.

Description: Use the text and illustrations in the Learner's Book to lead a class discussion about how giraffes may have come to have such long necks. Note: it is very important to stress that this is an imaginary example – a 'thought experiment' – and that there is no evidence that the story told here actually happened.

> **Differentiation ideas:** Everyone can take part in this discussion. Some learners may be able to suggest why it is not possible to find hard evidence for theories about what has happened in the past.

2 Activity: Does natural selection always produce change? (10–15 minutes)

Learning intention: To appreciate that natural selection does not produce change if there is no change in the genes of organisms or in the environment.

Description: Ask learners to think about the three questions on their own for a few minutes. Then ask them to discuss their thoughts with a partner. When everyone is ready, ask for ideas to share with the class, and discuss the issues with them. The discussion should conclude that natural selection does not always produce change in a population, but that if there is a change in the environment then it may do.

> **Differentiation ideas:** Some learners may find it difficult to imagine a population of organisms and to follow their idea through the three questions without help. You could make a suggestion to start them off, or pair them with another learner who is full of ideas.

Learners who need a further challenge could be asked: 'Sometimes, genes change unpredictably, producing new features in an individual. Could this affect natural selection?'

> **Assessment ideas:** Use suggestions, comments and answers from learners to judge how well they understand the processes of natural selection.

3 Camouflaged caterpillars (30–40 minutes)

Learning intention: To experience how natural selection might work within a population.

Resources: Per class:

*   cooked pasta shapes (e.g., spirals or short tubes), coloured by dipping into food dye; half of one colour and half of another colour.
*   six identically shaped and sized pieces of card, with three matching each of the two colours of pasta shapes
*   access to an outside area where birds visit.

Description: Carry out this experiment as a whole-class activity. Ask learners to put the pieces of card outside on the ground. Then place the pasta shapes on the cards. If the colours are green and blue, then:

*   on one of the blue cards place blue pasta
*   on one of the blue cards place green pasta
*   on one of the blue cards place a mix of blue and green pasta
*   on one of the green cards place blue pasta
*   on one of the green cards place green pasta
*   on one of the green cards place a mix of blue and green pasta.

Learners should then move away from the card, and watch to see how birds react to the shapes. If bird activity is sufficient, then they may be able to count how many of each colour are pecked by the birds on each coloured card.

> **Practical guidance:** This experiment is only likely to yield interesting results in conditions where there is plenty of bird activity. If this is good then learners can count and record the number of pecks on each colour of pasta on each piece of card. This can yield very interesting results, which generally show that birds have a preference for shapes that have a colour that contrasts with the background.

However, as with all experiments in a natural environment, it is not possible to be sure of getting decent results, let alone expected ones, so be prepared to adapt the plans or to accept that no useful results have been obtained. It is also strongly recommended that you try it out first!

> **Differentiation ideas:** Everyone can be involved in this experiment. Make sure that all learners are encouraged to be actively involved. Some learners may need help in constructing a table in which they can record their results.

Learners who would benefit from a further challenge could link any results from this experiment to the peppered moth story (described in Topic 7.4 of the Learner's Book). You could also ask them: 'Imagine that there is a population of pale green caterpillars that live on pale green leaves. A new variety of tree appears, which has dark green leaves. Suggest how natural selection could eventually result in a population of dark green caterpillars.'

Plenary ideas

1 Question loop (5–10 minutes)

Resources: A set of cards, each with a question about a topic covered in this unit, plus an answer to a different question.

Description: Give out a card to each learner, pair or group. Ask a learner to read out their question. The learner with the card with the answer to that question reads out the answer, and then reads out their own question.

> **Assessment ideas:** Listen for learners wrongly identifying the correct answer to a question. If a wrong answer is given, ask: 'Do the rest of you think that is the correct answer?' 'Why is that answer not correct?' 'Who thinks they have the correct answer?'

2 Mind map (20–30 minutes)

Resources: Large sheets of paper, coloured pens.

Description: Ask the class: 'What have you learnt about in this unit?' Construct a list of their ideas on the board.

Settle learners in pairs, or groups of three or four. Ask them to construct a mind map of everything they have learnt in this unit. They can use the ideas you have written on the board, or they can use their own ideas.

If time allows, you can ask each group to explain their mind maps to other groups.

> **Assessment ideas:** Ideas from the class about what they think they have learnt in this unit will help to tell you how well they have understood the topics covered.

Homework ideas

1 Workbook Exercises 7.4A–C

2 Worksheets 7.4A–C

Topic worksheets

• Worksheets 7.4A–C, Development of antibiotic resistance in bacteria

PROJECT GUIDANCE

This project addresses the following learning objectives:

9SIC.01 Discuss how scientific knowledge is developed through collective understanding and scrutiny over time.

9SIC.02 Describe how science is applied across societies and industries, and in research.

9SIC.03 Evaluate issues which involve and/or require scientific understanding.

9SIC.04 Describe how people develop and use scientific understanding as individuals and through collaboration, e.g. through peer review.

9SIC.05 Discuss how the uses of science can have a global environmental impact.

This is a challenging project. By the end of Stage 9 many learners are likely to be ready to take on this challenge, especially if they have had plenty of experience of tackling similar projects during their science course.

However, some may need more guidance than is given in the Learner's Book. For these learners, you could suggest search terms for them to use, or even provide a list of websites for them to visit. You will need to do your own research first, to find websites that are easily accessed from the country in which you are working and that provide information at a level that you think your learners will be able to understand.

The project addresses the Science in Context learning objective, *Discuss how scientific knowledge is developed through collective understanding and scrutiny over time.* A short list of five steps is suggested for research, ranging from Mendel's discoveries in the 1860s through to the culmination of the Human Genome Project in 2001. There are, of course, many other steps that could be investigated, and you may like to add others or substitute some of those listed in the Learner's Book with your own preferences. You may be able to find an example of important work done by scientists in your own country.

It is obviously best if different groups work on different steps. However, the groups will also need to talk to each other in order to answer the question about how earlier discoveries enabled the step that they are researching to take place. This is perhaps the most interesting and most challenging aspect of this project.

The final reports may vary from very simple to very complex. Encourage brevity: it is far better for learners to write a short report that they understand, rather than a long one that includes a lot of disconnected information that has been lifted from the internet with little filtering or understanding.

〉8 Rates of reaction

Unit plan

Topic	Learning hours	Learning content	Resources
8.1 Measuring the rate of reaction	2-4	Measuring the rate of reaction; explanation of why the rate of reaction changes	**Learner's Book:** Questions 1–7 Activity: What makes a good graph? Think like a scientist: Measuring the rate of reaction. **Workbook:** Exercise 8.1A, Showing the change in rate of reaction on a graph Exercise 8.1B, Changes in the rate of reaction Exercise 8.1C, Explaining observations **Teacher's Resource:** Worksheet 8.1, Interpreting a graph Template 1: Peer assessment: What makes a good graph?
8.2 Surface area and the rate of reaction	2-3	Investigating the rate of reaction when the surface area of one of the reactants is changed; finding the surface area of different shapes; carrying out a practical investigation safely	**Learner's Book:** Think like a scientist: Burning iron Activity: Calculating the surface area Think like a scientist: Investigating the effect of surface area in the rate of reaction **Workbook:** Exercise 8.2, Surface area and the rate of reaction **Teacher's Resource:** Template 2: Self-assessment: *Investigating the effect of surface area on the rate of reaction*
8.3 Temperature and the rate of reaction	3-4	Investigating the effect of temperature on the rate of reaction; carrying out a trial run and preliminary practical work to help plan an investigation; carrying out an investigation safely	**Learner's Book:** Questions 1–2 Think like a scientist: The effect of temperature on the rate of reaction – trial run (preliminary and investigation) **Workbook:** Exercise 8.3A, Explaining changes in the rate of reaction Exercise 8.3B, Temperature and the rate of reaction **Teacher's Resource:** Worksheets 8.3A–C, True or false?

Topic	Learning hours	Learning content	Resources
8.4 Concentration and the rate of reaction	3-4	The effect of concentration on the rate of reaction; planning an investigation; using particle theory to explain the results of an investigation	**Learner's Book:** Questions 1–2 Think like a scientist: Investigating the effect of concentration on the rate of reaction (planning and investigation) **Workbook:** Exercise 8.4A, Concentration and the rate of reaction Exercise 8.4B, Which results are which? Exercise 8.4C, As fast as possible **Teacher's Resource:** Template 3: Group discussion: *Investigating the effect of concentration on the rate of reaction*
Cross-unit resources			**Learner's Book:** Check your Progress Project: Gas for sale **Teacher's Resource:** Template 4: Project price list Language development worksheets 8.1 Matching words and meanings 8.2 Correcting statements

BACKGROUND/PRIOR KNOWLEDGE

This unit focuses on the rate of reaction and the factors that affect this rate. It brings together many reactions that learners have met before. The practical work is the main focus of each topic and it gives learners a chance to practise the skills they have acquired over the whole course. Learners will need to plan investigations, choose equipment, carry out risk assessments and carry out practical tasks in a logical and accurate manner. Some of the practicals and the way in which they are carried out will be familiar, and some not. Learners will need to use most of their thinking and working scientifically skills in this unit.

There is an opportunity to assess the various practical skills in class and much opportunity for group work.

TEACHING SKILLS FOCUS

Peer- and self-assessment

Learners who do not undertake peer- or self-assessment tend to have little idea as to how good or otherwise their own work is, especially if they see their grades as acceptable. If you have tried the various suggestions given in the previous units, the next step would be to look at who is assessing each learner's work.

- Are they always assessing/being assessed by the same person?
- Are they friends?
- Have they become used to this same level of work and think it acceptable?
- Have they got different ideas about how the assessed learner could improve their work?

Even when work is peer assessed by just one person every time, the assessment tends to be a secret between the two learners and they become used to that quality of work.

During this unit, aim to vary the pairs of learners who assess one another. Your class may have taken a while to adjust to peer assessment, but now feel relatively comfortable with working with one particular person, which is great to build their confidence with the whole idea of peer assessment, but now is the time to take it forward.

You could decide who will assess whom, based on your knowledge of the class, keeping in mind the levels of confidence, ability and general quality of the work. Bear in mind that some learners need to see a higher quality of work to understand what they should be aiming for, but you need to make sure they will not be overwhelmed or become disheartened.

You could draw names at random. You could split the class into groups of about six or eight and ask them to choose who they will assess and then ask them to swap with another person and assess their work; that way they will each get two sets of comments to think about. Before you attempt this, you would need to remind the learners why peer assessment is helpful, both to the learner whose work is being assessed and to the assessor. You would also need to remind them that they need to be helpful and kind. You need to stress the advantages of working with someone else.

It would also be helpful if, during this unit, you discuss with learners how they have found the peer-assessment process.

- Did they find it helpful?
- Did they find it stressful?
- Was it easy to spot where someone could improve their work or to spot a misunderstanding?
- Did it give them an insight into how others approach a task?
- Did peer assessment help them to move towards self-assessment and a critical, fair assessment of their own work?

You could do this as an exit plenary task but it would probably need to have more than 10 minutes allocated to it. The results of this feedback to you would be very useful in helping you think about how you will use self- and peer assessment in the future.

Topic 8.1 Measuring rates of reaction

LEARNING PLAN

Learning Objectives	Learning intentions	Success criteria
9Cc.01 Use word equations and symbol equations to describe reactions (balancing symbol equations is not required).	• What is meant by the rate of reaction and how it changes.	• Be able to state how the rate of reaction changes.

CONTINUED

Learning Objectives	Learning intentions	Success criteria
9Cc.04 Describe the effects of concentration, surface area and temperature on the rate of reaction, and explain them using the particle model. **9TWSm.03** Use symbols and formulae to represent scientific ideas. **9TWSp.05** Make risk assessments for practical work to identify and control risks. **9TWSc.02** Decide what equipment is required to carry out an investigation or experiment and use it appropriately. **9TWSc.04** Take appropriately accurate and precise measurements, explaining why accuracy and precision are important. **9TWSc.05** Carry out practical work safely, supported by risk assessments where appropriate. **9TWSc.07** Collect, record and summarise sufficient observations and measurements in an appropriate form. **9TWSa.02** Describe trends and patterns in results, identifying any anomalous results and suggesting why results are anomalous. **9TSWa.05** Present and interpret results, and predict results between the data points collected.	• How to measure the rate of reaction. • Use graphs to calculate the rates of reaction and compare them at various points. • Understand why the rate of reaction changes.	• Carry out an investigation safely. • Measure the rate of reaction. • Use graphs to discuss and measure the rate of reaction. • Explain why the rate of reaction changes.

LANGUAGE SUPPORT

Learners will use the following words:

anomalous result: a measurement or reading that does not fit in with the pattern of the other results; such a result is not necessarily wrong, but it should be checked

gradient: the steepness of a slope, in this case on the graph

collecting a gas over water: a way of collecting a gas given off in a reaction

collision: what happens when two or more objects bump into one another

Common misconceptions

Misconception	How to identify	How to overcome
Some learners do not understand that the rate of reaction changes during a reaction.	Ask directly and look closely at their written answers to questions about the rates of reaction.	The use of the model behaviour of particles should help.
Some learners find the interpretation of graphs very difficult.	Learners will not be able to answer questions and will find the use of graphs very hard.	This needs to be practiced and individual help given. The use of Worksheet 8.1, Interpreting graphs, could help.

Starter ideas

1   Getting started (10 minutes)

Learning intention: To revise the ways in which you can tell that a reaction has taken place.

Description: Ask learners to list as many examples as they can of the ways in which they can tell that a reaction has taken place. This should be done with a partner. Ask them to suggest ways that they could measure how quickly a reaction takes place. Share their ideas with the class.

2   What do these graphs show you? (10 minutes)

Learning intention: To focus the learners on the information they can get from graphs.

Resources: Three or four graphs sketched on the board, such as:

- water temperature after being heated for a number of minutes (see Graph 1)
- mass of water when left to evaporate over a number of days (see Graph 2)
- the volume of acid needed to neutralise increasing volumes of alkali (see Graph 3)

Graph 1

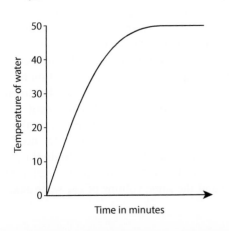

Graph 2

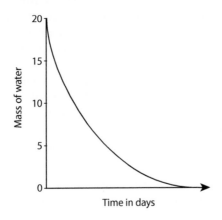

Graph 3

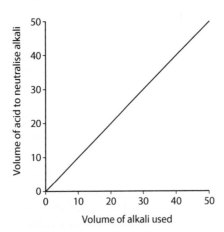

Description: Ask learners to decide what these graphs tell them and to discuss this with a partner and then have a class discussion. This could be a good introduction to the graph work in this section.

Main teaching ideas

1 The rate of reaction (30–40 minutes)

Learning intention: To introduce ideas about what the rate of reaction is and how to measure it.

Resources: Safety glasses, magnesium ribbon, dilute sulfuric acid, conical flask fitted with a bung and delivery tube, gas syringe, clamp stand, calcium carbonate, dilute hydrochloric acid, top pan balance, graph paper.

Description: You could introduce the ideas of what the rate of reaction is and ways to measure it by following the information given in the Learner's book. You may decide to carry out demonstrations of the way to measure the rate of reaction using the two methods shown in the Learner's Book. If you do this, it would be a good idea to get learners to be your assistants and to follow instructions and, as you go through the practical, discuss various aspects of safety, organisation and accuracy. You could spend some time looking closely at the results and graphs. This may be a good opportunity to look at how much support the class need with graph work.

⟩ **Practical guidance:** Try to involve the learners as much as possible.

⟩ **Differentiation ideas:** You could use the least confident learners as your assistants and give them as much praise and support as possible.

Give those learners who need a challenge some results from similar investigations and ask them to plot graphs and comment on the rates of reaction.

⟩ **Assessment ideas:** You could use the questions in the Learner's Book to assess knowledge, and to inform you of how much support the class will need.

2 What makes a good graph? (20–30 minutes)

Learning intention: To revise the finer points of plotting graphs.

Resources: Poster materials and/or computer access.

Description: This is a good opportunity to think about the reason why graphs are used and what they can be used for. You can tailor this discussion to your learners' abilities and any difficulties they have with graphs.

You may choose to have the initial discussion as a whole-class activity and you could lead the discussion by asking questions such as: 'How do you know which variable goes on which axis?' 'What are your top tips for graph plotting?'

You could follow the suggestion in the Learner's Book and ask learners to discuss with a partner why they may need to plot a graph of their results when they carry out an investigation. You could prompt them also to discuss the things that make a good graph, using the suggestions from the Learner's Book.

Once the presentations have been completed, learners could do their presentations to another pair and do a peer assessment using Template 1, or you could choose to have the whole class do peer assessments.

⟩ **Practical guidance:** Set fixed times for discussion and for the production of the presentation.

⟩ **Differentiation ideas:** Think about how you pair the learners so that everyone makes a contribution. You could help those who find graphs difficult by asking prompt questions such as: 'What is important about the way you mark the points on your graph?'

⟩ **Assessment ideas:** The peer assessments as detailed above could be used.

3 Think like a scientist: Measuring the rate of reaction (50 minutes)

Learning intention: To carry out an investigation safely to measure the rate of reaction.

Resources: This will depend on what you have available and the method you or the learners choose. These are likely to include some of the following: safety glasses, calcium carbonate, hydrochloric acid, stopwatch, conical flask fitted with delivery tube, thistle funnel and bung, beehive shelf, measuring cylinder, glass trough or very large beaker, conical flask fitted with bung and delivery tube to a gas syringe, clamp stand, top pan balance, conical flask. See the diagram in the Learner's Book.

Description: The learners are asked to measure the rate of reaction between calcium carbonate and hydrochloric acid. There are three common methods and the choice depends on what equipment you have available. You could allocate different methods to different groups, if you have no restriction on equipment. Learners are asked to make their own list of equipment, carry out a risk assessment and draw up a results table **before** they begin the practical task. You may need to discuss the need to repeat the experiment: if you plan to do this, it will be necessary to use the same mass of calcium carbonate and the same volume of the same acid.

> **Practical guidance:** Plan how you will provide the equipment so that there is no crowding at collection points.

> **Differentiation ideas:** As you circulate, you need to keep a look out for those who have organisational problems, especially when starting the reaction as the learners need to do a number of things at the same time. You will need to offer practical help and practical suggestions to some learners. Ask learners to consider how they are avoiding risks and are trying to make their results as accurate as possible. For those learners who need to be stretched, ask them how they can ensure their results are reliable and to consider how they could do this if they repeated the investigation, for example, using the same mass of calcium carbonate, etc.

> **Assessment ideas:** You could use this task to assess practical skills. You could use their graphs to assess their skills and/or the quality of the results they obtained.

Plenary ideas

1 **Explaining the changes in the rate of reaction (10 minutes)**

Description: Ask learners to write an explanation for why the rate of reaction changes over time, using particle theory. Ask them to swap with a partner and see how they can improve their answers. Feed back to the class.

Reflection ideas: How can I make my explanations clearer?

2 **Making practical work accurate (10 minutes)**

Description: Ask learners to think for a minute about how they made their practical work as accurate as possible. Then spend 3 minutes discussing this with a partner and writing a list of points. Feed back to the class.

> **Assessment ideas:** You could use the questions in the Learner's Book.

> **Reflection ideas:** Ask learners to think about what they could do in the future to improve the accuracy of their practical work.

Homework ideas

1 Workbook Exercises 8.1A–C

Topic worksheet

• Worksheet 8.1, Interpreting a graph

Topic 8.2 Surface area and the rate of reaction

LEARNING PLAN

Learning Objectives	Learning intentions	Success criteria
9Cc.04 Describe the effects of concentration, surface area and temperature on the rate of reaction, and explain them using the particle model. 9TWSp.05 Make risk assessments for practical work to identify and control risks. 9TWSc.02 Decide what equipment is required to carry out an investigation or experiment and use it appropriately.	• Investigate the rate of reaction when the surface area of one of the reactants is changed. • Carry out an investigation using the reaction between calcium carbonate and dilute hydrochloric acid. • Consider how changing the shape of a material can affect the surface area.	• Safely investigate the rate of reaction when the surface area of one of the reactants is changed. • Carry out an investigation using the reaction between calcium carbonate and dilute hydrochloric acid. • Explain how changing the shape of a material can affect the surface area.

CONTINUED

Learning Objectives	Learning intentions	Success criteria
9TWSc.07 Collect, record and summarise sufficient observations and measurements in an appropriate form. 9TWSa.01 Evaluate the strength of the evidence collected and how it supports, or refutes, the prediction. 9TWSa.02 Describe trends and patterns in results, identifying any anomalous results and suggesting why results are anomalous.		

LANGUAGE SUPPORT

Learners will use the following words:

surface area: the total area of the surface of an object

There is very little new vocabulary in this topic. You could use this as an opportunity to review more general scientific vocabulary.

Common misconceptions

Misconception	How to identify	How to overcome
Some learners do not understand that there is a relationship between the surface area and the rate of reaction.	Ask direct questions.	The 'hands on' *Activity: Calculating the surface* area will help. You could also try giving the learners a piece of modelling clay and asking them to make different shapes and see the effect on the surface area.

Starter ideas

1 Getting started (10 minutes)

Learning intention: To explore the idea of surface area and how the surface area can be changed by rearranging material.

Resources: Learner's Book or children's construction blocks.

Description: Ask learners to find the surface area of each of the six faces of the Learner's Book or any suitable cuboids you may have. They should record the surface area for each face and then calculate the total surface area.

With a partner, ask them to arrange their two books (or construction blocks) so that they are touching face-to-face and have the least possible total surface area. What is this total surface area? Then ask them to arrange the books so that they are touching face-to-face but have the largest possible total surface area. What is this total surface area? How does changing the arrangement of the books affect the total surface area?

2 Variables (10 minutes)

Learning intention: To revise the three types of variables.

Description: Ask the learners in pairs to explain what independent, dependent and control variables are. Ask them to give examples from suggested practical work they have done in the past.

Main teaching ideas

1 Think like a scientist: Burning iron (20–30 minutes)

Learning intention: To demonstrate the effect of surface area on the reaction rate when iron is burnt in air.

Resources: Safety glasses, tongs, Bunsen burner, heatproof mat, spatula, iron nail, iron wool, iron filings.

Description: The learners are going to burn an iron nail, iron wool and iron filings. The point is to see how the reaction is different due to the difference in surface area. You may want to demonstrate this first, at least the way to attempt it rather than actually doing it, and make the safety points.

You may want to go through the surface area theory points from the Learner's Book before they do this task or you could go through those as a summing-up of the task.

> **Practical guidance:** Safety glasses must be worn. Make sure the learners are aware that the iron wool and iron filings can spark, and lighted iron can drift off from their workstation, so make sure they only use small amounts and are careful with the task.

> **Differentiation ideas:** If you are carrying this out as a demonstration, only use the least confident learners as your assistants and question them and the class as they carry out the task. If you do this as a whole class experiment, you will need to offer help and guidance especially about the safety aspects to those learners who are less dextrous or less organised.

Those learners who need a challenge should be able to carry out this task with little supervision as long as you are sure they are working safely. Ask these learners to think of other examples of where surface area has an impact on the rate of reaction, for example, cutting up onions or apples so that they cook more quickly.

> **Assessment ideas:** You could use *Think like a scientist* questions 1–3. You could also ask questions as you circulate during the practical to assess the observation skills and/or understanding of the safety aspects.

2 Activity: Calculating the surface area (20 minutes)

Learning intention: To ensure learners understand the issue of measuring the surface area and how that can be changed by altering the arrangement of the components.

Resources: 27 simple child's construction blocks per group, ruler.

Description: Follow the instructions and diagrams in the Learner's Book to arrange the blocks in various ways and to measure the surface area.

You may choose to do this activity as a paper and pen exercise by telling the learners that each block shown in the illustrations is $1\,cm \times 1\,cm \times 1\,cm$ (a 1 cm cube) They can then do all the calculations based on this information.

> **Differentiation ideas:** For those learners who need support, it is often worth spending time doing this task in a practical way, as they can then really understand the idea of changing the shape and changing the surface area by working 'hands on'.

You could use blocks that are rectangular for those learners who need a challenge. The way in which these are arranged may well show a much bigger impact on the surface area.

> **Assessment ideas:** You could use activity questions 1–9.

3 Think like a scientist: Investigating the effect of surface area on the rate of reaction (30 and 45 minutes for the first part and the practical)

Learning intention: To carry out a practical task safely and with care and precision.

Resources: This will depend on the method chosen or available in your setting. The glassware options are shown in the Learner's Book. If you are able, learners could use different methods.

You will also need safety glasses, dilute hydrochloric acid and calcium carbonate chips in two different sizes.

Description: This task could be done in two separate lessons: the first part where the method is chosen and questions 1–6 are answered could be done together, and then the practical task, results collecting and graph drawing in a second lesson. It is essential that the learners answer questions 1–6 before carrying out the practical task.

> **Practical guidance:** You will need to circulate and give help and support to learners as they do this task.

> **Differentiation ideas:** Some learners may find it difficult to take accurate readings every 30 seconds, so you may need to give more help and support to them. Those who work faster and need a challenge may have time to repeat their experiments or to try the experiment with 5 g of powdered calcium carbonate.

> **Assessment ideas:** You could use *Think like a scientist* questions 1–11. You could also assess practical skills, such as organisation, safety and accuracy, by watching the various groups undertake the practical task.

You could ask the learners to undertake a self-assessment of the way they carried out the investigation using Template 2.

Plenary ideas

1   Making more or just being faster? (10 minutes)

Resources: Graphs from the experiments.

Description: Ask learners, in pairs, to look closely at the graphs from the *Think like a scientist* activity. What evidence do they have that tells them the reaction has happened more quickly? What evidence is there that the same volume of gas is produced when they have used 5 g of large chips or 5 g of small chips? Feed back to the class. This is a very

important point to make and one that is often misunderstood by learners who mistake speed for more gas.

> **Reflection ideas:** If you use the same mass of large and small calcium carbonate chips and the same volume and type of acid each time, do you make more carbon dioxide when the reaction is quicker?

2   Pyramid ideas (10 minutes)

Resources: Triangles drawn on paper as shown.

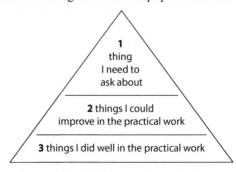

Description: Ask learners to answer the questions and hand in the pyramids as they leave.

> **Reflection ideas:** This is a self-assessment task that will help learners to reflect on their practical work skills.

Homework idea

1   Workbook Exercise 8.2

Topic 8.3 Temperature and the rate of reaction

LEARNING PLAN		
Learning Objectives	**Learning intentions**	**Success criteria**
9Cc.04 Describe the effects of concentration, surface area and temperature on the rate of reaction, and explain them using the particle model.	• Investigate the effect of temperature on the rate of reaction.	• Investigation carried out safely and accurately.

CONTINUED

Learning Objectives	Learning intentions	Success criteria
9TWSp.04 Plan a range of investigations of different types to obtain appropriate evidence when testing hypotheses. 9TWSp.05 Make risk assessments for practical work to identify and control risks. 9TWSc.02 Decide what equipment is required to carry out an investigation or experiment and use it appropriately. 9TWSc.03 Decide when to increase the range of observations and measurements, and increase the extent of repetition, to give sufficiently reliable data. 9TWSc.04 Take appropriately accurate and precise measurements, explaining why accuracy and precision are important. 9TWSc.05 Carry out practical work safely, supported by risk assessments where appropriate. 9TWSc.07 Collect, record and summarise sufficient observations and measurements in an appropriate form. 9TWSa.02 Describe trends and patterns in results, identifying any anomalous results and suggesting why results are anomalous. 9TWSa.04 Evaluate experiments and investigations, including those done by others, and suggest improvements, explaining any proposed changes. 9TSWa.05 Present and interpret results, and predict results between the data points collected.	• Use a trial run and preliminary work to inform the planning of an investigation. • Explain the effect of temperature on the rate of reaction using particle theory.	• Plan of investigation informed by the use of the trial run and preliminary work. • Particle theory used to explain the effect of temperature on the rate of reaction.

Use the terms repeatedly as you speak to learners. Encourage learners to use them as they respond to your questions, and as they talk to each other. Use them in written and oral questions.

Common misconceptions

Misconception	How to identify	How to overcome
Some learners do not think there is any need for a trial run or any preliminary work.	Learners will probably ask 'What's the point of this?' or treat the task less than seriously.	Directly ask them to say which range and temperature intervals they will use and then ask how they know these will work. The practical does take a long time if the steps are followed, but the learners need to understand and appreciate that this is the way in which scientists carry out their work.

Starter ideas

1 Getting started (10 minutes)

Learning intention: To recap what learners understand by the rate of reaction and how and why it changes as the reaction proceeds.

Description: Ask learners to write down what they mean by the phrase 'rate of reaction'. This should be done in silence and be time limited (perhaps a minute). They should then compare their statement with a partner and discuss their answers, forming one statement. The two learners should then be asked to discuss how the rate of reaction changes as the reaction progresses and write an explanation of why this happens. Some of the statements should then be shared with the class.

2 Ways of measuring the rate of reaction (10 minutes)

Learning intention: To review the various ways to measure the rate of reaction that learners have met so far.

Description: Ask the learners, in pairs, to identify the different ways of measuring the rate of reaction. They could do this by drawing a quick sketch of the equipment used and/or a brief description.

Feed back to the class.

Main teaching ideas

1 Think like a scientist: The effect of temperature on the rate of reaction – Trial run (20 minutes)

Learning intention: To set the scene for the practical work and to introduce the reaction and safety procedures.

Resources: Safety glasses, test tube with stopper, clamp stand, white card with a cross marked on it, timer or stop clock, sodium thiosulfate solution (0.1 mol/dm³), dilute hydrochloric acid (1 mol/dm³ or less), access to a large beaker containing solid sodium hydrogen carbonate.

Description: You may want to introduce this reaction to the class using the method with beakers shown in the Learner's Book. If you demonstrate this and/or the method for the trial run, you could spend some time dealing with the experimental issues and the safety issues, as indicated below.

Learners need to understand the reason for undertaking a trial run (to allow them to practise carrying out the procedure) and what it will help them to do better in the investigation that will follow.

Follow the instructions in the Learner's Book.

⟩ **Practical guidance:** At this concentration, hydrochloric acid is an irritant. In this reaction, sulfur dioxide is produced, so care must be taken. Sulfur dioxide is a corrosive and toxic gas. The investigation should take place in a well-ventilated room. Particular care is required if you have learners with asthma or other respiratory issues. The reacted solution should be disposed of in a plastic container with a solution of sodium hydrogen carbonate. The solution must be alkaline (universal indicator solution can be used to check this – add more sodium hydrogen carbonate if necessary). This can then be poured down the drain.

⟩ **Differentiation ideas:** You could support those learners who are less confident with practical skills and reassure them that the whole point of this trial run is to help them practise the method, so that it will help them in the investigation. While you circulate, ask questions such as: 'Why are you doing that?' 'Can you explain to me about disposing of the used solution?'

Those learners who need a challenge can be left to attempt this with little guidance, as long as you are sure they are working safely. To stretch them, ask questions such as: 'Can you explain to me how this will improve how accurate your readings are?' 'What is the advantage of doing it this way?', What improvement can you suggest?' (in this case ask them to try it out).

⟩ **Assessment ideas:** *Think like a scientist* questions 1–2 could be used for assessment.

2 **Think like a scientist: The effect of temperature on the rate of reaction – Preliminary work (30–40 minutes)**

Learning intention: To show that preliminary work can be useful to find a suitable range and interval for the temperatures to use in the investigation.

Resources: Safety glasses, test tube with stopper, clamp stand, white card with a cross marked on it, timer or stopwatch, sodium thiosulfate solution

(0.1 mol/dm^3), dilute hydrochloric acid (1 mol/dm^3 or less), access to a large beaker containing solid sodium hydrogen carbonate, thermometer, water bath (this could be a beaker containing water at a particular temperature that is checked regularly, adding hot water to maintain the temperature if needed. You could use some insulation material to help reduce temperature changes) access to hot water and/or means of heating water.

Description: Learners could carry this out at a few different temperatures to establish the interval needed. The students could try temperatures above $55\,°C$. You would need to get them to avoid doing this in the full investigation, as the reaction is so fast that the timings may be unreliable. If you are short of time, you could set specific temperatures for groups to try and feed back to the class. You could do this as an assisted demonstration if you are really short of time, but take the opportunity to use learners as assistants and keep up a discussion and questions about what is being done and why. Stress the safety aspects of this reaction. At the end of the practical session you will need to have a class discussion about what you have found out, and how you will use this in the full investigation.

⟩ **Practical guidance:** You may need to help learners to understand that the temperatures need to be accurate and to be maintained during the test.

At this concentration, hydrochloric acid is an irritant.

In this reaction sulfur dioxide is produced, so care must be taken. Sulfur dioxide is a corrosive and toxic gas. The investigation should take place in a well ventilated room. Particular care is required if you have learners with asthma or other respiratory issues. The reacted solution should be disposed of in a plastic container with a solution of sodium hydrogen carbonate. The solution must be alkaline (universal indicator solution can be used to check this, add more sodium hydrogen carbonate if necessary). This can then be poured down the drain.

⟩ **Differentiation ideas:** You could support those learners who are less confident with practical skills and reassure them that the whole point of this preliminary work is to help them identify the range and interval of temperatures needed in the investigation. You could allocate specific temperatures to various groups to try, perhaps the higher temperatures to those groups who work more quickly and accurately. You could restrict those who are less confident with practical skills to a few specific temperatures.

While you circulate, ask questions such as: 'Why are you doing that?' 'Can you explain to me about disposing of the used solution?' Those who work more quickly could be asked to try a larger range of temperatures.

During feedback make sure that you include information from all groups of learners.

⟩ **Assessment ideas:** *Think like a scientist* questions 3–8 could be used for assessment.

3 Think like a scientist: The effect of temperature on the rate of reaction – Investigation (60 minutes)

Learning intention: Plan and carry out an investigation safely.

Resources: Safety glasses, test tube with stopper, clamp stand, white card with a cross marked on it, timer or stopwatch, sodium thiosulfate solution (0.1 mol/dm^3), dilute hydrochloric acid $(1 \text{ mol/dm}^3$ or less), access to a large beaker containing solid sodium hydrogen carbonate, thermometer, water bath (this could be a beaker containing water at a particular temperature that is checked regularly, adding hot water to maintain the temperature if needed. You could use some insulation material to help reduce temperature changes), access to hot water and/or means of heating water.

Description: It would be helpful if the detailed plans could be done as homework and checked before the lesson. You could issue a class method and set of temperatures to be used if you are short of time. You will need to circulate and keep a careful watch on all aspects of safety with the investigation. Feedback on the results the learners have obtained may take some time and you may choose to do this in a subsequent lesson.

⟩ **Practical guidance:** At this concentration, hydrochloric acid is an irritant.

In this reaction, sulfur dioxide is produced, so care must be taken. Sulfur dioxide is a corrosive and toxic gas. The investigation should take place in a well-ventilated room. Particular care is required if you have learners with asthma or other respiratory issues. The reacted solution should be disposed of in a plastic container with a solution of sodium hydrogen carbonate. The solution must be alkaline (universal indicator solution can be used to check this, add more sodium hydrogen carbonate if necessary). This can then be poured down the drain.

⟩ **Differentiation ideas:** You could support those learners who are less confident with practical skills and reassure them. While you circulate ask questions such as: 'Why are you doing that?' 'Can you explain to me about disposing of the used solution?' 'What have you found out?' 'How reliable do you think your results are?' Some learners may need more hints and support in answering these questions but in a smaller group they may have the confidence to answer.

Most learners carrying out this task should need little or no support and guidance as long as they are working safely. You could suggest that they take readings at closer intervals and ask them how this will impact their results.

⟩ **Assessment ideas:** *Think like a scientist* questions 9–12 could be used for assessment.

Plenary ideas

1 Explaining why increasing the temperature increases the rate of reaction (10 minutes)

Resources: Learner's Book.

Description: This topic is very full with practical work and you may find it difficult to allow time for a normal plenary. You could ask learners to read through the section 'Looking at typical results' in the Learner's Book and to answer questions 1 and 2. They could do this in pairs. You could also ask them to read through the section about explaining the effect of temperature and to explain it in their own words. This could be also be done in pairs. Feed back to the class.

2 How did it help me? (10 minutes)

Description: Ask learners to write down how doing the trial run helped them to carry out their investigation.

Ask them to write down how doing the preliminary work helped them carry out their investigation.

Ask them to leave their notes as exit cards so that you can assess how well they have understood the ideas.

Homework ideas

1 Workbook Exercises 8.3A–B

Topic worksheets

• Worksheets 8.3A–C, True or false?

Topic 8.4 Concentration and the rate of reaction

LEARNING PLAN

Learning Objectives	Learning intentions	Success criteria
9Cc.04 Describe the effects of concentration, surface area and temperature on the rate of reaction, and explain them using the particle model. **9TWSp.03** Make predictions of likely outcomes for a scientific enquiry based on scientific knowledge and understanding. **9TWSp.04** Plan a range of investigations of different types to obtain appropriate evidence when testing hypotheses. **9TWSp.05** Make risk assessments for practical work to identify and control risks. **9TWSc.02** Decide what equipment is required to carry out an investigation or experiment and use it appropriately. **9TWSc.03** Decide when to increase the range of observations and measurements, and increase the extent of repetition, to give sufficiently reliable data. **9TWSc.04** Take appropriately accurate and precise measurements, explaining why accuracy and precision are important. **9TWSc.05** Carry out practical work safely, supported by risk assessments where appropriate. **9TWSc.07** Collect, record and summarise sufficient observations and measurements in an appropriate form. **9TWSa.02** Describe trends and patterns in results, identifying any anomalous results and suggesting why results are anomalous.	• Investigate the effect of concentration on the rate of reaction. • Plan and carry out an investigation safely. • Explain the findings in terms of particle theory.	• Be able to plan an investigation. • Carry out an investigation into the effect of concentration on the rate of reaction safely. • Explain the effect of concentration on the rate of reaction using particle theory.

LANGUAGE SUPPORT

Learners will use the following words:

concentration: a measure of how many particles of a substance are in a fixed volume of a solution

dilute: adding water to a solution dilutes it as there are fewer particles of the solute in a fixed volume of the solution

Explain each of the terms clearly to learners when you use them for the first time. You can also get learners to say the terms with you a few times. Encourage learners at all times to use the new terms, including when they are talking during activities or describing differences between elements, compounds and mixtures. The three ideas described in the Main teaching ideas for this topic give opportunities for learners to practice using the key words correctly. The language development worksheets give opportunities to match terms with their meanings. The *Words that begin with* task described in the Getting started section of this topic will help to reinforce the key words and their definitions for learners.

Common misconceptions

Misconception	How to identify	How to overcome
Some learners see little or no reason to plan their investigation and try to get on with the task straight away.	Be aware of those learners who try to give only the briefest of outlines for a plan.	Insist on a well structured plan. Make a feature of the plans and reward those who plan well.

Starter ideas

1 **Getting started (10 minutes)**

    Learning intention: To set the scene for the practical work.

    Description: Ask the learners to discuss with a partner what they think would happen if they carried out an experiment with marble chips (calcium carbonate) using the same mass of chips at equal temperatures, but with different concentrations of acid. Ask them to explain the reasons behind their ideas. Share ideas with the class.

2 **Words that begin with (10 minutes)**

    Learning intention: To improve scientific vocabulary.

    Resources: Learner's Book

    Description: Write the word, concentration, vertically on the board. Challenge learners to find scientific words starting with those letters. You could restrict learners to words connected with this particular topic or give them a wider choice of vocabulary. You could allow access to the Learner's Book or not.

Allow up to 5 minutes, and ask for ideas from learners. Check that they have an idea what the word means. You can award points for a correct word and extra points if no one else has this word.

Make sure learners do not just go for difficult words they do not know the meaning of, although some learners love to find the hardest words they can. This can be a real boost to their scientific vocabulary, especially if this technique is used regularly.

Main teaching ideas

1 **Think like a scientist: Investigating the effect of concentration on the rate of reaction – Planning (30–40 minutes)**

    Learning intention: To plan an investigation and to use group discussion to help do this.

    Resources: Learner's Book, Template 3.

Description: Divide the class into groups of no more than three. Explain the idea of the investigation, using the diagram as a starting point. Talk through the suggestions for things to be discussed given in the Learner's Book.

While learners are discussing this, circulate and ask them to explain the points they are making. Ask groups if there is anything else they can think of that needs to be mentioned to improve their plan. You could use Template 3 so that learners can record the outcomes of their discussion. This may be especially useful for those learners who find investigation planning a challenge.

It would be a good idea to think carefully about how you will group the learners, perhaps use some of the ideas from the teaching focus on group work in Stage 7.

> **Practical guidance:** See advice above regarding groups; you could have mixed-ability groups or similar-ability groups.

> **Differentiation ideas:** See above regarding the use of Template 3; some learners may not need to use this at all. The level of support and questioning you give while circulating during their discussions will depend on the different groups you have in the class.

> **Assessment ideas:** You could use *Think like a scientist* question 1 – writing the plan, to assess their progress. The plan could easily be used as a homework task and done as individuals or as groups.

2 Think like a scientist: Investigating the effect of concentration on the rate of reaction – Investigation (40–60 minutes)

Learning intention: To carry out an investigation safely.

Resources: Safety glasses, marble chips, dilute hydrochloric acid, water, measuring cylinders (to collect the gas and to measure the volume of acid used), beakers and marking pen to label the different concentrations of acid, conical flask fitted with a bung and delivery tube, large container for collecting the gas over water, top pan balance, timer.

Description: You could allow the learners to follow their own plans for the investigation. You may choose to allow them to follow the instructions in the Learner's Book. Learners will probably need help to ensure that they make up the different concentrations of acid accurately; the table in the Learner's Book will help them but the practical aspect may need support from you. You could provide them with ready-made dilutions of acid to save time, but it is a good idea for them to realise how those dilutions are made. It would be sensible, if you have limited time, to do this as a class exercise and use learners as assistants; use the least confident learners and use this as an occasion to try to build their confidence.

There may not be time for the results to be double-checked.

> **Practical guidance:** You will need to be very careful with the dilutions of acid and ensure that these have been correctly labelled.

> **Differentiation ideas:** The level of practical support you provide will vary with the practical skills of the learners. You may need to provide the different dilutions of acid for some groups. You could do the dilutions as suggested above.

Most learners carrying out this task should need little or no support and guidance as long as they are working safely. You could suggest that they take readings using dilutions at closer intervals and ask them how this will impact their results.

> **Assessment ideas:** You could use *Think like a scientist* question 2–7 to assess their progress. You could also use the practical as an opportunity to assess their practical skills.

You could also ask the learners to explain why they obtained these results and to use particle theory to explain their findings.

Plenary ideas

1 Lucky dip words (10 minutes)

Resources: Cards in a box with all the key words from this unit written on them.

Description: You draw a word out and each group (of no more than three) has to discuss the definition. Learners should write on a mini-white board or piece of paper and hold it up for you to see. Discuss with the class.

This could be done as a revision activity.

> **Reflection ideas:** How does a good scientific vocabulary help me to make more progress?

2 Increase/decrease (10 minutes)

Resources: Dice, cards with the following words written on them:

- concentration
- temperature
- surface area

Description: Draw a card to give you the variable. Throw the dice: even numbers mean that variable increases, odd numbers that variable decreases. Ask learners to do thumbs up for increasing the speed of a reaction and thumbs down for slowing a reaction.

Homework ideas

1 Workbook Exercises 8.4A–C

PROJECT GUIDANCE

This project addresses the following learning objectives:

9SIC.02 Describe how science is applied across societies and industries, and in research.

9SIC.03 Evaluate issues which involve and/or require scientific understanding.

This project is designed to allow learners to put into practice the ideas about increasing the rate of reaction and to put themselves in the place of chemical manufacturers.

This project could be introduced by demonstrating the manufacturing process and asking learners to highlight the points where they may be able to increase the rate of reaction and to reduce the loss of the carbon dioxide gas so that profits can be maximised. Stress the fixed time allowed for this task and make sure all groups are aware of the time as the task proceeds. You can choose the time allowed depending on the time you have available.

Arrange the learners into small groups of three or four. You can use the price list in the Learner's Book or give them a price list based on your local currency by modifying Template 4.

You could give them 'money' made from paper or card if that helps to keep track of how much they have 'spent' and 'earned'.

You could ask each group to assign one person to be in charge of each aspect, such as budget and accounts; manufacturing; risk assessment; reporting. Each task should not be done exclusively by this person however.

It will be important that you circulate and observe what each group is doing and watch for any excellent or poor technique.

Some learners or groups may be tempted to present you with test tubes full of air and expect payment, so be prepared to test each tube before you allow payment. You could test random tubes if you prefer, just as a purchaser might do with items they have bought.

At the end of the task, you need to spend some time on a feedback session, so that the various groups can present their reports and their accounts.

>9 Electricity

Unit plan

Topic	Learning hours	Learning content	Resources
9.1 Parallel circuits	3-4	The difference between series and parallel circuits; how current flows in a parallel circuit	**Learner's Book:** Questions 1–5 Activity: Measuring current in parallel circuits Think like a scientist: Making predictions about current **Workbook:** Exercise 9.1A, Current flow in parallel circuits Exercise 9.1B, Facts about parallel circuits Exercise 9.1C, Understanding current in parallel circuits **Teacher's Resource:** Worksheets 9.1A–C, Mistakes in circuits Template 1: Results table and graph axes for *Measuring current in parallel circuits*
9.2 Current and voltage in parallel circuits	3-4	Compare current and voltage in series and parallel circuits; the effects of adding cells and lamps to current and voltage in circuits	**Learner's Book:** Questions 1–6 Activity: Measuring voltage in a series circuit Think like a scientist: Measuring current in a parallel circuit **Workbook:** Exercise 9.2A, Voltage Exercise 9.2B, Current and voltage Exercise 9.2C, Changes in current and voltage **Teacher's Resource:** Worksheets 9.2A–C, Measuring current and voltage Worksheets 9.2D–E, Current and voltage in parallel circuits Template 2: Results table and graph axes for *Measuring voltage in a series circuit*

Topic	Learning hours	Learning content	Resources
9.3 Resistance	3-4	How resistance affects current in a circuit; calculate resistance from voltage and current	**Learner's Book:** Questions 1–4 Activity: Working out resistance Think like a scientist: Current and voltage in a resistor **Workbook:** Exercise 9.3A, Describing resistance Exercise 9.3B, Calculating resistance, voltage and current Exercise 9.3C, Ohm's law **Teacher's Resource:** Worksheets 9.4A–C, Resistance Template 3: Results table and graph axes for *Working out resistance*
9.4 Practical circuits	2-3	Draw circuit diagrams that include symbols for cells, switches, resistors, variable resistors, ammeters, voltmeters, lamps and buzzers; make circuits that include some or all of these components	**Learner's Book:** Questions 1–4 Think like a scientist: Designing and building circuits **Workbook:** Exercise 9.4A, Variable resistors Exercise 9.4B, Uses of variable resistors Exercise 9.4C, Comparing circuits
Cross-unit resources			**Check your Progress** **Project:** Circuits for schools and houses **Teacher's Resource:** Language development worksheets 9.1 Electricity vocabulary 9.2 Correcting the statements

BACKGROUND/PRIOR KNOWLEDGE

Learners should recall the circuit symbols for a cell, lamp, buzzer, ammeter, switch and how to represent connecting wires. Learners should also recall how to draw series circuits with these components and the functions of each of these components.

Recalling that current is the flow of electrons will help in understanding how current splits and comes together again in parallel circuits.

Understanding changes in energy will be useful for considering voltage.

TEACHING SKILLS FOCUS

Giving feedback

Many teachers say that giving feedback to every learner during every lesson is very time-consuming and so is not possible. In addition, parents or school leaders may wish to see written evidence that feedback has been given, which is even more time-consuming to do during the lesson.

CONTINUED

Some strategies are suggested here that will facilitate the process of giving feedback and also provide recorded evidence that the feedback has been given.

- In group-work situations, such as during experiments or when collaboratively working on worksheets, feedback can be given to groups, but the individuals within the group are addressed. For example, a group of learners has come up with a good strategy for collecting results. 'I like your method of doing … (making eye contact with each learner in the group briefly). That works well because … .' By making eye contact with each member of the group, each learner feels they have received individual feedback.

- In individual work situations where the teacher's time is taken up with tasks other than giving feedback, ensuring that learners can receive feedback in the next lesson may still be effective.

- If possible, use digital assessment tools and apps, many of which are now free. Use a search engine to look for 'free digital assessment tools'. Learners really engage well with these and many are very quick and easy to use effectively. If smart phones are not allowed in school then learners can use these from home. Direct contact details of learners should not be used and social media should not be used. Only ever make contact with learners through the educational or assessment apps.

- Where written evidence needs to be shown for feedback to every learner, try introducing an ink stamp or sticker system. The stamp or sticker should be quite small so it can be placed onto a learner's page and be seen to apply to one part of their work. An example of a phrase on a stamp or sticker could be 'Feedback was given here.' This example can be used to show where feedback was given, but it puts responsibility on the learner to remember what that feedback was. Having one quite generic stamp or sticker is much simpler to use than having more, but some teachers may be comfortable with more.

Try a combination of strategies for giving feedback. Remember, one piece of effective feedback will have far more learning impact than the fifteen corrections that you would really like to give!

Other teaching skills focus ideas are given in other units of this Teacher's Resource.

Topic 9.1 Parallel circuits

LEARNING PLAN

Learning Objectives	Learning intentions	Success criteria
9Pe.01 Describe how current divides in parallel circuits. 9TWSm.03 Use symbols and formulae to represent scientific ideas. 9TWSp.03 Make predictions of likely outcomes for a scientific enquiry based on scientific knowledge and understanding.	• Recognise and understand the difference between series and parallel circuits. • Understand how current flows in a parallel circuit.	• Recognise and draw circuit diagrams for parallel circuits. • Describe how current divides at a branch of a parallel circuit. • Predict values of current before or after branches in a parallel circuit.

CONTINUED

Learning Objectives	Learning intentions	Success criteria
9TWSp.04 Plan a range of investigations of different types to obtain appropriate evidence when testing hypotheses.		
9TWSc.01 Sort, group and classify phenomena, objects, materials and organisms through testing, observation, using secondary information, and making and using keys.		
9TWSc.03 Decide when to increase the range of observations and measurements, and increase the extent of repetition, to give sufficiently reliable data.		
9TWSc.04 Take appropriately accurate and precise measurements, explaining why accuracy and precision are important.		
9TWSc.05 Carry out practical work safely, supported by risk assessments where appropriate.		
9TWSc.07 Collect, record and summarise sufficient observations and measurements in an appropriate form.		
9TWSa.01 Evaluate the strength of the evidence collected and how it supports, or refutes, the prediction.		
9TWSa.02 Describe trends and patterns in results, identifying any anomalous results and suggesting why results are anomalous.		
9TWSa.03 Make conclusions by interpreting results, explain the limitations of the conclusions and describe how the conclusions can be further investigated.		

LANGUAGE SUPPORT

Learners will use the following words:

connected in series: components that are attached in a circuit end-to-end with no branches so that all the current flowing out of one component flows into the next; there are no branches in a series circuit

parallel circuit: circuit with branches where current can flow through more than one route

branches: parts of a parallel circuit where the current divides

connected in parallel: components that are attached across each other, so that the terminals of one component are connected to the terminals of the other

Common misconceptions

Misconception	How to elicit	How to overcome
Current is the same in all parts of a parallel circuit.	After learning about current in parallel circuits, ask learners to comment on the current through the cell and through the branches of a simple parallel circuit.	Learners may have had difficulty grasping that current is the same in all parts of a series circuit. This may now be committed to memory, so dealing with the difference in parallel circuits could be challenging. Main teaching idea 3 should help to overcome this.

Starter ideas

1 **Getting started (5 minutes)**

   Learning intention: To recall information about circuits from Stage 7.

   Description: At Stage 7, the word 'series' may not have been used because the distinction with parallel circuits was not needed. At this stage, learners can just be told to draw circuit diagrams just as they did before.

   The answer to part **c** may show that learners think current decreases around a series circuit.

2 **Turn the lights on (5 minutes)**

   Learning intention: To show learners a practical application of a parallel circuit.

   Resources: Room with a light switch that controls more than one lamp.

   Description: Show learners that the light switch operates more than one lamp. Remind learners that sometimes one of the lamps is not working, yet the others continue to work. Ask how the lamps may be connected to allow this to happen. If a series circuit is suggested, then learners should be asked what will happen if one lamp fails.

The correct answer is not required at this stage, as the idea is to start learners thinking that there is another way to connect components, other than in series.

Some learners may think that series is the only possible way to connect components.

Main teaching ideas

1 **Activity: Measuring current in parallel circuits (15–30 minutes, depending on number of circuits)**

   Learning intention: To allow learners to connect ammeters in various positions in parallel circuits and determine how current divides.

   Resources: See Learner's Book.

   Description: See Learner's Book.

   ⟩ **Differentiation ideas:** Learners needing support can be asked to describe the pattern in the results.

   Learners needing a challenge could be asked to suggest reasons for the differences in current based on the numbers of electrons flowing through each part of the circuit in a given time.

> **Assessment ideas:** Learners can work in groups to compose a summary or general rule that applies to current in parallel circuits.

2   **Think like a scientist: Making predictions about current (15–30 minutes, depending on number of circuits)**

Learning intention: See Learner's Book. This should be done after the activity Measuring current in parallel circuits.

> **Differentiation ideas:** Learners needing more support could work with parallel circuits that have identical branches, so each branch has the same current.

Learners needing more of a challenge could move on to work with circuits that have different numbers of lamps in each branch. How would the current through a branch with two lamps compare to a branch with one lamp (it will be lower, or half). The focus should still be on the current dividing between the branches and adding together again.

> **Assessment ideas:** Learners can be observed while working and asked about their predictions during the investigation.

3   **Modelling electron flow (10+ minutes)**

Learning intention: For learners to act the role of electrons in a parallel circuit.

Resources: Method for marking the path of a 'circuit' on the floor.

Description: Learners will be 'electrons' in a 'circuit' that follow a path around the room. Start with a series circuit, which can just be a circular or square path. Learners walk around in single file, all at the same constant speed and with no passing. This shows current (number of learners passing one point in a given time) is the same all the way around.

Next, introduce a branch, so learners walk around in single file then at the branch learners alternately go left or right, then merge in turn at the end of the branch.

In each branch, the number of learners passing one point in a given time will be fewer than (half of) that in the part of the circuit that is not branched.

Safety: There must be a clear path with no tripping hazards; learners must not walk around in a circle until they become dizzy.

> **Differentiation ideas:** Learners can volunteer to be 'ammeters' where they stand in one place and count the number of other learners passing their position.

For learners needing support, the teacher can tell them when to start and stop counting; the time interval itself is not important but is equal for all counters. Learners needing a challenge can use a timer to record their own time interval. These can then be standardised to the number of learners passing per minute.

> **Assessment ideas:** Learners can be asked to comment on the current in the branched and unbranched parts of the circuit.

Plenary ideas

1   **Top tips for parallel circuits (5 minutes)**

Resources: Paper and pencils.

Description: Learners work in pairs to devise a series of 'top tips' to advise others when learning this topic. This should be more than a list of facts, but rather suggestions of how to remember or understand.

> **Assessment ideas:** Learners can share their top tips with the class.

2   **What I learned today (1–5 minutes, depending on number of statements)**

Resources: Paper and pens.

Description: Learners to list a minimum of four things they the learned in the lesson.

> **Assessment ideas:** This activity can be done in notebooks for assessment at the same time as the next homework or as exit slips.

Homework ideas

1   Questions from the Learner's Book

2   Workbook Exercises 9.1A, 9.1B, 9.1C

3   Worksheets 9.1A–C

Topic worksheets

•   Worksheets 9.1A–C, Mistakes in circuits

Topic 9.2 Current and voltage in parallel circuits

LEARNING PLAN

Learning Objectives	Learning intentions	Success criteria
9Pe.02 Know how to measure current and voltage in series and parallel circuits, and describe the effect of adding cells and lamps.	• Compare current and voltage in series and parallel circuits.	• Describe and draw circuit diagrams to show how ammeters and voltmeters are connected in circuits.
9TWSm.03 Use symbols and formulae to represent scientific ideas.	• The effects of adding cells and lamps to current and voltage in circuits.	• State that the voltage across the cell in a series circuit is the same as the total of the voltages across each of the components.
9TWSp.01 Suggest a testable hypothesis based on scientific understanding.		
9TWSp.03 Make predictions of likely outcomes for a scientific enquiry based on scientific knowledge and understanding.		• State that the voltage across the cell in a parallel circuit is the same as the voltage across each of the branches.
9TWSp.05 Make risk assessments for practical work to identify and control risks.		• Make correct predictions about the effects on current and voltage of adding cells and lamps to both series and parallel circuits.
9TWSc.02 Decide what equipment is required to carry out an investigation or experiment and use it appropriately.		
9TWSc.03 Decide when to increase the range of observations and measurements, and increase the extent of repetition, to give sufficiently reliable data.		
9TWSc.04 Take appropriately accurate and precise measurements, explaining why accuracy and precision are important.		
9TWSc.05 Carry out practical work safely, supported by risk assessments where appropriate.		
9TWSc.07 Collect, record and summarise sufficient observations and measurements, in an appropriate form.		
9TWSa.01 Evaluate the strength of the evidence collected and how it supports, or refutes, the prediction.		

CONTINUED

Learning Objectives	Learning intentions	Success criteria
9TWSa.02 Describe trends and patterns in results, identifying any anomalous results and suggesting why results are anomalous. **9TWSa.03** Make conclusions by interpreting results, explain the limitations of the conclusions and describe how the conclusions can be further investigated. **9TWSa.04** Evaluate experiments and investigations, including those done by others, and suggest improvements, explaining any proposed changes. **9TSWa.05** Present and interpret results, and predict results between the data points collected.		

LANGUAGE SUPPORT

Learners will use the following words:

voltage: a quantity that is related to either the energy supplied by a power supply or the energy changed by a component, although voltage is not the same as energy

volts: the unit of voltage, V

rating: the maximum current or voltage that can be safely used without damaging a component

voltmeter: a meter that is connected in parallel with a component in order to measure the voltage across that component

Common misconceptions

Misconception	How to elicit	How to overcome
Voltmeters are connected in series with components.	After learning about voltage, ask learners to draw a circuit diagram to show how a voltmeter can be used to measure the voltage across a cell.	Learners have used and drawn circuit diagrams for ammeters that are connected in series with components. They will naturally think that voltmeters are connected the same way. Take care to always use the phrases 'The current *through*…' and 'The voltage *across*…' Allow learners to see the effect of connecting a voltmeter in series with a component such as a lamp. The voltmeter will read zero and the lamp will not light. Safety: Learners should not connect ammeters in parallel with components, and especially not across cells or batteries.

Starter ideas

1 Getting started (5 minutes)

Learning intention: To allow learners to recall ideas about current from Stage 7.

Resources: Paper and pens.

Description: Learners can work in groups, pairs or individually to answer the questions.

Learners may have forgotten the word electron. While the charge of the electron is not mentioned here, many learners incorrectly think that positive charges move when current flows.

2 Why does the lamp get dimmer? (5–10 minutes)

Learning intention: To remind learners of the effect of adding lamps in series.

Resources: A simple circuit with a cell and a lamp, another identical lamp.

Description: Show learners that the lamp lights from the cell. Questions can be asked to assess prior understanding of current. Ask learners to predict the effect of adding the second lamp in series with the first. Demonstrate that the lamp becomes dimmer. Ask why this happens.

Learners may (correctly) say that the current though two lamps is less than through one lamp. They may also (correctly) make reference to the energy from the cell being shared between two lamps rather than all given to one lamp.

The correct answer is a combination of both, although beyond the scope of the curriculum. As the current decreases, energy from the cell is delivered more slowly to the lamps (the voltage across each lamp also decreases). This is the concept of electrical power and should not be introduced at this stage.

The misconception of current being 'used up' in a series circuit is very common, so learners think that the current decreases in a stepwise manner as it passes through each lamp.

Main teaching ideas

1 Activity: Measuring voltage in a series circuit (20+ minutes)

Learning intention: To show learners how to connect voltmeters, and that the voltage across each of the components in series adds up to the voltage across the cell.

Resources: See Learner's Book.

Description: See Learner's Book.

> **Differentiation ideas:** Learners needing support can be reminded that the voltage across each of the components in series adds up to the voltage across the cell. Learners can then be asked to make simple predictions about voltage values either across the cell or across one of the components.

Learners needing a challenge can be reminded that voltage is a quantity related to energy and then asked to explain the observations in terms of energy.

> **Assessment ideas:** Learners can be asked to write an equation to summarise their results. (The voltage across each of the components in series adds up to the voltage across the cell.)

2 Think like a scientist: Measuring current in a parallel circuit (20+ minutes)

Learning intention: To measure current at different positions in a parallel circuit, and to discover the relationships between the current values.

Resources: See Learner's Book.

Description: See Learner's Book.

> **Differentiation ideas:** Learners who need support can be asked the describe what happens to the current as it flows from the unbranched part of the circuit to a branch.

Learners who need a challenge can be asked to make predictions about current values in various parts of the circuit.

> **Assessment ideas:** Learners can be asked to write an equation to summarise their results. (The current through each of the parallel branches adds up to the current through the cell or unbranched part.)

3 Explaining the difference between current and voltage (15–20 minutes)

Learning intention: To help learners understand the difference between current and voltage.

Resources: Small identical objects (for example, beads, counters or balls of scrap paper), path for learners to walk around the room.

Description: Current and voltage are abstract concepts, so modelling can help some learners to understand the difference. Care must be taken, as no model is perfect and often breaks down when applied to another situation.

Allocate one learner, possibly seated at a desk, to be the 'cell'. This learner will hand out the small objects to those that pass. An equal number is given to each person. The small objects represent electrical energy. Only the 'cell' can give these objects.

Allocate another learner, possibly seated at another desk, to be a 'component' such as a lamp. Learners walk in a circuit, collecting 'energy' at the cell and giving this energy to the 'lamp'. Learners must return to the 'cell' carrying no 'energy'. This can be extended to two lamps in series where each passing learner gives half their 'energy' to the first 'lamp' and half to the second 'lamp'.

More 'cells' can be added, each giving the same quantity of energy to each passing learner.

Care must be taken in this analogy not to imply that voltage is the same as energy. In this analogy, voltage is the number of 'energy' objects given to, or given up by, each walking learner. The full definition of voltage is beyond the scope of the curriculum at this stage.

> **Differentiation ideas:** Learners who need support can be asked what the model shows about current in a series circuit. Is it the same all the way around, or does it decrease to zero after the last lamp?

Learners who need challenge can be asked to describe how this model can be extended to parallel circuits. For example, two lamps in parallel with the cell.

> **Assessment ideas:** Ask learners:

- What do the walking learners represent? (electrons)

- What does the speed of walking represent? (current)

- What does the number of objects gained or given up represent? (voltage)

- How, in this model, can a battery eventually stop working? (all the 'energy' objects have been given out)

Plenary ideas

1 What did my partner learn? (3–5 minutes)

Resources: Small, rectangular pieces of paper, approximately 10 cm by 5 cm.

Description: Learners work in pairs and each tells the other what they learned in the lesson or topic. Each learner then summarises, in bullet points, what their partner told them.

> **Assessment ideas:** Read the statements to see what has been learned. If anything is missing, recap next lesson.

2 Current and voltage true or false (5 minutes)

Resources: Small pieces of paper.

Description: Each learner writes one or more statements of their choice about current or voltage that can be true or false. The statements are swapped for others to decide whether they are true or false. The answered statements are then swapped back again for checking or discussion.

> **Assessment ideas:** The teacher should randomly check some of the statements and their intended answers before they are swapped.

Homework ideas

1 Questions from the Learner's Book

2 Workbook Exercises 9.2A–C

3 Worksheets 9.2A–C

Topic worksheets

- Worksheet 9.2A, Measuring current and voltage

- Worksheet 9.2B, Current and voltage in series circuits

- Worksheet 9.2C, Current and voltage in series circuits

- Worksheet 9.2D, Current and voltage in parallel

- Worksheet 9.2E, Current and voltage in parallel

- Worksheet 9.2F, Current and voltage in parallel

Topic 9.3 Resistance

Learning Objectives	Learning intentions	Success criteria
9Pe.03 Calculate resistance (resistance = voltage ÷ current) and describe how resistance affects current. 9TWSm.03 Use symbols and formulae to represent scientific ideas. 9TWSp.01 Suggest a testable hypothesis based on scientific understanding. 9TWSp.03 Make predictions of likely outcomes for a scientific enquiry based on scientific knowledge and understanding. 9TWSc.01 Sort, group and classify phenomena, objects, materials and organisms through testing, observation, using secondary information, and making and using keys. 9TWSc.04 Take appropriately accurate and precise measurements, explaining why accuracy and precision are important. 9TWSc.07 Collect, record and summarise sufficient observations and measurements, in an appropriate form. 9TWSa.02 Describe trends and patterns in results, identifying any anomalous results and suggesting why results are anomalous. 9TWSa.03 Make conclusions by interpreting results, explain the limitations of the conclusions and describe how the conclusions can be further investigated. 9TSWa.05 Present and interpret results, and predict results between the data points collected.	• Discover how resistance affects current in a circuit. • Calculate resistance from voltage and current.	• State what happens to current in a circuit when resistance increases or decreases. • Recall the unit of resistance. • Recall and use the equation resistance = voltage ÷ current.

LANGUAGE SUPPORT

Learners will use the following words:

resistance: in an electrical circuit, anything that tends to slow the flow of current

ohms: the unit of resistance, symbol Ω

filament: the high resistance wire used in some lamps and in some radiant heaters

Ohm's law: the relationship where

$$resistance = \frac{voltage}{current}$$

resistor: an electrical component designed to have a particular resistance value that is higher than an equivalent length of copper wire

Common misconceptions

Misconception	How to elicit	How to overcome
Increasing resistance makes current increase.	After learning about resistance, ask learners about the effect of increasing resistance on current.	The *Think like a scientist* investigation should overcome this. Alternatively, set up a simple series circuit with a cell, a resistor and an ammeter. Replace the resistor with another resistor of either higher or lower value and observe the change in current.

Starter ideas

1 Getting started (5 minutes)

Learning intention: To allow learners to recall the difference between conductors and insulators and remind them that current does not flow equally easily in all materials.

Description: Learners can work individually or in pairs.

2 Adding lamps in series (5 minutes)

Learning intention: To assess prior understanding of the effect of adding more lamps on the current in a series circuit.

Description: Draw a circuit with one lamp and one cell. Ask learners the effect on the current when another cell is added in series (current decreases). Ask learners why they think this happens.

The correct answer about resistance is not required, as this will be covered later in the topic. Learners may express ideas about it being more difficult for current to flow, or maybe have the idea that the job of the cell in pushing electrons is made more difficult. These are correct concepts.

Main teaching ideas

1 Activity: Working out resistance (20–30 minutes)

Learning intention: For learners to measure current through, and voltage across, resistors and then calculate resistance.

Resources: See Learner's Book.

Description: See Learner's Book for instructions. Learners should be aware that resistance cannot be measured directly, but must be derived from these two quantities. (Some multi-meters can display resistance, but these work by measuring current and voltage.)

> **Differentiation ideas:** Learners needing support can be reminded of the order in which to divide the quantities: always voltage divided by current, and not always the larger number divided by the smaller.

Learners needing more of a challenge can choose other components and calculate the resistance of those.

> **Assessment ideas:** Learners can check each other's calculations of resistance.

2 Think like a scientist: Current and voltage in a resistor (10–20 minutes)

Learning intention: For learners to investigate the relationship between current and voltage in a resistor.

Resources: See Learner's Book. A variable resistor can be used instead of adding more cells; variable resistors are introduced in the next topic.

Description: See Learner's Book. The investigation can be introduced as one similar to that done by Ohm, leading to the development of Ohm's law.

> **Differentiation ideas:** Learners needing support could be asked to read intermediate values from their graph. For example, if 1.5 V cells have been used, what would be the current when the voltage is 2.0 V?

Learners needing a challenge can attempt *Think like a scientist* question 4 in the Learner's Book and explain their choices of lines.

> **Assessment ideas:** Learners can discuss the answers to the Learner's Book questions in groups or individuals can volunteer answers to the class.

3 Analogies for resistance (10–20 minutes)

Learning intention: To help learners understand the concept of resistance.

Description: Resistance, current and voltage are quite abstract concepts and can be difficult for many learners to understand. Analogies can be used to make the concepts more concrete.

Ask learners to recall the way current was modelled with them walking around a 'circuit' in the class. If this has not been done before, it can now be done for the first time. Remind learners that they represent electrons and their speed is the current. The energy, or effort, for walking is voltage.

Now ask learners to imagine doing the same activity while walking in the shallow end of a swimming pool. How would it be different? The analogy here is that the water provides resistance to their movement, so slows the current. In order to keep the current the same as on land, more effort (higher voltage) would be needed.

Give learners one other analogy, such as riding a bicycle on hard ground and then in soft sand. Then ask learners to make their own analogies.

> **Differentiation ideas:** This activity will differentiate by outcome. Learners can be divided into mixed-ability groups, but ensure all members of a group have a role assigned to them.

Learners who need a challenge may not be given the one additional analogy.

> **Assessment ideas:** Learner groups can compare analogies.

Plenary ideas

1 Remembering the equation (2–5 minutes)

Description: Learners work in pairs to think of a mnemonic to help remember the equation relating resistance, voltage and current.

> **Assessment ideas:** Assessment is part of the activity.

2 Was it easy or difficult? (2–3 minutes)

Resources: Paper and pens.

Description: Learners recall three ideas or concepts from the lesson and rank each as easy, medium or difficult to understand or remember.

> **Assessment ideas:** Learners can compare each other's output from this activity and discuss.

Homework ideas

1 Questions from the Learner's Book

2 Workbook Exercises 9.3A–C

3 Worksheets 9.3A–C

Topic worksheets

• Worksheets 9.3A–C, Resistance

Topic 9.4 Practical circuits

Learning Objectives	Learning intentions	Success criteria
9Pe.04 Use diagrams and conventional symbols to represent, make and compare circuits that include cells, switches, resistors (fixed and variable), ammeters, voltmeters, lamps and buzzers. 9TWSm.03 Use symbols and formulae to represent scientific ideas. 9TWSc.01 Sort, group and classify phenomena, objects, materials and organisms through testing, observation, using secondary information, and making and using keys. 9TWSc.02 Decide what equipment is required to carry out an investigation or experiment and use it appropriately. 9TWSc.03 Decide when to increase the range of observations and measurements, and increase the extent of repetition, to give sufficiently reliable data. 9TWSc.07 Collect, record and summarise sufficient observations and measurements in an appropriate form. 9TWSa.04 Evaluate experiments and investigations, including those done by others, and suggest improvements, explaining any proposed changes.	• Draw circuit diagrams that include symbols for cells, switches, resistors, variable resistors, ammeters, voltmeters, lamps and buzzers. • Make circuits that include some or all of these components.	• Draw circuit diagrams that include symbols for cells, switches, resistors, variable resistors, ammeters, voltmeters, lamps and buzzers. • Build circuits that include some or all of these components, using circuit diagrams.

LANGUAGE SUPPORT

Learners will use the following words:

dimmer: in circuits a control used to adjust the brightness of a lamp, usually a variable resistor

volume: in this context, a control used in audio equipment for adjusting the loudness of the sound output, or the loudness of sound

variable resistor: a component whose resistance can be changed

fixed resistor: a component whose resistance should be constant under specified conditions

Common misconceptions

Misconception	How to elicit	How to overcome
Voltmeters are connected in series with a component and not in parallel with that component.	Learners draw circuits with voltmeters in series.	Always refer to the voltage *across* a component and the current *through* a component, drawing attention to the use of the words 'across' and 'through', as these refer to where the quantities are being measured.

Starter ideas

1 Getting started (5 minutes)

Learning intention: To allow learners to recall how to draw circuit diagrams correctly.

Description: Learners should work individually, but can swap answers for peer assessment.

2 Quick-fire circuit symbols (5 minutes)

Learning intention: To allow learners to recall the circuit symbols they have learned so far.

Resources: Prepared slides or cards with circuit symbols drawn for cell, lamp, buzzer, ammeter, voltmeter, resistor, open switch and closed switch.

Description: Each slide or card is shown to the class for a very short time. Learners then write the name for the component. The next is shown, and so on.

As an alternative, learners can work in pairs, make their own cards and show them quickly to each other.

Some learners may use the term 'battery' when the word 'cell' is required.

Main teaching ideas

1 Think like a scientist: Designing and building circuits (20+ minutes)

Learning intention: To allow learners to draw circuit diagrams and then build circuits for specified purposes.

Resources: See Learner's Book.

Description See Learner's Book.

> **Differentiation ideas:** The activity will differentiate by outcome. Learners needing support can be given help to draw the circuit diagrams for the circuits specified in the Learner's Book. Learners needing more of a challenge can design their own circuits and describe the purpose for which these circuits could be used.

> **Assessment ideas:** Learners can be asked to describe how their circuit works.

2 Variable resistors (10–20 minutes)

Learning intention: To show learners how a variable resistor works.

Resources: For teacher demonstration: variable resistor, power supply, ammeter and lamp.

For learner activity: resistance wire, crocodile clips and access to other laboratory equipment.

Description: Many school components that can be used as variable resistors are actually potentiometers. These have three terminals and can be used as variable resistors, usually by connecting the middle terminal and one of the end terminals. Many school variable resistors are also called rheostats, but neither this nor the word 'potentiometer' should be used with learners.

These work by having a strip of resistance material or a coil of resistance wire along which an electrical contact can be moved. Moving the contact changes the length of resistance material in a circuit: the longer the length, the greater the resistance.

This should be shown and explained to learners, then the effect demonstrated in a simple circuit. As the resistance is increased, the brightness of the lamp decreases and the current also decreases.

The potentiometer and varying the voltage in a circuit is beyond the scope of the curriculum at this stage.

> **Differentiation ideas:** For an activity that differentiates by outcome, learners could work in groups to design and make their own variable resistor using resistance wire, crocodile clips and their own choice of other equipment with varying levels of support. Groups can then demonstrate their variable resistor working.

> **Assessment ideas:** Learners can be asked questions such as: 'What will happen to the resistance when the length of the wire is doubled?'

3   Making an ohm meter (20+ minutes)

Learning intention: To build circuits and understand how meters can be calibrated to do different jobs.

Resources: Cells or batteries, wires and connectors, ammeters (preferably analogue), selection of resistors of values known to the teacher.

Description: An ohm meter, or resistance meter, uses an ammeter to measure the current through an unknown resistor with a known voltage. The cell or battery is connected in series with the ammeter and the unknown resistance. As resistance = voltage ÷ current, the ammeter can be re-calibrated in ohms. The ammeter is still measuring current but as voltage is constant, resistance is inversely proportional to current. For example, with a 1.5 V cell, a current of 0.5 A means the resistance is 3 Ω (1.5 ÷ 0.5). That means the ammeter reading of 0.5 A in this case can be changed to 3 Ω to make an ohm meter.

Safety: Learners' designs should be checked to ensure that the ammeter is not to be connected in parallel with the cell or battery.

Learners can therefore make their own ohm meter and use this to measure the values of some resistors. Learners could use tape and pens to make a new temporary scale in ohms for their meter, or make a conversion chart.

> **Differentiation ideas:** Learners needing support can be helped with either the design of the circuit or with the current to resistance conversion, or both.

Learners needing a challenge should be asked to design the circuit and calculate the current to resistance conversion themselves.

> **Assessment ideas:** Learners could be asked to explain how their ohm meter works, or to calibrate the scale for a different voltage of battery.

Plenary ideas

1   One minute each (3–5 minutes)

Description: Learners work in pairs. Each has a minute to tell the other what they learned in the lesson or topic. The teacher should time this so all learners in the class are working to the same times at once.

> **Assessment ideas:** Individuals can volunteer to tell the class what their partner told them. The teacher should confirm with the other partner that this was relayed correctly.

2   Two plus two (5 minutes)

Resources: Paper and pens

Description: Learners work individually and write two things they enjoyed about the lesson or topic and the two things they found most challenging.

> **Assessment ideas:** This can be done as an exit slip activity or in books to be seen next time books are taken in.

Homework ideas

1   Questions from the Learner's Book

2   Workbook Exercises 9.4A–C

PROJECT GUIDANCE

This project addresses the following learning objectives:

9Pe.01 Describe how current divides in parallel circuits.

9Pe.02 Know how to measure current and voltage in series and parallel circuits, and describe the effect of adding cells and lamps.

9Pe.04 Use diagrams and conventional symbols to represent, make and compare circuits that include cells, switches, resistors (fixed and variable), ammeters, voltmeters, lamps and buzzers.

9SIC.02 Describe how science is applied across societies and industries, and in research.

9SIC.03 Evaluate issues which involve and/or require scientific understanding.

The aim of the project is to allow learners to put electrical circuits into everyday contexts and to allow creativity and encourage logical planning.

Learners should start by collecting resources for their model building and then planning what is to be designed. How many rooms will there be? What will be the purpose of the building: house, school, etc?

Before putting the electrical components into the building, the circuit should be planned and drawn using a circuit diagram. Once the components are in place, this can be modified and adapted. All circuit diagrams should be kept so that a record of the development of the project is available. Learners should be encouraged not to think that an original idea was 'wrong' and should be discarded. When presenting their project, they can make reference to the development stages and how new ideas were incorporated.

Learners can decorate their rooms to make the model more realistic, but this should not become a distraction from the main focus, which is the electrical circuit.

The final stage of the project should have a fully working model that the learners can demonstrate, and should have a complete circuit diagram for the final construction.

> Glossary

advantageous feature – a feature of an individual that gives it a better chance of survival than other individuals in the population

alignment – the orientation of objects or the way things are lined up according to some external influence

alkali metals – metals in Group 1 of the Periodic Table that produce alkalis when they react with water

amplitude – the maximum distance moved by a particle in a wave as measured from the position of the particle when there is no wave; the heightof a wave, or graph of a wave, from the mid-point to the top

anomalous result – a measurement or reading that does not fit in with the pattern of the other results; such a result is not necessarily wrong, but it should be checked

atomic number – the number of protons in an atom; each type of atom has a unique atomic number

bases – metal oxides are known as bases

bladder – an organ in which urine is stored before removal from the body

branches – parts of a parallel circuit where the current divides

carbonate – a salt that is made from carbonic acid

chemical bond – ways in which elements are joined together to form compounds

chloride – a salt that is made from hydrochloric acid

chlorophyll – a green pigment present in chloroplasts, which absorbs energy from light and helps to transfer it to the carbohydrates made in photosynthesis

chromosomes – long thread-like structures, found in the nuclei of cells, which are made of DNA and contain genes

citrate – a salt that is made from citric acid

colder – used to describe an object at lower temperature than another

collecting a gas over water – a way of collecting a gas given off in a reaction

collision – what happens when two or more objects bump into each other

collision theory – one of the theories for the formation of the Moon; sometimes called the giant impact hypothesis

concentric – circles or arcs of circles with a different radius but having the same centre

concentration – a measure of how many particles of a substance are in a fixed volume of a solution

conduction – method of thermal energy transfer where more vigorously vibrating particles cause neighbouring particles to vibrate by colliding; conduction works best where particles are close together: in solids and liquids

connected in parallel – components that are attached across each other, so that the terminals of one component are connected to the terminals of the other

connected in series – components that are attached in a circuit end-to-end with no branches so that all the current flowing out of one component flows into the next; there are no branches in a series circuit

conserved – in this context, conserved means the total quantity of something is kept the same

continental coasts – the outlines of the continents that form the boundary between land and sea or ocean

convection – method of thermal energy transfer where more vigorously vibrating particles cause expansion and decrease in density in a liquid or gas; the less dense material then rises because it floats, setting up a convection current

convection current – method by which all of a liquid or gas becomes heated through convection; particles flow through the material due to differences in density

covalent bond – a link formed when atoms share electrons to form a molecule

created – to be made from nothing or from something different

crucible – a piece of laboratory equipment; a container that is heated directly at high temperatures

crystallisation – the process of turning into crystals

crystallise – to form crystals

density – the property of a material or object that is mass per unit volume; calculated as $\frac{mass}{volume}$ and usually has the units g/cm³ or kg/m³

destroyed – cease to exist

dilute – adding water to a solution dilutes it as there are fewer particles of the solute in a fixed volume of the solution

dimmer – in circuits, a control used to adjust the brightness of a lamp, usually a variable resistor

displacement reaction – a reaction in which a more reactive metal 'pushes out' a less reactive one from a compound

DNA – the chemical from which genes and chromosomes are made; its structure constitutes a code that determines the proteins made in a cell

dot and cross diagram – a way of showing atoms sharing electrons to form a covalent bond

egg cell – the female gamete of an animal

electron shells – the layers of electrons arranged around the nucleus of an atom

electronic structure – the arrangement of electrons in the shells or levels around the nucleus of an atom

electrostatic forces – forces of attraction between particles with opposite electrical charges

endothermic reaction – chemical reaction in which energy is transferred from the environment

energy levels – the layers or shells of electrons are referred to as being at different energy levels

erodes – wears away

excretion – getting rid of waste materials from the body; specifically, these waste materials have been inside the body (so do not include the egestion of faeces)

exothermic reaction – a chemical reaction in which energy is transferred to the environment

expand – become larger

fertilisation – the fusion of the nucleus of a male gamete with the nucleus of a female gamete

fertiliser – a substance containing minerals required by plants, which can be added to soil

fetal – to do with the fetus

fetus – a developing child while still within the uterus; specifically, the term embryo is used for the first few weeks, and fetus from about 11 weeks onwards

filament – the high resistance wire used in some lamps and in some radiant heaters

fixed resistor – a component whose resistance should be constant under specified conditions

formula – uses chemical symbols to show how many atoms of different elements are present in a particle of an element or compound (the plural is formulae)

fossil record – the collection of remains of dead animals and plants from millions of years ago that provide evidence of what conditions were like in those times

frequency – the number of complete vibrations of an object in 1 second

gametes – specialised cells that contain only half the normal number of chromosomes (that is, one set rather than the usual two sets) and that join together during sexual reproduction to produce a zygote

genes – lengths of DNA on a chromosome, which contain a code that determines which proteins a cell makes; this in turn determines some of the characteristics of the cell and of the organism

genetic differences – differences between the genes of different organisms

gradient – the steepness of a slope, in this case on the graph

graphite – a form of carbon used as the 'lead' in pencils

halogens – the elements found in Group 7 of the Periodic Table

hollow – an object that has a space filled with air on the inside

hotter – used to describe an object at a higher temperature than another

inheritance – the passing on of genes (DNA) from parents to offspring

interference – the effect produced when two or more waves meet

intermolecular forces – the forces between molecules

ion – an atom with a net electric charge due to the loss or gain of one or more electrons

ionic bond – a link formed between two or more ions to form a compound

ionic compound – a compound formed when the ions of a metal and a non-metal react together

irregular – of a three-dimensional shape, having a volume that cannot be calculated using a simple equation

jigsaw – a type of puzzle where a complete picture is made by fitting smaller interlocking pieces of the picture together

kidneys – a pair of organs in the upper abdomen, which filter the blood and produce urine

lattice – a regular, repeated, three-dimensional arrangement of atoms, ions or molecules in a metal or other crystalline solid

layers – a form of material where one sheet of material is placed on top of another

light intensity – a measure of the quantity of light energy falling onto an object

limestone – a sedimentary rock made from calcium carbonate

loudness – the intensity of a sound; very quiet sounds are difficult to hear, whereas very loud sounds can be painful and damaging to the ears

macromolecules – giant molecules

mass extinction – the complete loss of a very large number of species

mass number – the number of protons and neutrons in an atom added together

meteorite – part of a meteor that reaches the Earth's surface

meteoroids – objects in space that are smaller than an asteroid

meteors – a meteoroid when it moves through the Earth's atmosphere

molecule – a particle formed when atoms are bonded together with covalent bonds

molten – in a liquid state

natural selection – a process in which only the best-adapted individuals survive and reproduce, passing on the genes that produce their advantageous features to their offspring

nebulae – a cloud of dust and gas in space (the singular is nebula)

neutralisation – to change an acid or alkaline solution to one that has a pH of 7

nitrate – a salt that is made from nitric acid

noble gases – the elements found in Group 8 of the Periodic Table

northern hemisphere – the part of the Earth that is north of the equator

Ohm's law – the relationship where resistance $= \dfrac{\text{voltage}}{\text{current}}$

ohms – the unit of resistance, symbol Ω

ores – rocks or minerals that contain a metal compound

oscilloscope – electronic equipment used to display a waveform on a screen

parallel circuit – circuit with branches where current can flow through more than one route

peak – the top of a wave graph where the line is at its highest; also known as a crest

Periodic Table – a table of all the elements placed in order of their atomic number

photosynthesis – a series of chemical reactions that take place inside the chloroplasts of plants, in which carbon dioxide and water react together using light energy; the products are glucose (and other carbohydrates) and water

pitch – the highness or lowness of a musical note

porous – a solid that has tiny holes allowing water to soak through

precipitate – an insoluble solid formed when two soluble substances react

preliminary work – some practical work you do before an investigation to find out how you will carry it out. For example, you might find out the range or interval of the independent variable that you need to use

radiation – method of thermal energy transfer that uses waves and does not depend on particles; occurs through a vacuum, through gases and through transparent solids

random – not predictable or not following any pattern

rating – the maximum current or voltage that can be safely used without damaging a component

reactivity – how quickly or slowly a chemical reacts compared with another

reactivity series – a list of metals in order of how reactive they are; the most reactive are at the top of the list and the least reactive at the bottom

regular – of a three-dimensional shape, such as a cube or cuboid, having a volume that can be calculated using a simple equation

reinforce – in this context, where interference results in an increase in amplitude

renal – to do with the kidneys

resistance – in an electrical circuit, anything that tends to slow the flow of current

resistant – an adjective describing an organism that it is not harmed by a chemical that kills others – for example, bacteria, for example, can be resistant to antibiotics and weeds can be resistant to herbicides

resistor – an electrical component designed to have a particular resistance value that is higher than an equivalent length of copper wire

root hairs – specialised cells in the outer layer of a plant root that increase the surface area through which water and minerals be absorbed from the soil

salt – a compound formed when a metal reacts with an acid, for example, magnesium chloride

sex inheritance – the way in which the sex of a child is determined by the inheritance of X and Y chromosomes from its parents

slush – partly-melted snow

solid – in this context, an object that has no space filled with air on the inside

southern hemisphere – the part of the Earth that is south of the equator

sperm cell – the male gamete of an animal

stable – firmly fixed

stellar nurseries – places within some nebulae where stars are formed

stomata – microscopic holes in the surface of a leaf (usually on the underside) through which gases diffuse into and out of the air spaces inside the leaf (the singular is stoma)

sulfate – a salt that is made from sulfuric acid

surface area – the total area of the surface of an object

system – in this context, a system is a place where an energy change or transfer occurs and where no energy enters or leaves that place

the law of conservation of energy – the principle that energy cannot be created or destroyed, only changed or transferred

the law of conservation of mass – the principle that there is no loss or gain of mass in a chemical reaction

transpiration – the loss of water vapour from the leaves of a plant

trial run – a test run of an investigation to check that you can carry it out correctly

trough – the bottom of a wave graph where the line is at its lowest

urea – an excretory product made in the liver from excess amino acids

ureter – a tube that carries urine from the kidneys to the bladder

urethra – a tube that carries urine from the bladder to the outside of the body

urine – a liquid produced by the kidneys, which contains urea and other waste substances dissolved in water

variable resistor – a component whose resistance can be changed

variation – differences between individuals belonging to the same species

vigorously – with a lot of movement and a lot of energy

voltage – a quantity that is related to either the energy supplied by a power supply or the energy changed by a component

voltmeter – a meter that is connected in parallel with a component in order to measure the voltage across that component

volts – the unit of voltage, V

volume – in this context, a control used in audio equipment for adjusting the loudness of the sound output, or the loudness of sound

wilted – of a plant, having lost so much water that the soft tissues (especially leaves) lose their firmness and flop over

xylem vessels – specialised cells in which all cell contents and end walls have disappeared, leaving an empty tube through which water is transported

yield – the quantity of useful crop obtained at harvest

zygote – the new cell that is formed when a male gamete fuses with a female gamete; it contains one set of chromosomes from the male gamete and one set from the female gamete